IDEOLOGY AND PARTICIPATION

Volume 3, Sage Library of Social Research

SAGE LIBRARY OF SOCIAL RESEARCH

Ideology and Participation

Douglas E. Ashford

Volume 3
SAGE LIBRARY OF
SOCIAL RESEARCH

SAGE PUBLICATIONS   Beverly Hills   London

To Karen

320.01
A825i

For information address:

SAGE PUBLICATIONS, INC.
275 South Beverly Drive
Beverly Hills, California 90212

SAGE PUBLICATIONS LTD
St George's House / 44 Hatton Garden
London EC1 8ER

Printed in the United States of America

International Standard Book Number 0-8039-0256-5 (C)
0-8039-0197-6 (P)

Library of Congress Catalog Card No. 72-98028

FIRST PRINTING

14-4200

TABLE OF CONTENTS

IDEOLOGY AND PARTICIPATION

Volume 3, Sage Library of Social Research

PREFACE

So much has been written, and so much remains to be understood, about the relation of thought to action that I undertook this effort with severe reservations. My earlier work on Africa and Asia persuaded me that transforming vision into reality is a much more precarious task than present thinking in Western social science recognizes. The shattered hopes and forgotten dreams of the less-developed countries are equalled only by the bloodshed and violence that have so tragically overtaken one new nation after another for the past decades. In our own countries, citizens are also preoccupied with violence, and the destinies of the democratic regimes seem shrouded in ambiguity.

The weaknesses I see in the theory and concepts prevailing in our analysis of ideology can be described in several ways. I have been especially influenced by S. F. Nadel and other anthropologists who have tried to grapple with the nature of public life and authority. Behavioral models, and some versions of systems models, have helped us see the relation of differentiation to political change and ideas, but these modes of analysis are not well suited for the study of structural transformations and expanding self-awareness, two issues that seem at the root of many political crises in the world today. Finding the origins of power obscure, we have drifted into thinking it must be highly determined. Using ecological maps, we can trace the contours of authority in society, but such analysis provides at best a disembodied notion of civic order. The impact of psychology on politics has been great, but the approach by its very concentration on the individual tells us little about collective support for authority as it is actually manifested in public institutions and processes.

In thinking about these problems, I have become increasingly aware that many societies, perhaps all, forego the advantages of material progress in various ways and make more substantial efforts to maintain their symbolic identity than sociological theory acknowledges. In politics, it may be as important to know how equality is made possible as to know how superiority is justified. The possibility of restructuring hierarchies and engaging in reciprocal interaction makes politics as a discipline possible. Western social science, and here I would include figures as different as Marx and Weber, starts from assumptions that put aside basic questions about the restructuring of power in an ongoing society and culture. Political solidarity and integration are the dimly perceived residuals in an elitist, determined world. The public is deprived of reason; civic order depends on the benevolence of an elite; the authority buttressing political institutions is derived more from the apprehensions of a perverse citizenry than from their collective expression and shared values.

My hope is to encourage students of politics to speculate about the reversal of all these propositions. Publics have a curious way of persisting as elites are changed, and some may even achieve their goals, as V. O. Key believed. Civic order may persist despite the blunders and hypocrisy of the privileged rather than because of their peculiar foresight. The apathy of many citizens must be measured against the abuse of office and cynical manipulation of power that seems to plague both industrial and agrarian societies. Political hierarchies are essential, but should our theories and concepts about the use and transformation of authority depend so heavily on the wisdom and reliability of the powerful?

Political science is beginning to rethink the arguments about the decline of ideology. In part, this is because we are just beginning to realize that, without some propositions about the effect of ideas on action, we cannot say much about publics, civic order, or legitimacy. If ideas, values, and aspirations become real only when blessed by the powerful, change is severely limited, and ideology, however conceived, cannot have independent effects. Much of the work on political socialization, political culture, and political mobilization starts out with the view that power is its own reward and that political destiny is permanently fixed in men's minds. I have tried to extricate some of these concepts from their highly determinist, elitist bearings. To do so, we must develop concepts that permit political culture to vary from established authority; that make it possible to undergo political mobilization while maintaining individual and collective leverage on political goals and values; that enable us to see something more challenging in political socialization than a carefully tutored, passive public.

I would have difficulty recalling the names of the many scholars and colleagues whose ideas and writing helped in shaping this book. It would be consistent with my views on ideology and participation to note that, in the absence of an academic community, my evaluation—or that of anyone— would be impossible. I hope the reworking of my own views contributes to the vitality of such a community. I have benefited directly from two institutions that are trying to nourish critical attitudes among scholars, the Center for International Studies of Cornell University and the Institute of Development Studies of Sussex University. Needless to add, I am indebted to all my friends who find authority tempered by civility.

September 1972

—Douglas E. Ashford

Chapter I

IDEOLOGY AND PARTICIPATION

Ideology concerns the interaction of ideas and behavior around a shared set of political values. Many discussions of ideology have dwelt on the origins and uses of ideology, but this inquiry will be more concerned with how psychological and cultural elements of individual and group behavior relate to the manifestation of the shared values, especially as they appear in political life. In addition, the study will be interested in how political ideologies affect political participation and contribute to the success or failure of democratic political systems.

There are, of course, various terms to describe how ideas and behavior interact in politics. Doctrines and creeds refer to more dogmatic, rigid forms of ideology and generally imply some kind of inflexible standard for judging behavior. More recently, political science has adopted the notion of belief systems, suggesting that individual attitudes and perception could be conceived as having latent structural qualities which might not be explicitly recognized in the values governing political life. Thus, the relatively high levels of confidence expressed in the political system in Western democracies might be considered an element of our belief system, although democratic values themselves do not explicitly postulate political efficacy as a value to be achieved. A third, even looser, usage is to think of ideology as the disconnected, almost accidental, outcome of diverse opinions and reactions coalescing in some way to affect events and problems. The pluralist approach to politics tends to take this randomized view of ideology.

The more systematic study of individual and collective behavior over the past fifty years has told us a good deal more about the interdependence of ideas and values in our daily experience. Though many of the classic problems of ideology remain, we are in a much better position to understand how ideas and values interact, and one of the aims of this study is to bring some of this knowledge to bear on the analysis of ideology. As the illustrations indicate, how one sees ideas and values interacting in political and social life is one way of approaching the study of ideology. Assumptions of this kind suggest how values may or may not affect political life in the society concerned. A dogmatic relationship involves a rigid separation of approved behavior from unacceptable behavior, and this should be apparent in observing relatively fixed patterns of individual and group action. The more abstract notion of a belief system acknowledges that the interdependence of ideas and values has both manifest and latent dimensions. The more ambiguous view is almost devoid of structure in relation to behavior or values. By permitting no assumptions about either behavior or values, the relevance of ideology to political events escapes systematic inquiry of any kind.

The analysis of ideas and behavior as an interdependent dimension of political systems is, of course, only an aspect of the study of ideology. The particular problems raised in this study leave out much of ontological and ethical discussion that has conventionally been included in trying to evaluate ideologies in the abstract. Lest this be taken as an unacceptable disclaimer, it should be noted that this does not imply that all values are equally virtuous or that all behavior is equally acceptable. Indeed, the thread running through this study is that the values associated with democratic political life have more than an ethical defense. One of the unfortunate effects of the behavioral emphasis in political studies has been the neglect of the ways in which ideas do influence behavior. My intent is to redress the balance by suggesting that *how* ideas and behavior are structured in individual and group responses to political life is an essential link between political philosophy and political action.

The historical and philosophical study of ideology has found itself removed from the mainstream of political science in part because little attention has been given to the immense variation among individuals and groups in actual political systems. More attention to the interdependence of ideas and behavior under varying political conditions directs and seeks to restore to ideas their proper importance. Ideas have independent effect on political life, but this can only be discovered by looking more closely at the conditions where this seems to have occurred. By working from assumptions that permit this possibility, we should be concerned not only with the analytical pattern of interaction between ideas and behavior in politics, but with the contextual quality of such interaction. The analysis of interaction in the highly diverse world we confront requires that the problem of analyzing ideology be considered in stages. The first might be how patterns of participation, influenced by personality and cultural factors, provide the *context* for ideological interaction.

Those who write ideologies and a good deal of the commentary on ideologies give little attention to contextual problems. Marx was a notable exception. His outline of the stages of transformation of societies provides a *longitudinal* context. Because ideologies are advanced in historical time and often in periods of historical stress, the time context is perhaps the most common one used to state how ideas and behavior are manifested in political situations. But it is also the most difficult one to deal with in precise, empirical terms. Elaborate records exist only since the invention of printing, and many early records are destroyed and unaccountably biased. Systematic records and large data pools date from the turn of the century. Hence, it is difficult to test theories about the interaction of ideas and behavior for earlier periods.

A second contextual problem in discussing ideology is the *level* of society of greatest concern. Traditional writing on ideology has been most concerned with leadership: how leaders use ideas to preserve their power, and how to justify central authority in political systems. Bachrach (1967) has suggested, for example, that democratic theory has been distorted in pluralist politics in order to defend and consolidate elites. A similar argument is made in Lowi's (1969) interpretation of the New Deal reforms in America, where values are seen as perpetuating political inequality while claiming the virtue of equalitarian principles. The elitist emphasis in the study of ideology has neglected the fact that group and individual behavior is shaped by ideas. Pluralism, for example, proceeds on the assumption that the principles and motives of interacting groups in society are equally acceptable in a political system—which then becomes a kind of marketplace for ideas. As more careful studies are done of groups like the American Medical Association or the National Rifle Association we find that these assumptions are often incorrect (Connelly, 1971).

The systematic study of politics enables us to approach the problem of levels of interaction with greater confidence than in the past. Survey research has added immensely to our understanding of how citizens view their governments. Small group studies tell us much about the transmission of ideas in face-to-face situations. Organizational theory and case studies provide a wealth of information about the values of larger collectivities in the political system. The study of communications has almost become a separate discipline and is closely-related to how ideas, as well as opinions and information, are shaped and transformed in transmission. Behavioral research has made a contribution to our understanding of the relationships between ideas and behavior which cannot be ignored. Most important is an understanding that the level of interaction itself makes a substantial difference in how ideas will influence action. The easy assumption that elites manipulate ideas, which, in turn, assigns all other members of the political system to an ambiguous and often ineffective category of "mass" is no longer acceptable. People interact in a number of settings—their families, their jobs, their communities, and their political institutions. Ideas and behavior are not expressed and reconciled identically at these various levels of activity. The behavioral persuasion may be remiss for trying to hold ideas and values constant, though this is hardly uniformly the case nor is it equivalent to saying that values are irrelevant. But behavioral studies have also added immeasurably to our ability to understand how ideas affect behavior in the diverse settings that exist in every society.

A third contextual problem in the analysis of ideologies and their effects on people is *comparative*. Until the end of the nineteenth century, ideologies were generally analyzed in the European context and only as part of the Western cultural and philosophical tradition. Comparisons among ideologies were most often made along a left-right spectrum based largely on the formal content of the ideology. Thus, ideologies were considered alike or similar largely in relation to their intentions to promote change, to favor displaced classes, and to redistribute power. While the liberal ideology prevailed in Europe, roughly from the French Revolution until World War I, comparing ideologies was not too difficult. All the recognized nations of the world were industrializing, and the Concert of Europe was the limit of most analysts' interests. Two factors generated interest in comparing how ideologies relate to behavior, the rise of Marxism, and the spread of nationalism to the Third World.

Marxism introduced a number of new assumptions about the effects of ideology on people. These views could be tested by observing the conditions and mentality of workers.

Moreover, Marxists were intensely involved with the application of their ideology to the industrial nations of Europe. Having constructed an ideology with longitudinal characteristics, they wanted to know if a socialist society might first emerge in Germany, Britain, or elsewhere. As indications of deep unrest in Russia appeared, they were perplexed by the implications of an essentially industrial ideology emerging in a peasant society. Socialist ideas also appealed to the growing nationalist movements of the Third World and began to be interpreted in relation to the diverse cultural and historical circumstances of these countries. The early nationalist leaders came in contact with Marxists in European capitals and universities, and naturally found the Marxist critique of capitalist power harmonious with their goals.

Trying to compare how ideas affect behavior, then, was by no means simply a scholarly pastime. The emergence of fascism showed that, under some conditions, the oppressed were as fervently nationalist as were the privileged. In 1914, the German Social Democrats voted to support the Kaiser's war. In Britain, Joseph Chamberlain was able to arouse workers to vote for conservative, Tory policies. In America, the strong anti-capitalist strain in the Populist movement was subdued. Marxism provided a new stimulus for the comparative analysis of ideology by highlighting how diverse might be the institutional, social, and psychological conditions confronting an ideology. New explanations were needed that more explicitly took these conditions into account. Lenin revised Marxism to explain the dominance of a party vanguard in Russia. The Webbs devised a pragmatic view of socialism that looked to internal reform and local control to foster socialism in Britain. Michels (1959) surveyed socialism on the continent and concluded that the oligarchic tendencies in political organizations made the implementation of new policies and the diffusion of power impossible.

The purpose of this book, then, is not to analyze the ideas raised by socialism, fascism, or liberalism in the abstract or as purely philosophical questions, but to examine how we might understand the interdependence of ideas and behavior in political life. To do this one cannot avoid the distinctions noted thus far. The historical circumstances surrounding the introduction of new ideas affects outcomes. The level of society with which one is most concerned affects the concepts and evidence that one uses to evaluate ideology. The comparison of ideas and behavior across nations is basic to understanding how both temporal and structural forces influence the manifestation of ideological goals and principles. These are the three major contextual problems in the analysis of ideology.

SOME PROBLEMS

I have hitherto advanced no definition of ideology, but have only attempted to sketch the kinds of problems an understanding of ideology involves. Much analysis is done of ideas or behavior in isolation, but relatively little of how they interact, especially at the level of political systems. Political thought has concerned itself with the first, and the general study of political institutions with the second. Political thought tends to omit the ways people actually use ideas, while institutional studies often take political ideas for granted. The possibility of joining these two endeavors arises in large measure from the impact of other disciplines on political science. Psychology has had an increasing influence on political analysis since Lasswell, and studies of political identity, confidence, and motivation have now become commonplace. Anthropology has also begun to study more complex societies, and its concepts and theories have been widely introduced into politics in order to understand changes in the Third World.

In conjunction with the multiplication of comparative political studies (much of it under the shadow of psychocultural theories), political analysis can now bring to bear on the ways in which ideas and behavior interact more powerful concepts and a vast range of findings. Although each discipline continues to have its disputes over theory and concepts, enough has been learned so that the analyst of ideology need no longer be caught in the dichotomy of ideas and behavior. The application of the same idea over time does indeed produce widely differing results. Whether advanced by an individual or a group, ideas vary in their acceptance, persuasiveness, and clarity. In political systems, they are filtered and screened against the background of experience and expectations of the society. One of the first tasks of comparative politics is to improve our understanding of how this process of reconciliation and reaction to ideas takes place in existing societies.

On the other hand, political science would be misled into adopting a narrowly conceived behavioral approach. Concern with justice, equity, and virtue is found among the people of every nation, and every political system makes its moral overture to citizens. The legitimacy of nations rests on achieving some acceptable overlap between the leaders' purposes and the citizens' perceptions of these purposes. The support essential to the nation depends on the loyalty of people. The interdependence of experience and ideas constitutes the working relationship between people and their governments, and it is with the nature of this relationship that this study will be primarily concerned.

The need to devise better approaches to the analysis of how ideas and behavior interact becomes especially apparent in studying developing countries, and this has certainly influenced my view of what the study of ideology might contribute to political science. To the majority of citizens in the Third World, the nation is little more than an idea, often only partially articulated and highly abstract. As the revolutions and violence testify, these people have severe difficulties attaching concrete, specific meanings to their image of a nation. Political institutions are often irresponsible, parties often behave erratically, and all along the ideological spectrum political leadership seems more interested in preserving power than in improving the lot of the ordinary man. An interest in the Third World underscores the way in which *both* ideas and the behavior change rapidly. At one moment, political ideas may influence behavior change in radical ways, and at other times political ideas become expedient solutions to specific problems. Neither ideas alone nor the concrete expressions of advancement will build a country. In more methodological terms, it is absurd to assume that only ideas *or* behavior has causal significance in political change. A more accurate and infinitely more complex view is that the process of shifting between these two concerns represents the central problem of ideological transformation in developing countries, and in the more industrial countries as well.

If this study underscores the psychocultural roots of ideological transformations in political systems, it is because political science has tended to emphasize the behavioral component. Starting from the early work of Lerner (1958) and Deutsch (1961) on development, attention has been focused on how various ecological dimensions of change relate to very general characteristics of the political system. When a nation achieves a given degree of literacy, for example, it also moves toward increased urbanization. These ecological interdependencies have told us a good deal about the overall behavioral contours of the developing nation, but the approach leaves little room for political ideas, nor does it pretend to anticipate how nations will manage to define their goals. The ecological approach to studying political change has been widely criticized—on the one hand, for using methods too simple to analyze the interdependence of socioeconomic change, and, on the other, for simplifying the notion of a political system beyond recognition. Both of these criticisms are correct, but neither attacks the most fundamental problem in understanding how ideas and behavior relate. Their interaction is not a *distributive* phenomenon, but a *structural* phenomenon.

The meaning of these terms can most easily be seen by thinking about the individual citizen's relation to the political system, although I shall later want to explore how similar relationships might be studied at various levels of collective activity. Having a certain degree of education, income, exposure to mass media, and the like, tell us virtually nothing about how citizens incorporate political values into their lives. At best, the ecological view tells us something about the potential limits of interaction by tracing more explicitly how a range of political alternatives correlates with a range of socioeconomic conditions. By comparing nations, Cutwright (1963), for example, is able to show how the communications system of some nations is deficient. But the approach itself reveals little about the points at which ideologically rooted dislocations occur in society. Even if sufficient data were available, analysis of distributions would still tell us little about how tolerable these disparities might be to the individuals and groups concerned. Unless we can say something about how disparities between ideas and behavior are indeed reconciled for the person or group *within* the given political system, we can make only the crudest estimate of the independent effect of political ideas in that system.

A more precise way of stating this problem is to say that an analysis of the interaction of ideas and behavior needs to make some allowance for *intrasystem variations.* There seems to be little controversy over the statement that there is a great difference between allocating an increase in national income to a privileged elite or to an isolated peasantry. In this case, the structural difference is clear, although most ecological analysis lacks the necessary data to deal with these problems. Much more difficult and much more controversial are questions about the distribution of justice, political influence, and loyalty to government in a political system. The ecological response, which is adequate for some purposes, handles these questions by observing that the political system persisted (or did not persist) during the period studied. It cannot specify how "more" loyalty, participation, or confidence might have been achieved under the *same* conditions because the critical areas where ideas and behavior overlap for citizens are treated in residual form. There is some hypothetical floor to the influence of ideas. Below this point, the political system collapses, an unmistakable empirical demonstration of failure; and above this point, the variations in the process of relating ideas and behavior is ignored. Ecological analysis of political development will not tell us very much about the interaction of political ideas and behavior for a simple reason: it cannot.

A major advance over the ecological view is the analysis provided by cross-national surveys. The model proposed by Almond and Verba (1963) tried to deal with the structural problem of a citizen's perception of politics by distinguishing between the inputs and outputs of government. A person who is positively oriented to both support and benefit from government is defined as a "participant," a person positively oriented only to benefits is defined as a "subject," and a person who does not respond positively to either support or benefit is defined as a "parochial." This ingenious model permits structural variation among individuals, but not within the system. Thus, British and Americans *as a whole* display more confidence and understanding of their political systems than do other countries. Distinctions can be introduced to show the variations among perception of different levels of government. One of the most interesting findings in *Almond and Verba* (1963) is that differences in perception of local and national government are smaller in Britain than in the United States, a psychological analog to the federal system and the relatively strong local governments of the United States.

But survey methods are still basically distributive. Two political systems may display very similar overall characteristics when citizens are observed in the aggregate. The significance of these findings in assessing how ideas and behavior interrelate in the system, however, is vastly different if the proportion of disenchanted is equally mixed in the various regions or subnational units of authority or if it is concentrated in one place or around one issue. Attitudes toward politics are similar in absolute levels in Britain and the United States, but Britain encounters different conflicts over democratic values, projects these values in very different institutions and under very different circumstances. Nor are the bases of comparison entirely reliable because the requirements and services of governments vary. Education is a local responsibility in Britain, but about two-thirds of the money spent on education comes from the central government. Health is almost entirely in the hands of Parliament. The major utilities (steel, transport, and coal) have been nationalized for nearly twenty years. When an Englishman says he "understands" his government, he means something very different by government than would an American. These are structural differences in individual perception of politics that are hard to allow for in survey research.

Thus far, my approach has argued that the analysis of ideology, at least in comparative politics, should concentrate on the ways by which individuals and groups adjust to the differences between their ideas and their circumstances. Interaction of the kind discussed here ceases when politics becomes purely visionary or wholly determined by past experience. Given the immense variation in personalities, group interaction, and institutionalized behavior in every society, it seems unlikely that either of these limiting conditions could be identified even if they were to occur. In every society, one can point to persons and groups invoking the past and defending habitual behavior, just as one can also find persons and groups advocating new ideas and distrusting their past experience. Rather than dwell on the conventional dichotomy of ideas and behavior in politics, this study will examine how we might begin to trace the structural characteristics of the ways in which reconciliation takes place in various political systems. One of my concerns is that, unless political and social analysts provide some way of describing how ideas and behavior interact, we shall not establish the independent effects of ideas, or, more precisely, the shifting nature of our dependence on ideas as we act as individual citizens and as groups in political life. The transformation of ideologies seems to me to be fundamentally a psychocultural phenomenon, more relevant to the context of political life and participation in particular, than to the rationalization of authority in a specific, institutional form.

SOME
DEFINITIONS

The model will be illustrated and elaborated further in Chapter II, but the reader may more easily relate some of the arguments raised above to the traditional view of ideology if we first look at some of the recent alternative definitions of ideology, several of which reflect the same concerns that are found in my critique. The dictionary gives a broad definition: "the integrated assertions, theories and aims that constitute a sociopolitical program." There are two important points in this definition. An ideology has a programmatic quality, indicating that policies can be derived from its statements. It also represents in some measure an integrated set of statements such that political goals and political values acquire a coherent and consistent form. But, in applying this definition to political systems, there might still be difficulties. Would one wish to consider the capricious and often ruthless political code of Stalinist Russia an ideology? Stalin's policies were influenced by such profound suspicions that—at least in the closing years of his rule—they could hardly be called a program. Likewise, the Nazi ideology in its most severe form would eliminate many of the distinctions of this definition, as Arendt (1958) has argued. One might also argue that the liberal ideology by virtue of its permissiveness and disconnected quality, especially in outlining a program for society, falls short of this definition.

A definition that appears to have more utility in explaining participation comes from Gould (and Kolb, 1964: 315): "Ideology is a pattern of beliefs and concepts (both factual and normative) which purport to explain complex social phenomena with a view to directing and simplifying sociopolitical choices facing individuals and groups." Gould makes explicit the individual and group reference of ideology. He incorporates the notion of choice affecting the whole society, but adds that the version of choice contained in ideology is condensed and simplified. Another important addition is that ideology contains both factual ideas—i.e., cognitive and logical elements—as well as normative ideas—i.e., moral and emotional elements. It is the simplification of social and political complexity which seems to be the special quality of ideological statements, and which appears crucial in understanding participation. Large populations do not reflect similar emphasis on the cognitive and affective dimensions of an ideology, nor do they apply these elements identically in different situations. Whether one is referring to an emergent political system or an industrial society, some sort of generalized scheme about the political system can be found. Indeed, Geertz (1964: 63-64) calls ideology a "schematic image of social order."

Johnson's definition (in Sills, 1968: 71) is more conventional in its highlighting of the possible distortions arising from ideologies. He defines ideology as "selected or distorted ideas about a social system or a class of social systems where these ideas purport to be factual, and also carry a more or less explicit evaluation of the 'facts.' " I shall return to the problem of ideological distortion in the discussion of Mannheim below, but it may suffice for the moment to note that the degree of factual distortion depends very much on how firmly one believes factual truth can be established. Emphasis on distortion seems to arise in ideological analysis when one accepts the possibility of scientific truth and then assumes that it can serve as a meaningful measure of how political systems operate. A number of questions might be raised about whether this view is itself an accurate account of scientific truth. Scientists have very lively debates over their own objectivity, and the history of science suggests that the same facts take on very different meaning, even within a "scientific" framework, when viewed by different investigators (Kuhn, 1962; Bridgman, 1959). More important, the distortion view tends to minimize the importance of psychological variables in any schematic version of how society makes choices or establishes its goals.

More psychological emphasis is found in Erikson's view of ideology, which he sees as a problem of religious and scientific as well as political thought. He defines ideology as "the tendency at a given time to make facts amenable to ideas, and ideas to facts, in order to create a world image convincing enough to support the collective and individual sense of identity" (Sills, 1968: 82). Like most psychologists, Erikson recognizes that there is some sort of exchange going on between facts and ideas as personalities and groups respond to both internal needs and situations. He avoids the dichotomization of facts and values by accepting the existential nature of the problem. To the prejudiced, Jewish inferiority or black shiftlessness is a "fact," and highly elaborate theories claiming scientific validity have been assembled to explain these "facts." Such ideas become part of an individual's schematic sense of reality just as firmly as does the law of gravity. They have both affective and cognitive significance to the individuals and groups adhering to them. Erikson is closer to the theory of ideology advanced here in his emphasis on analyzing how people make the shift between facts and ideas, rather than starting from the view that either can be satisfactorily isolated in human experience in order to define and study the other.

Shils (1968: 67) has provided what is perhaps the most complete definition of ideologies, calling them one form of "comprehensive patterns of cognition and moral beliefs about man, society and the universe in relation to man and society." He feels that ideologies are more specific than "creeds" or "outlooks," which he might attach to pluralist thinking. He also feels that ideologies convey schematic versions of society more insistently and more programatically than what he calls "systems of thought and movements." The distinguishing feature of ideologies in Shils' mind seems to be the generation of emotional intensity, although his list of ideological qualities goes well beyond the affective element of patterns of belief. He speaks of the ideology's explicitness of formulation, the intended integration of the political system around moral or cognitive beliefs, acknowledged affinity with the past or contemporary conditions, receptivity to novel elements, imperativeness attached to observe certain forms of conduct, the authority of promulgation, and association with an organization intended to realize the pattern of beliefs. How these qualities relate to each other, or may place limits on each other, is not discussed; although the implication is that, as emotional intensity along any of these dimensions increases, it will increase for all other dimensions as well. Many of the propositions that might be derived from this typology could, of course, be tested, and some suggestions in this direction will be made in later chapters of this book.

Shils' list of the elements of an ideology raises one of the most difficult problems in attaching psychological concepts to political behavior and participation. Though it is not explicit in his listing, the implication is that emotional insecurity or attraction would operate in the same direction along all or most of these elements. The better-articulated ideology would be more open to novelty, openness to novelty would diminish authoritativeness of promulgation; less emphasis on an authoritative source would, in turn, encourage flexibility in devising institutions. A person who had a positive emotional response to one of these elements in an ideology might be supposed to be positively attracted to an emotionally consistent position on other elements. This is consistent with a Freudian view of emotion which has influenced our thinking about how the transference and projection of feelings takes place. Similar reasoning can be found in the analysis of more remote objects of feeling, such as the political system. *The Civic Culture* (Almond and Verba, 1963), for example, assumes that those responding positively to local and national government indicate more attachment to the system in question than does a positive feeling toward one of these objects.

There are a number of reasons why this assumption about individuals should not be uncritically extended into analysis of political systems. In Third World countries, a chronic difficulty is that more emotional attachment is directed to subnational groups. Sunni Muslims' quarrel with Sufi Muslims; Punjabis suspect Bengalis; Kachin tribesmen distrust

Buddhist rulers, and so on. Political events and leaders are remote from most citizens, and one can doubt if emotional attachments take this undirectional form. In fact, ideologies try hard to adapt to the emotional ties of a population. Marx's notariety in no small part stems from his attack on organized religions. Nassar, Boumediene, and Ayub all took pains to show that their ideological positions were not inconsistent with Islam. In industrial nations, ideologies generally avoid statements about families except for bland approval of the virtues of home and hearth. Where highly emotional relationships do enter directly into ideology, as in the case of Nazi view of the family, this tends to occur only where very intense emotions can be successfully attached to politics.

In trying to analyze the psychological and cultural roots of ideology, it is important to keep in mind that political systems are very distant from citizens. Intense feeling is aroused only in fairly specific situations and over fairly specific issues. There are immense differences in intensity and persistence between emotional responses to family, friends, and community, and to elites and parties. How ideologies respond to basic emotional ties is, of course, important in their acceptance and rejection, but the position taken in this study is that there has been too easy generalization about emotion and politics. While ideologies require emotional approval, in practice there are differences in the emotional intensity aroused and in the degree of consistency expected as they are translated into political action. At least one study, done in Boston (Levin, 1962), indicates that citizens may even feel negatively oriented toward their local governments while retaining positive feelings toward the national government.

The definitions of ideology have raised a number of points that are central in my approach to understanding ideological transformations. The individual and group response has both emotional and cognitive content. Ideologies have a programmatic aspect, which with varying degrees of insistence and conformity, adherents press into action. Ideologies help men see the relationships between themselves and more remote frameworks—their country, their world, and their universe. Ideologies are a way of dealing with the complexity of the political and social environment, often giving the citizen an acceptable simplification of processes and people he has neither the time nor the ability to observe firsthand. Ideologies are an important source of what Erikson has called "psychosocial identity," enabling the citizen to discover complementarities between his personality and the various roles he performs, especially in political relationships. Ideologies are, in Shils' phrase, a justification of "transcendant authority" in society.

Ideologies have a good deal to say, then, about how citizens should behave, and the behavior of citizens provides a measure of how widely an ideology is accepted. Ideology could be analyzed in either of these more static versions, prescriptive or descriptive. Another way of looking at ideology, and the one pursued here, is that it is the range of adjustment possible in a political system that is most important to specify. The detailed formulation of appropriate behavior, in Nazism, for example, means that behavioral complexities are rigidly and forcefully excluded. The permissive, flexible acceptance of diverse behavior in, for example, liberalism obscures the direct manifestation of ideology. As noted above, I shall be most concerned with the *interaction* of our ideas and behavior in politics, in part because the logical extremes of this relationship seem to me to be relatively easy to identify and have effects that are relatively easy to anticipate. It is through the study of the changing relationship over time, among levels of political and social activity, and across nations that we may learn about ideological transformations. To dogmatically transform an ideology into behavior is not too interesting a problem, and sufficient terror can accomplish this goal. On the other hand, an intricate pattern of authority, political or otherwise, that did not generate some abstract ideas about its origins, justification, and purpose would hardly be imaginable. My own view is that men in the modern world will all have and need ideologies. How we reconcile and change these two "realities" is my central problem.

Thus, when I speak of ideological transformation in this study, I shall not be referring to either political ideas or behavior alone, but to the ways in which they appear to be interdependent. What behavioral research has shown about such interdependence can be useful in helping us understand how ideologies affect action in more remote settings, such as the political system. If in the course of passing a message around a room, its meaning is radically changed, what then happens when messages are sent from London to Piddinghoe or from New Delhi to Bisapur? If children with aggressive tendencies moderate their behavior in more democratically oriented groups, how then does the citizen adjust to the participatory injunctions of democratic elections? If productivity falls where workers feel alienated and distrustful of their employers, what then does this teach us about apathy toward government itself? The range and complexity of human reactions established by behavioral inquiry should caution us in making any simple models about the interaction of ideas and behavior in political systems. Above all, the accumulated research tells us not to convert our theories and concepts into simple measures, though much conventional writing on ideology uses measures that would be totally unacceptable in systematic research. The fact that individuals and groups can be threatened, coerced, and fooled into approving certain ideas is hardly novel, nor does it require very sophisticated analysis to figure out how to make ideas dominant in this sense. If the framework selected for assessing the nature of the interaction of ideas and behavior is crude, our conception of the significance of ideas is likely to be crude as well. The restoration of ideology as a proper and crucial element in our understanding of political life, in my view, requires recognition of the complexity and diversity of men themselves. Ideological conviction has neglected behavior, just as enthusiasm for a more precise understanding of behavior has neglected ideas.

REFERENCES

ALMOND, G. and S. VERBA (1963) The Civic Culture. Princeton: Princeton Univ. Press.

ARENDT, H. (1958) The Origins of Totalitarianism. New York: Meridian.

BACHRACH, P. (1967) The Theory of Democratic Elitism: A Critique. Boston: Little, Brown.

BRIDGMAN, P. W. (1959) The Way Things Are. New York: Viking.

CONNELLY, W. E. [ed.] (1971) The Bias of Pluralism. New York: Atherton.

CUTWRIGHT, P. (1963) "National political development." Amer. Soc. Rev. 28: 253-268.

DEUTSCH, K. (1961) "Social mobilization and political development." Amer. Pol. Sci. Rev. 55 (September): 493-514.

GEERTZ, C. (1964) "Ideology as a cultural system," in D. Apter (ed.) Ideology and Discontent. New York: Free Press.

GOULD, J. and W. L. KOLB (1964) A Dictionary of Social Science. New York: Free Press.

KUHN, T. S. (1962) The Structure of Scientific Revolutions. Chicago: Univ. of Chicago Press.

LERNER, D. (1958) The Passing of Traditional Society. New York: Free Press.

LEVIN, M. B. (1962) The Alienated Voter: Politics in Boston. New York: Holt, Rinehart & Winston.

LOWI, T. J. (1969) The End of Liberalism. New York: W. W. Norton.

MICHELS, R. (1959) Political Parties. New York: Dover.

SILLS, D. [ed.] (1968) International Encyclopedia of the Social Sciences. New York: Macmillan and Free Press.

Chapter II

IDEOLOGY: INDEPENDENT OR DEPENDENT FACTOR?

In the language of social science, the distinction between dependent and independent factors or variables is basic. Independent factors are those conditions, characteristics, or events which can be shown to have regular relationships to human activity more often than would occur by chance. The factors used to describe whatever activity is being investigated are dependent. This method of reasoning is by no means unique to social scientists with carefully controlled experiments in human behavior. In somewhat looser form, the attempt to think systematically influences all our analysis of society and history. Thus, Moore's (1966) magnificent analysis of the emergence of totalitarian and democratic regimes over long periods of historical change employs a very simple theory, but one of very great scope in terms of its transferability from one society to another. He argues that in those societies undergoing rapid socioeconomic change, the formation of durable links between the preindustrial elite and the new middle class "explains" whether democratic or total-itarian forms of government resulted. A workable coalition between the main beneficiaries of industrialization, the bour-geiousie, and the aristocratic survivors of an earlier age tends to postpone and inhibit wider participation.

Moore's theory is essentially a class theory with the form of government the dependent factor and the coalition of classes the independent factor. Thus, in Britain, the new merchant and banking community overthrew the Stuart monarchs and with the help of a professional soldier, Crom-well, tried to establish a middle-class dominance. The British Restoration of 1660 institutionalized the dependence of the monarchy and the various immunities of the House of Commons (Hill, 1961). In the Meiji Restoration, on the other hand, the Japanese reformers drew back from a full-scale institutional renovation, and many traditional forces re-mained at work in Japanese society, the Emporer retained his supernatural status, and the industrial and bureaucratic leaders from the new middle class insulated themselves against further change toward more participation (Ward, 1968). There is no easy formula for extracting the signifi-cance of ideas in either of these complex historical situations, but it can be argued that in both instances the ideological transformation was consistent with the way that new class linkages appeared. In the Putney debates and constitutional experiment in Britain, liberal thought developed, later to be formed into an intricate system of analysis by Locke and Hume. In the less open, but no less intense, controversy following the Tokugawa regime, the Japanese leaders decided to revive a number of elements from Shintoism and to strengthen Emporer worship.

Class-based theories tend to minimize the independent effects of ideas, saying that classes adopt those ideas that best serve their self-interest. The restructuring of political thought tends to become a consequence of class conflict and a power struggle between materially defined interests. The Classic statement of this position in contemporary social science is Lipset's (1960: 97-178) interpretation of extremism of the left and right. The oppressed and the privileged share a common pattern of thinking, the poor because they wish to make a claim on society and the rich because they wish to preserve their claim on society. In this line of reasoning, ideas tend to become a residual element. An ideology is devised to relieve both the feelings of threat among the elite and the feelings of deprivation among the outcasts. The Nazi experience added to the credibility of this theory, Hitler himself being an outcast of German society who managed to ally himself with the industrial and social elite of the country. The Nazi party in its early stages drew heavily on the unemployed, desperate "lumpenproletariat" of German cities (Neumann, 1942). But there is also evidence that Nazism had strong middle-class support as well and that many substantial citizens found Nazi ideas attractive (Dahrendorf, 1967: 386-411).

The Nazi example is important in helping clarify how the contextual issue, raised in Chapter I, influences whether or not we see ideas as independent factors in political systems. If one analyzes Nazism longitudinally, in terms of its origins and seizure of power, the ideas seem to be the result of disenchantment and despair at the upper and lower fringes of society. If one examines the levels of German society, it appears that the ideology was embraced with a consistency that suggests it influenced Germans to behave in a brutal fashion regardless of their interests and earlier convictions, thus having some independent effects that could be attributed to the ideology. If one takes another step back and investigates authoritarian appeals in the depression across nations, the result is at best mixed. Mussolini fashioned a fascist coalition in Italy that was successful, while in France the fascist maneuverings of the Croix de Feu were repulsed by a Common Front under Blum and in England the Mosleyites remained a lunatic fringe and never came close to taking power. Each of these explanations deserves more investigation, but the immediate point is that the context in which one sets out to explain the interaction of ideas and behavior influences whether or not ideas will appear to have

independent effects. To say, as I will, that *both* independent
and dependent effects may be observed is not an evasion, but
a recognition of the complexity of the problem.

   At the root of most discussions of ideas and action are two
fundamental problems. These problems could no doubt be
traced back in political thought, but this is not the aim of
this study, though they are certainly of classical dimensions.
The first is how individual identity can be manifested in
social and political organization, most clearly reflected in
Marx's thought. Marx was much less interested in political
activity or, in the strict sense, political ideas than in the
nature of man's relationship to social order. How power was
perceived, how political relationships might be explained, and
even how to build political institutions were to him secondary problems. In fact, he wrote relatively little about politics
as we think of it except for his statements and advice to
European socialists, which must be interpreted in light of
how he saw economic forces impinging on social problems at
that time. What he saw as practical politics comes largely
from later commentary of Engels and, of course, from the
bitter disputes that raged among socialist thinkers since the
turn of the century. But at the root of Marx's thinking is how
individual and social identity come into focus, a problem
which contemporary society has by no means resolved, and
which might be restated as whether the individual or society
have independent effects in the interaction of ideas and
experience.

   A second and equally formidable problem connected to
the analysis of ideology is the effect of scientific knowledge
on men's ability to control their destiny in both their individual and collective choices. If ideas have a logic that escapes
human control and human values, then the question of the
interaction of ideas and behavior becomes meaningless. My
own view has already been suggested above and is drawn
from the very interesting work that has been done on the use
of paradigms and the nature of discovery in science. The
problem is basically that described in the sociology of knowledge literature, though the use of "sociology" in this context

may itself prejudge the question. The political thinker commonly associated with our ability to use ideas to influence social and political life is Mannheim (1936). While I make no pretense of solving the intricate philosophical problem of the nature of ideas, the discussion of how ideas and behavior interact must recognize the problem, and how one makes assumptions concerning it will strongly influence the more specific issue of this study.

WHO WINS:
MAN OR SOCIETY?

Given the massive output of Marx in his lifetime, it is not surprising that each person can find pretty much what he wishes in Marx's thought. A good deal of his writing has not been translated into English. In addition, his work touched a chord which struck a number of nineteenth-century concerns, and so this aspect of his writing has no doubt been exaggerated. The ideas of social class and materialism weighed heavily on the minds of nineteenth-century political leaders and the rapidly growing middle class of the first nations to industrialize. The popular version of Marx generally ignores that his observations on class and materialism were a consequence of a much more profound philosophical analysis of how man and society interact. In this inquiry, Marx was primarily concerned with the individual and how his thought unfolds rather than the collectivity and how it imposes constraints on men. Marx never claimed to have discovered socialism, which began with the classical philosophers. What he did do was to give us a radically new perspective on how individuals deal with their sociopolitical environment. Joining his thoughts about man to social action was a subsequent, and to him a logical, sequence to his analysis of man himself.

Avineri (1968) sees Marx's thought growing out of his early reading of Hegel and argues that it changed relatively little from these early conclusions. Like the utilitarians, Marx objected to the separation of civil society from the state. By postulating the state as a separate concept from society, Hegel concluded that man's identity with sovereignty was the critical step in relating ideas to political action. Marx inverted Hegel by arguing that the political state—that is, civil society—precedes the "real" state, or organized authority in society. For Hegel, civil society is "material" and the state is "spiritual" so that man's attempt to link himself to the state becomes a wholly intellectual task. Marx reversed this argument, saying that man cannot be conceptually divorced from his social context. The liberal state tries to bridge this gap in a particular way, which Marx felt would not succeed, but this is a second step in his reasoning.

Marx was, of course, very close to the contemporary view of how social systems should be viewed. There are only relative advantages and disadvantages to different kinds of social and political organization, at least until man finds the state no longer necessary. But the focal point for Marx is very much man's development. Avineri (1968: 33) describes this by observing that Marx made society into the predicate rather than the subject of the state. The activities that men engage in can be observed and felt without the state. Interaction is a reliable and real phenomenon even without political order and authority. The political system, which was not a major concern for Marx, comes out as a dependent factor generated in different ways in different kinds of society. In the realm of experience, there was no monopoly of political virtue, but a series of historical steps toward a society where authority would not be needed. In each of these stages, men's ideas were pitted against society in a characteristic way. But the dynamic element in this tension was the division of the private from the public self, an individual and not a social condition. Socialism was the final stage in this dynamic, historical process that would relieve the tension between man's self-image and society. In Marxian thought, the tension disappears not because one or the other set of factors dominates, but because the problem itself no longer exists in a truly socialist society.

Capitalist society represents the situation Marx saw in the nineteenth century, and it is in the consideration of the dislocation between men's potential and existing conditions that Marx introduces most of the notions used to describe his thought today. But here again Marx has been widely misinterpreted. If property were indeed as immovably determining as often represented in ordering society, then Marx's own socialist vision would be precluded. Marx felt that the alienation of man from his conditions took a peculiar form in capitalist society, not that the feeling of isolation was unique to capitalist society. Avineri (1968: 47) calls this the imposition of an "anonymous arbitrator" between man and society and notes that Marx's logic led him to reject Mazini's valiant struggle to unite the Italian petty states. But it is the divorcing of ideas and action in the capitalist state that makes the uncontrollable, and eventually oppressive, state apparatus necessary. The state is, of course, only an adjunct of a social system based on property, and it is for this reason that the state as we think of it today was secondary in Marx's framework. The political system could only be a phantom force protecting those holding economic power, but not *because* economic power created the abuse of power. The disparity between man's potential and his present state originates in the alienation that comes inescapably from a society based on property.

Naturally, those receiving a disproportionate share of the society's surplus will use the state, and any other mechanism, to protect their privileges. Marx never denied self-interest; he claimed that as an organizing principle of society it cannot work. It is at this point that he departs from the utilitarians and from liberal apologists such as Weber (Gerth and Mills, 1947: 196-266) since that time. To Marx, the bureaucracy was the political expression of the division of labor, almost the exact opposite of Weber's argument that bureaucracy made possible the impartial, uniform application of authority. The strength of the bureaucracy was one of the few indicators of the need for revolution that Marx provided. In Britain and the United States, a less powerful bureaucracy might not obstruct the transition to a socialist society, but more highly bureaucratic states might require revolution. This is not too far removed from Moore's argument that where the preexisting elite manages to ally itself with the new middle class, of which the bureaucracy is a major part, the political system will tend to become totalitarian. Through the bureaucracy, the state becomes the "anonymous arbitrator" of society and the instrument of the capitalist elite.

Man's struggle to reconcile himself to the anonymity imposed on him by the capitalist economy has a dynamic quality not unlike the notion of how ideas and behavior interact advanced in this study. In a truly socialist society, however, the tension between the inescapable inequalities of society and the individual's perception of society is totally relieved. The search for consistency between thought and action ceases in what Marx calls the commonwealth. How do men achieve this ideal state of affairs? In a society released from material inequality, the disparity between what men find about them and the assertion of universality of their values disappears. In the victory of the proletariat the opposition of the classes ends, not because some forseeable institutional changes and psychological transformation takes place, but because the clash of these two problems no longer exists. For Marx the socialist society represented neither the emergence of "pure intellect" nor the acceptance of some ideal form of behavior. Indeed, he provided very little description of a socialist society because in the framework of social action he envisaged this was not a serious problem and in the logic of his theory such a description could not be provided.

Thus, class consciousness as defined by Marx is widely misinterpreted in the popular mind. Workers could only begin to transform capitalist society by becoming aware of their oppression, but the outcome of this new awareness was not carefully described. The emancipation from a class-ridden society, however, placed the same demand on the proletariat that it does on the privileged. Awareness makes class unnecessary as a principle of social organization and as a way of calculating self-interest. Avineri (1968: 65-95) points out that Marx's economic values are derived from a humanist belief that man changes nature, and that cognition can shape reality. The socialist society is the analog at the collective level of Kant's view of the virtuous individual, being able to will that one's values become universal. Achieving this ideal state of affairs depends on the awareness of the existing class, the proletariat, which does not need its opposite in order to define its existence. But, in a capitalist society, the proletariat risks corruption just as much as the middle and upper classes. The notion that material self-interest only misleads the elite is incorrect, for it can also prevent the worker from achieving the awareness that is prerequisite to building a socialist society.

One does not need to look too closely at the AFL-CIO or the British T.U.C. to find that awareness among workers has had much difficulty reconciling society to Marx's universalism. The important point for this analysis is that the reconciliation of man and his environment that Marx foresaw does not entail a strict, behaviorist position. In capitalist society men were conditioned and coerced by their environment, their inequality, and their state, but a socialist society is posited on the liberation of men from such conditioning. Such conditioning would, in Marx's view, never disappear in capitalist society. In fact, it would become more acute, because such a society needed cooperation in production, while denying mutuality in the use of the products of cooperation. Though not central to understanding how ideas and behavior relate in Marx's thinking, resolving the contradiction in the productive system of society is critical to Marx's analysis and explains why he gave such great attention to the labor theory of value. For Marx it was not too difficult to explain how materialism distorts society, and Avineri points out that Marx actually wrote very little on materialism as such. What was critical to his theory was to show how socioeconomic organization could escape the dilemma of capitalist production and avoid the increasing alienation of the workers from this mode of production.

Looking at some of the specific views of Marx helps us understand how ideas and activity might be reconciled. He supported the cooperative movement and the Homestead Act because they diminished the importance of property in the determination of choice. However, he opposed the nationalization of industry because in a capitalist society this would only transfer the concentration of economic power to a new elite and enhance the ability of the elite to use labor surplus to reinforce the state. Precisely this argument has been used to criticize the effects of nationalization in Britain (Kelf-Cohen, 1958), and the state corporation managers are more often than not simply the capitalist owners in state positions. The same reasoning led Marx to conclude that terror must not be used to achieve a socialist society, which is why he denounced the Jacobins. In the revolutions of 1848 he opposed attempts at armed uprising, and during the Paris Commune of 1871 he congratulated the leaders on avoiding terror. A socialist state is not the same as a socialist society. An effort to build a socialist society through political coercion would fail just as surely as an attempt to redistribute the product of society under capitalist structures. Most important, both these measures would delay the emergence of class consciousness and, hence, prevent men from discovering a truly socialist solution to reconcile their individual and social problems.

Marx's concern with economic theory, then, is a consequence of his analysis of how men manifest their ideas. In this respect, Marx has more profound psychological implications than economic implications, and his view of perception and motivation is not inconsistent with the approach advanced in my view of ideology and political change. His humanism resisted the notion that ideas were wholly determined by conditions, but he accepted the conditioning of ideas that occurs in societies where men are divorced from the product of their labor. Whether or not one accepts his dialectic for the discovery of a socialist society does not affect the analysis of how self-awareness and social responsibility interact. The French Revolution marks the creation of tension between civil society and the state, not its resolution. The political rights and dignity acquired under democratic government are a step toward a similar transformation of economic rights and obligations. Bourgeois society is an essential step toward full self-realization in a socialist society. When self-awareness can be extended from the political realm to the socioeconomic realm, a classless society will be possible, and the state, now the bulwark of the capitalist elite, will no longer exist. Thus, the logical consequences of Marx's analysis of man and society are clear, and by no means the key ideas in his theory. The essential dynamic is the struggle to manifest ideas by shaking off habits and the constraints of an unjust economic order, a notion that is entirely consistent with much contemporary psychological theory.

Neither ideas nor conditions regularly dominate in Marx's analysis, but constantly shift. Circumstances differ in the stages of social development, and so the critical conditioning elements themselves change. Capitalist society is only one phase, characterized by economic exploitation and coercion, which seeks to counter-act self-realization among the oppressed. Likewise, the function of ideas changes with time, as do the possibilities of achieving a more satisfying concept of how ideas and circumstances may be reconciled. The political universalism of democracy can be extended to socioeconomic life only if the individual can free himself from his habits and develop sufficient self-awareness. This view of man is not too different from Maslow's categories of human needs which place self-realization very high, nor is it inconsistent with Erikson's (1963) theory of the transformation of personality through the stages of life. The theory of ideological transformation advanced in this study is, then, much the same as Marx's concern with how individuality and society are mutually changed, and shares Marx's view that the process of individual change must be given more emphasis if we are to understand how ideas are manifested in society.

WHO KNOWS:
SUBJECT OR OBJECT?

The rise of the modern nation was coincident with philosophical inquiries that destroyed the harmony between man and his universe found in classical and early Christian thought. While we cannot unravel this philosophical dispute in the limits of this study, the breakdown of the beliefs postulating universal values over man and nature produced the dilemmas now investigated under the rubric of the sociology of knowledge. The scientific revolution, and particularly the emergence of modern psychology, brought the laws of man and the laws of nature into opposition. With the discovery of laws about the physical universe, it was a short step to begin to find similar regularities about the social universe. Pure intellect no longer sufficed to uncover the truth about man, because man could indeed be considered in two very different ways.

With the destruction of classical harmony, it becomes most important to know, as Wirth notes in his preface to Mannheim (1936: xxii-xxiii), what man takes for granted and "the most elemental and important facts about a society are those that are seldom debated and generally regarded as settled." Fact and value, object and subject, interest and truth become relational problems in such a world, and how men define the relationship becomes central to understanding social and political order. The sociology of knowledge is the study of how individual and social conditions influence the discovery and acceptance of ideas, a problem that acquired central importance in politics with Marx, and that is the central theme of Mannheim. If interests, motives, and emotions put into doubt the validity of pure intellect, it follows that the beliefs and values incorporated in an ideology may reflect the distortions and untruths of the powerful or the dispossessed.

Mannheim felt that the rapid social change put in motion by the scientific and industrial revolutions intensified the conflict between thought and experience as they are translated into ideology. In his works (1936: 7), "social mobility . . . destroys the earlier illusion, prevalent in a static society, that all things can change, but thought remains eternally the same." The democratization of society elevated the aspirations and thoughts of the lower class to the importance once attributed only to priests, magicians, and Brahmins. Vertical mobility brought conflict about ideas into the open, and the "monopoly of the ecclesiastical interpretation of the world" was broken. Once a different set of assumptions or principles could be applied in studying thought and experience, the subject and the object, it was apparent that "the subject was by no means such a safe point of departure for the attainment of a new conception of the world as had previously been assumed" (Mannheim, 1936: 16). For Mannheim, the study of ideology, then, was very closely related to the general problem of the sociology of knowledge. The sociology of knowledge is the more general study of distortion of knowledge as objects present themselves to subjects in different social settings, while ideological investigations are concerned with "the process of individual self-clarification" (Mannheim, 1936: 47).

The relativity that Mannheim saw in the unfolding of knowledge and in the shaping of ideologies does not mean that he then abandons men to a willful, capricious subjectivity or to a rigid, arbitrary kind of social causality. He recognized that systematic inquiry of social and political problems was possible, but he explicitly rejected a simple positivist view. It would be a serious misinterpretation to classify Mannheim as a behaviorist. In discussing social inquiry, he writes (Mannheim, 1936: 18-19), "The interconnections of meaning . . . are not recaptured by a mere further perfection of formalization through the discovery of correlations and functions." Our understanding of ideology and the biases and distortions it may introduce into society is not likely to be furthered according to Mannheim by either the retreat into a pseudo-scientific approach to experience or into an attempt to resurrect the fiction of "the isolated and self-sufficient individual." His position is more sensible and more specific, suggesting that we learn more about how men acquire their political values through the study of political socialization and reference groups. In this way he anticipated what has indeed become a major area of social investigation, but he did not regard such investigation as a retreat from the continuing conflict of ideas and action in society.

Social inquiry can help us clarify how conditions influence our ideas, but it is in the continuing struggle itself that ideologies are tested and refined. In this respect, it would probably be fair to consider Mannheim (1936: 19) a social activist: "The most important role of thought in life consists, however, in providing guidance for conduct when decisions must be made." Man cannot escape making decisions involving good and evil, subjective desires and demonstrated needs, agreed truth and uncertain assumptions. In describing how ideas are shaped in conflict, Mannheim arrives at his now classic formulation of "ideology" and "utopia." The conflict between theory and politics is inescapable, just as, for Marx, the realization of the denial of universal values in capitalist society seemed inescapable. The interaction of decisions and political experience to reveal the true origins and intent of ideologies is an essentially Marxian element in Mannheim's thinking, a kind of intellectual dialectic that is found in every society. The interaction of politics and theory is twofold. On the one hand, those concerned with examining facts cannot be restricted by political necessity, and, on the other hand, crises affecting political life may determine the course of scientific and social investigation itself.

Developing a full awareness of an ideology, then, is handicapped by what Mannheim called "physical repression" and "psychic annihilation." The meaning of these terms can be seen in the early reactions to scientific learning itself which often became heresy and led to persecution. The interaction of power and knowledge continues in modern-day disputes over the proper use of nuclear discoveries, the huge data banks accumulated by governments, and use of drugs and narcotics. Decisions on problems such as these are the way that ideologies are unmasked and that the future search for knowledge is guided. Mannheim (1936: 38) felt that each encounter would produce a political struggle because "every theoretical refutation was gradually transformed into a much more fundamental attack on the whole life-situation of the opponent." He continued, "Basically it was in political struggles that for the first time men became aware of the unconscious collective motivations which had always guided the direction of thought." From the struggle there tend to develop two "slogans": the intensely interest-bound interpretation of the powerful who "are simply no longer able to see certain facts which would undermine their sense of domination," and the wishful thinking of the oppressed who are "so strongly interèsted in the destruction and transformation of a given condition of society that they unwittingly see only those elements in the situation which tend to negate it" (Mannheim, 1936: 40).

The phrases that Mannheim attached to the study of ideologies are not his most important contribution to political analysis. Both ideology and utopia suffer from common distortions, caused by the inability of the advocates of each to arrive at shared subjective and agreed objective meanings in their discussion of society. For Mannheim, the important question was how to achieve the "systematization of doubt" needed to penetrate the meanings and intentions of political opponents. Understanding how our social and individual experience influences the formulation of ideology was the key problem for Mannheim and explains his interest in the sociology of knowledge. Current ideological disputes were to him centered on "particular" and "total" views, and these distinctions do more to clarify the problems of understanding ideology than do the slogans commonly attached to his name, which are both "calculated attempts to dupe others to self-deception." His analysis of particular and total ideological viewpoints indicates how we might discover how ideas are "a function of him who holds them, and of his position in the social milieu" (1936: 64-70). Unlike many contemporary critics of ideology, Mannheim was not tempted to abandon the effort to understand how ideas are shaped in society, nor was he content to assign ideology to some vague, residual significance in social behavior.

As the term suggests, the particular notion of ideology considers only part of an opponent's ideology as distorted, while the total view condemns the opponent's entire *Weltanschauung* and reasoning. The particular conception of ideology emphasizes intentional distortion of ideas to accomplish specific purposes, and therefore tends to reduce to a psychology of interests. The total view of ideology considers the distortion of ideas a function of a historical epoch or entire intellectual perspective, much like Marx, leaving little room for variations in motivation and perception. By placing stress on the individual as the bearer of ideas, the particular notion underestimates the impact of social and historical circumstances on ideas, while the total conception sees the social group as paramount. The particular notion of ideology is, of course, similar to the liberal view of the conflict of ideas in society, and the total notion is derived, as Mannheim notes, from the German historical school of political thought. Mannheim argued that the two approaches to the use of ideas were themselves evolving, and that the study of ideology should be focused on the revelation of "false consciousness" which tends to perpetuate the exaggerations of both the subjective and objective excesses in current ideological interpretations.

The epistemology of the transformation of ideology goes beyond the scope of this study, but it should be noted that Mannheim, like Marx, saw the resolution of ideological differences taking place in political conflict itself. The analysis of the actual decisions of governments and the increasing participation of citizens make men aware of the ways in which ideas are being used. For example, Mannheim observes that it was Marx's attack on the utopian socialism of Simon, Owen, and Fourier that shifted socialist thinking away from extreme subjectivity and introduced a concern with social and historical conditions. Moreover, Mannheim felt that Marx pointed the way toward a fusion of the particular and total views of ideology by attaching "such decisive significance to political practice conjointly with the economic interpretation of events, that these two became the ultimate criteria for disentangling what is mere ideology from those elements in thought which are more immediately relevant to reality" (1936: 75). But his respect for Marx did not prevent Mannheim from seeing that Marxist thought is itself a total view, and must be scrutinized for the same excesses he found in most interpretations of ideas in society.

Mannheim's conclusions on the study of ideology as a process of interacting individual and social change is essentially the approach used in this book. He wrote, "The task of a study of ideology, which tries to be free of value-judgments, is to understand the narrowness of each individual point of view and the interplay between these distinctive attitudes in the total social process." It is important to understand the way in which he used "value-free." Mannheim (1936: 81) rejected *both* the purely subjective view of ideas as the product of intellect alone and the purely objective notion that scientific knowledge might isolate the truth about society. He attacked the positivists and, much like Mill, also rejected a methodological retreat to avoid the full complexity of understanding ideology. For him ideology was a function of subjective and objective elements of society in interaction. Through the study of political socialization, family practices, and reference groups, we might learn more about social influence on ideas, but these institutions are themselves changing. Through the examination of political conflict, the adaptation of the political system, and the decisions of authorities, we might learn more of how ideas are being used by men in power, taking into account the tendency of men in power to resist change and the tendency of men seeking power to induce change by distorting ideas.

Value-free, then, does not mean eliminating choice and expression from the study of society, but recognizing the complex process of interaction by which ideas are manifested in social and individual behavior. Ideology is transformed by social forces and by individual expression. For this reason,

Mannheim distinguished between what he called "relativist" and "relational" approaches to the study of ideology. The relativist treats an intellectual statement or a social condition as a determining factor in the analysis of ideas, while investigating how the remaining dependent factors may vary. The relationist considers neither intellect nor social conditions as independent factors, recognizing "that all of the elements of meaning in a given situation have reference to one another and derive their significance from this reciprocal interrelationship in a given frame of thought" (Mannheim, 1936: 86). Men are constantly redefining the meanings of terms, and society is constantly being restructured to attach new meanings to norms and values. There are multiple conceptions of reality, and each results in a distinct mode of thought. Had not the term "functionalist" become so replete with meanings, it might describe Mannheim's view of how ideology should be studied in a relationist context. It is the interdependence of subjective and objective meanings that is the proper study of ideology, which I have referred to above as the transformation of ideology. In the next section, I will propose a simple paradigm which may help in organizing our analysis of this process of interaction, though it hardly does justice to the refinements of Mannheim's approach.

CONGRUITY AND
IDEOLOGICAL TRANSFORMATION

In this section, I will present a paradigm to help us distinguish how individual and institutional expressions of political values are structured in political systems. Many of the assumptions relevant to such a paradigm have been raised in the discussion above of Marx and Mannheim. One of the most difficult problems in the transformation of ideas, which Marx saw clearly, is making citizens aware of the conditions limiting the expression of values in society. Whether or not one accepts a Marxian view of how these constraints are identified and operate in society, it is clear that institutions are constantly in the process of being redefined by their members and by society. An essential step in this process is developing consciousness of the conditions relevant to the institution in question. Black nationalism, for example, began when black people realized that the values of American institutions were applied very differently to different races. The rates of unemployment, the different levels of income, the disparities in educational opportunity are inescapable evidence of discrimination in institutions whose primary values rest on assertions of equality. There have been two processes at work in the redefinition of American political values. One is the emergence of an awareness among black people of the proportion of the injustice, and another is the restructuring of American society that made these disparities increasingly evident. There were, in Mannheim's context, both subjective and objective dimensions of the disparity. The first was brought about by Malcolm X (1964) in his appeal for dignity among blacks, and the second by the concentration of crime, misery, and human waste in central cities. The effects of racial discrimination became known at the levels of both individuals and institutions.

No one can deny that American values have been changed by the black nationalist movement. Schools are run differently, jobs are assigned differently, and voting procedures are changed. The value is the same in only the abstract, intellectual sense, but individual and collective behavior intended to manifest equality in American society has changed. The more important question that involves the transformation of American ideas is how to describe this change. One way to do so is to observe that the differences among individuals, black and white, and the differences among institutional norms have changed in the direction of greater congruence. Within American society individuals have enlarged their view of what constitutes individual dignity and freedom and institutional norms have also shifted in the same direction. Thus, it is correct to say that there is now more congruence between individual values and institutional norms in American society. Individual and institutional values are more evenly reflected in American society, in part because the behavioral disparities once subsumed under very similar primary values have been reduced.

Every political system has some congruence of behavior between individual values and institutional norms. If citizens and institutions were to be totally disparate in the manifestation of social and political values, there would be no observable polity. This idea has been most fully developed by Eckstein in this theory of stable democracy. Particularly in the realm of political values there is a high degree of congruent behavior throughout British society. The cabinet, the parliament, pressure groups, and voluntary associations display what Eckstein (1961) has called "isomorphic authority patterns." The British are remarkably agreed on how to behave in political situations, often noted in the high degree of deference accorded political leaders and public officials. But perhaps the crucial difference of British society is that it has been able to maintain congruence with respect to the exercise of power while imposing few stringent requirements on individuals and institutions in other respects. There are also a high degree of individual freedom and highly differentiated institutions. Though they may reflect British deference in their internal political relationships, they are not part of the central political hierarchy of the system.

However, it is important to recall that British society has not always reflected such agreement on how political values should be manifested. In the turbulence of the seventeenth century, monarchial rule and middle-class values came into direct conflict. The capriciousness of the Stuart monarchs in waging war, bestowing privileges, and raising taxes became increasingly unacceptable to the new bourgeousie concentrated in London. The Puritan revolution occurred when the values of the new commercial and professional class and the norms generated to pursue their activities in institutional form could no longer survive under monarchial rule. Hill (1961: 299) summarizes the effects of Cromwell's Commonwealth as providing the Englishman freedom "from arbitrary arrest, from taxation which he has not voted, from conscription, from government interference with his economic activity, from religious persecution." The reduction in Crown property, the diminished authority of the Established Church, the professionalization of the army, the independent legal status accorded firms and banks are the historical evidence of how individual values and institutional norms were brought into working alignment, largely under the influence of the new liberal ideology.

In the course of the seventeenth century, then, institutional norms and individual values regained shared behavioral meaning. Individual citizens found activity in institutions that met with their approval, and institutionalized behavior reflected norms that could be shared by a large proportion of British citizens. Restoring congruence was a two-directional phenomenon, and both individual values and institutional norms changed. Much of the coherence and eventual stability of this change came from the liberal ideology so eloquently expounded in the Putney debates and later formalized by Locke. Essential to an understanding of ideological transformation is the recognition that change takes place at two or more levels. In order that the new ideology could be manifested in Britain, there needed to be a change in *both* citizens and institutions, though the institutional dimension might be more highly differentiated. The failure to incorporate two levels of change in most attempts at analysis of ideological change has much to do with the mistaken impression that ideology is not relevant. Unless a comparison is made between the individual's perception of the ideology and the institutional reflection of the ideology, the significance of shared behavior cannot be assessed.

The problem can be considered either longitudinally or cross-sectionally. In terms of time, the congruent behavior linking individual values and institutional norms under a rubric called the "liberal ideology" has clearly changed in Britain. The ideology has been transformed by citizens becoming more active, the emergence of an industrial society, the growth of parliamentary institutions, and numerous other factors. British liberalism of 1660 is not British liberalism of 1832 or 1945. The same conclusion can be drawn from a cross-sectional analysis. Britain has an established church whose national significance appears in endless ceremonies, the school system, and the most basic local authority unit, the parish. At the institutional level the Church of England remains an important norm of British society, but at the individual level only about a third of British citizens attend the Church of England and roughly two-thirds claim membership. The situation in France is very different. The Catholic Church is an important institution in France, and almost nine-tenths of all Frenchmen consider themselves Catholics. However, even fewer attend Mass regularly than attend church in England and the deviance from church norms in France is proverbial. The difference between the institutional significance of religion and individual adherence to religious values is different in the two societies. Religious values are manifested differently in the two societies in terms of the congruence of behavior that can be attributed to them by individuals and by the basic institutions. Drawing conclusions from the institutional norms and individual values about religion in Britain and France lead to very different results. Whether France is more religious than Britain, or vice versa, depends on the way importance is attached to the observed disparities between norms and values.

The comparison, either longitudinal or cross-sectional, is one way of evaluating the significance of religious beliefs in the society, and the same comparative method can be used to evaluate political ideologies. Where substantial uniformity of individual values or institutional norms (or both) can be achieved, the direct manifestation of the ideology is increased. Thus, it should be recognized that achieving sufficient congruent behavior to support the political system where individual values or institutional norms *vary* is different from congruence under conditions of substantial uniformity. A hypothesis might be advanced that, where ideologies tend to reduce individual or institutional variance, there will be a reciprocal effect. This has been one of the tenets of liberal ideology, though there is considerable controversy over whether liberal democracy in highly industrialized societies fosters such diversity among individuals or institutions. It is also one of the arguments for individual freedom. Diverse individuals tend to support and to generate diverse institutions, providing numerous ways by which individual values and institutional norms may increase congruent behavior in the society. The entire theory of incremental decision-making rests on assumptions that such diversity exists, and the main virtue of the incrementalist view is that hundreds of small decisions in diverse organizations enhance the participatory capacity of the society and respond to diversity. Part of Mills' (1959) argument about institutions in modern society is that diversity is foreclosed and the chain of widespread decisions broken by men controlling very influential central institutions.

The major difference between liberal and totalitarian ideologies is the amount of variance permitted in achieving congruence. The Nazi regime, for example, used an immense propaganda machine to increase individual uniformity among individual values. Moreover, some of the most basic emotions and needs of personalities were aroused by exploiting anti-Semitism. To be a good Nazi meant to subscribe uniformly to a rigid set of values and norms. Where congruent behavior is so carefully described, neither individual choice nor institutional adaptation are acceptable means of bringing values and norms into a working relationship. Thus, it seems correct to argue that the important difference between liberal and totalitarian regimes is not necessarily the amount of control achieved by bringing values and norms into a mutually supporting relationship, but the tolerable variance permitted in the political system. There are numerous ways of describing the uniformity of totalitarian regimes, but it is the rigid limitations on how values and norms might interact in the political system that is rooted in the ideology. The totalitarian use of ideology ensures that political ideas will not be transformed by narrowly prescribing appropriate behavior for both individuals and institutions. The transformation of the ideology by individual leadership or social forces is precluded by such prescriptions.

One of the reasons political science has not been able to attribute independent significance to ideology is the excessive concern with the achievement of power and influence, which may in fact not differentiate among liberal, socialist, and totalitarian regimes in a meaningful way. Each may achieve sufficient congruence between values and norms to persist and even to encourage adaptation within the system. The critical difference is how much diversity of individuals and institutions is possible. Ideologies that advance theories of institutional infallibility reduce variance among norms. Likewise, ideologies exploiting individual insecurity and fear restrict the kinds of behavior that citizens may attach to political ideas. It is the tolerance of conflict, experimentation, and deviance among individuals and institutions that distinguishes ideologies. To maintain a political system under these conditions is a more difficult task than under rigidly uniform criteria of relevant behavior. So long as political science uses absolute measures the "power," Nazi Germany is much like France or Britain. But the crucial question is whether power can be transformed and redefined within the system, to which I shall turn in later chapters. For the moment it is important to underscore how much variance is possible among citizens and institutions in order to achieve similar degrees of congruence. For this problem we require, as Mannheim noted, a paradigm that takes into account both subjective and objective dimensions of society. The following tabulation sketches several alternatives for the accommodation of diversity in the manifestation of ideology in both individual and collective endeavor.

	Permissible Variance of Behavior			
Citizens	Hi	Hi	Lo	Lo
Institutions	Hi	Lo	Hi	Lo

As has been suggested above, ideologies that stress individual participation and place few constraints on institutions represent the situation of high variance in manifesting values and norms. The totalitarian ideologies are the opposite extreme in requiring minimal variance from both citizens and institutions as activities are linked to the ideology. The mixed situations represent what I consider the most frequently found uses of ideology in developing countries. In the first case, political ideas accommodate a good deal of individual diversity, but institutions do not figure importantly in the ideology. Countries of this kind are often labelled "pragmatic modernizers" where individual initiative is relied upon to change the society, and institutional norms are less explicitly defined. To the extent that norms become a residual of individual action, institutions tend to represent the interests of the powerful and so in fact may reflect very little variation in the expression of national values. The key distinction is that institutional norms are not explicitly treated in the ideology. Turkey, Tunisia, India, and Japan have at some points in their development used ideology in this way.

In the second situation, the variance in behavior at the individual level is more narrowly defined, and intensive propaganda and educational efforts may be made to convey to citizens the appropriate range of behavior in interpreting political ideas. Institutional norms may vary considerably, however, and are more directly attached to the ideology. Examples of this use of ideology tend to come from the "intensive modernizers" such as China, Tanzania, and Cuba. In these countries, monumental efforts have been made to restructure institutions, often seriously disrupting the society. Compared to the pragmatic modernizers, the intensive modernizers use ideology to radically change institutions. Perhaps the most important distinction between the pragmatic and intensive modernizers as they seek to evolve an ideology centers on institutional choices. The pragmatic use of ideology does little to facilitate institutional change, and political institutions tend to fall into the hands of the new middle class, the army, and the landlords. The intensive modernizers are constantly discussing the relation between institutions and political ideas, and institutional norms are more clearly linked to the political behavior considered appropriate from citizens. The pragmatic modernizers tend to make decisions about institutional norms by default and under immediate pressure, while the intensive modernizers try to anticipate institutional developments and seek a way of making decisions about institutions coherent in terms of the prevailing ideology. In Mannheim's terms, the intensive modernizers have a "total" ideology and the pragmatic modernizers a "particular" ideology. The latter places emphasis on individual variance in manifesting political ideas, and the former places emphasis on institutional variance.

My interest in ideology, then, is not the minimal amount of acquiesence to central authority necessary for a state. There are many ways of extracting observance of authority, and many of them have little relevance to political ideas. Nor is my concern only with the accumulation of institutionalized behavior, whose norms may then be interpreted as the national ideology. If ideologies were solely the property of states, there would be no new ideology, and the reinterpretation of political ideas in light of experience and social change would not be a problem. I am using "ideology" to refer to both the activity individuals can attach to political ideas and the norms found in collective endeavor intended to manifest political ideas. Moreover, I am suggesting that an important way of discriminating among ideologies is to examine how much tolerance of conflict and diversity there is at *both* the level of individual values and institutional norms. Ideologies have been used to support and to erode authority, and it is not this quality of political ideas that seems to me to be their crucial significance in political life. Political ideas are important because they generate a sense of civility, of how men as citizens individually and collectively relate to one another in a political system.

Geertz (1963: 156) has written that "civic society requires a sense of the public." What we mean by the "public" is an ancient topic in the study of politics. What I am suggesting is that the public involves the range of politically relevant behavior possible in a system for both citizens and institutions. I am also arguing that it is difficult, if not impossible, to enjoy wide variance in such behavior without an ideology to provide coherence for both citizens and institutions. Ideologies provide a sense of civility by linking ideas to behavior. Rather than seeing ideologies arranged along a spectrum from left to right according to their abstract goals, it makes more sense to analyze them according to how much flexibility they may provide for citizens and institutions. As will be argued in subsequent chapters, narrowing the base of an ideology in political life is not difficult. The implementation of a totalitarian ideology is relatively easy, and, once established, it is easy to reinforce and protect those activities considered appropriate to it. It is in the multiplication of choice and the diversification of behavior that ideologies acquire significance by giving meaning to the word "public." The public of Nazi Germany was a narrowly circumscribed and stereotyped entity. The publics of France, Britain, and most democracies create an elusive and highly variable pattern of activity. Unless political science can begin to assess the differential meaning of ideology in political systems, it will retain its pejorative connotation and not be included among the basic concepts of the discipline. I feel this would be a grievous error because it would foreclose an important avenue for describing the public and the nature of civic order.

REFERENCES

AVINERI, S. (1968) The Political and Social Thought of Karl Marx. London: Cambridge Univ. Press.

DAHRENDORF, R. (1967) Society and Democracy in Germany. Garden City, N.Y.: Doubleday.

ECKSTEIN, H. E. (1961) A Theory of Stable Democracy. Princeton: Center for International Studies.

ERIKSON, E. H. (1963) Childhood and Society. New York: W. W. Norton.

GEERTZ, C. [ed.] (1963) Old Societies and New States: The Quest for Modernity in Africa and Asia. New York: Free Press.

GERTH, H. H. and C. W. MILLS [ed.] (1947) From Max Weber: Essays in Sociology. London: Routledge & Kegan Paul.

HILL, C. (1961) The Century of Revolution 1630-1714. London: Nelson.

KELF-COHEN, R. (1958) Nationalisation in Britain: The End of a Dogma. London: Macmillan.

LIPSET, S. M. (1960) Political Man. Garden City, N.Y.: Doubleday.

MANNHEIM, K. (1936) Ideology and Utopia. New York: Harcourt Brace.

MILLS, C. W. (1959) The Power Elite. New York: Oxford Univ. Press.

MOORE, B., Jr. (1966) Social Origins of Dictatorship and Democracy: Lord and Peasant in the Making of the Modern World. Boston: Beacon.

NEUMANN, F. (1942) Behemoth. London: Gollancz.

WARD, R. E. [ed.] (1968) Political Development in Modern Japan. Princeton: Princeton Univ. Press.

X, MALCOLM (1964) The Autobiography of Malcolm X. New York: Grove.

Chapter III

APOCALYPTIC IDEOLOGY AND

EMOTIONAL INSECURITY

Ideology has most frequently been associated with the arousal of very strong emotions. The intensity of such emotion has often been so great that men have been persuaded to commit acts of unbelievable hostility and cruelty in the name of national virtue. The excesses that have been justified on ideological grounds no doubt contributed to the disrepute of ideology in the postwar world, summarized in *The End of Ideology* (Bell, 1965). The reaction against ideology should be seen in historical perspective. The Western world had just emerged from a brutal and inhumane war costing millions of lives and, perhaps for the first time, had experienced the full force of emotional insecurities of the most basic kind exploited for political action. Under the shadow of Nazi Germany and with hopes of a new peace under the United Nations, ideology was understandably interpreted as a highly irrational and destructive force.

However, political and social systems have always required highly general statements of their aims and procedures. While it is no doubt true that much ideology associated with the nation has exploited human fears and insecurity, theories about ideology have undergone substantial revision in the past twenty years. Curiously enough, the revision was stimulated to a large extent by the emergence of the new nations, their justification for independence, and their search for identity. The proliferation of ideologies in Africa, Asia, and Latin America contributed to a new perspective on ideology and took national self-determination out of the legal context that had been advanced and thoroughly rejected, in Wilsonian times. The growth of new nations dramatically revealed the blend of cultural, social, and political elements in ideological statements. The difficult problems of political unification in the developing countries gave new emphasis to constructive features of ideology in generating solidarity and cohesion in a badly divided society.

In this chapter, we shall be primarily concerned with the affective aspects of ideology as they relate to individual beliefs, social norms, and cultural values. In Chapters IV and V, we shall deal with cognitive and evaluative aspects of ideology. Affect means the arousal of positive or negative feelings in the individual toward an object in his environment. Hence, the affective aspect of ideology is largely concerned with direction. Will the individual accept rules laid down by an authority? Is such and such a group loyal to the nation? Does the individual receive emotional gratification from participating in politics or belonging to the society? These are obviously some of the most rudimentary questions to be asked about political and social systems, and it should be noted that the affective element alone tells us very little about the intricacies of human behavior. For the individual, affect can be measured on a scale from total rejection to total submission; for collective action on a comparable scale, affect ranges from unquestioning acceptance of superior authority to complete rejection of authority.

Concentration on the affective or emotional aspects of ideological statements immediately raises some historic problems of politics. The many discourses in politics about legitimacy revolve around this elementary question of individual or group disposition toward a defined authority. Likewise, some of the basic problems of membership in the system constitute increasingly important issues in developing nations where tribal, regional, and even subcultural loyalties compete for loyalty with new governments. It is not coincidental that renewed interest in the role of ideology in developing nations should be accompanied with a new concern with the nature of citizenship and the meaning of national loyalty. In the industrial nations, the problems of treason, citizenship, and loyalty are surrounded with judicial institutions and procedures that, at least under normal conditions, tend to remove them from political controversy. But they clearly remain delicate and sensitive distinctions with profound emotional implications. A Hitler or a Senator McCarthy often succeeds in stimulating basic human insecurities and fears to generate loyalty of a very narrow and ruthless kind. Eliciting authoritarian responses in highly developed societies is clearly very different from the rudimentary nation-building problems of the developing countries, though, as will be argued in more detail below, it is important to detect when constructive political action shades into political manipulation.

The affective quality of ideology has severe limitations, which are most clearly revealed to psychological studies of perception under stress and personality studies under conditions of extreme anxiety. Those problems that generate more intense feelings, such as race, sex, and death, are more amenable to emotional interpretation in ideology. Hitler's highly successful manipulation of feelings about racial purity, reinforced by a number of social grievances and the dislocations created by the depression, is one of the most dramatic examples, but the themes of many of the most fundamental human fears and insecurities are seldom distant from any ideological code. The justification of death by dying for one's country, the sanctity of the home and personal habits, and continuing tension between racial and national identities are indicative of how basic human feelings intertwine with beliefs about the nation and the society. The same themes appear in the ideological statements of more recent nationalists, where national honor, the threat of corruption by external forces, and extreme sensitivity to issues of self-control and self-sufficiency frequently play on the most fundamental of human problems.

The methodological problems of observing affective influences on behavior suggest its shortcomings in more complex social relationships. The more intense is the feeling that can be stimulated, the more predictable are the behavioral consequences. For this reason, the use of affective devices is likely to occur under conditions of extreme stress. For example, the frequent use of sexual aggression themes in black nationalist literature in the United States suggests both the intense feelings that have been generated and also the predisposition of many black militants to violence. Predicting behavior under these conditions is not particularly difficult and tends to become almost a truism. The individual who feels sexually violated or threatened with extinction reacts strongly, but this is a relationship so fundamental to human existence that its relevance to more complex social and individual relationships is overpowering. Hence, the intensity of feeling tells us the direction that a person's action may take, but tends to be most useful under circumstances of such severe stress that prediction is not a difficult problem. It is precisely in those areas of human choice where alternatives are endowed with similar emotional significance that most political problems are found.

Under circumstances of affective neutrality or a diverse range of alternatives giving comparable emotional rewards, the intensity measure is not particularly useful. Most complex patterns of behavior in society and culture involve such complications. Put conversely, when collective problems can be reduced to basic emotional themes, the complexity of social relationships is itself reduced. In this respect, prejudice, hatred, and outrage are very attractive tools for individuals, and sometimes political leaders, who wish to simplify their problems; hence, the attraction of "neoimperialism" and conspiracy themes in many developing countries. If a nation's difficulties can be associated with external coercion or plots to destroy national dignity, the ordering of political behavior in relation to national government is vastly simplified. Extremes of political behavior have often been polarized around symbols, so that evocation of these symbols can override and control wide ranges of political behavior. The magnification of a single racial or religious distinction to govern all other relationships might be considered a definition of a totalitarian political system. The use of highly emotional themes in ideology tends to dichotimize behavior around the "pure" and the virtuous, usually with an apocalyptic vision of a new social order once the violation is totally rectified.

AUTHORITARIAN PERSONALITY AND IDEOLOGY

The effects of emotional insecurity on perception and behavior have been largely within the province of social psychology and psychoanalytic theory. Except for Lasswell's (1960) pioneering work in the 1930s, political and social research tended to concentrate on institutionally and legally defined problems until the rise of Hitler. The influence of Nazi Germany on the study of politics and society can hardly be exaggerated, though it is often forgotten a generation after World War II. The shock was much greater than the simple demise of the Weimar Republic, whose constitution was one of the most elaborate ever written and whose organization was, at least initially, carefully supervised by the victorious democratic powers of Europe. The internal contradictions of Weimar Germany might have been detected well before Hitler's rise to power. The traumatic effects of Nazi Germany were the ruthless display of inhumanity, the helplessness of the few elements of democratic political life before the Nazi organization, and the immense destructive force that could be unleashed by the appeal to hatred and fear. History is the final test of political and social analysis, and Hitler's Germany swept away the assumptions of rationality and moderation that had been built into our theories of social and political order.

To explain this monumental failure of democratic government became a major concern in the years immediately following the war. The inquiry led to an exploration of the ways in which personality relates to the collective activity which is one of the major contributions of contemporary social science. Talmon (1955) traced the continuing thread of irrationality in Western thought. Erich Fromm (1965) pointed the way for this inquiry with his extremely suggestive study of how Hitler exploited sadomasochistic weaknesses in German personality. His explanation is part of a larger theory of how the complexity and remoteness of modern industrial society generates feelings of aimlessness and powerlessness, encouraging profound individual alienation. Fromm did not make the reductionist error of simply transferring his theory of personality, essentially a neo-Freudian outlook, onto society. He recognized that both historical events and social differences facilitated Hitler's rise to power and became important intervening variables in the exploitation of personal insecurity through the Nazi ideology. Events between the wars generated severe feelings of insecurity in two social classes. The workers, whose hopes for democracy were raised in 1918, were disappointed and manipulated in Weimar Germany and overcome by "a deep feeling of resignation, of disbelief in their leaders, of doubt about the value of any kind of political organization and political activity." Their alienation removed the most serious obstacle to Hitler, though it should be recalled that a courageous group of Social Democrats were the only ones to vote against his installation in the Reichstag. The Nazi ideology had positive appeal to a mixed second group, largely lower-middle-class shopkeepers, artisans, and lesser bureaucrats. For them, particularly the disillusioned and unhappy youth of these groups, the Nazi ideology promised the self-assertion and fulfillment they found impossible in the interwar years. They ardently accepted the "spirit of blind obedience to a leader and of hatred against racial and political minorities [and] its craving for conquest and domination, its exaltation of the German people and the 'Nordic race' " (Fromm, 1965: 234-235).

Fromm interprets the alienation of these segments of German society as the essential prerequisite to Hitler's rise, while he himself made the final leap to power with the support of the industrialists and Junker landowners who were opposed to the very groups that Nazi ideology addressed most successfully. The ideology was a mixture of two paranoid responses, sadistic and masochistic reaction to failure and defeat. The themes are carefully laced throughout *Mein Kampf* (Hitler, 1943), sadism aiming at the "unrestricted power over another person more or less mixed with destructiveness" and masochism "aiming at dissolving oneself in an overwhelmingly strong power and participating in strength and glory" (Fromm, 1965: 246). The product was a typically ambivalent, authoritarian personality, craving power without knowing how to use it and yearning for submission to a leader whose apocalyptic vision became a substitute for individually meaningful action. As Fromm observes, the political practice of the Nazi regime confirmed the paranoid desires stimulated by the ideology and by social conditions. The believer recovered his individuality by complete submission to the regime and, in the final analysis, by self-annihilation, the total negation of the individual. The believers were betrayed personally by Hitler's own cynicism and fantasy and socially by the regime's aimless destruction that eventually ended in the defeat of Nazi Germany.

The powerful attraction of the emotional release promised by Hitler is corroborated in a number of social studies.

Bendix (1953) has shown how some five and a half million voters, half of them apathetic in 1928, came to the polls in 1930 to provide the Nazis with a grasp on the fragile democratic machinery of the Weimer Republic. Nearly two million new voters were eligible to vote in 1930, many of them undoubtedly fascinated by Hitler's easy promises of success and power and reflecting the disenchantment with their parents, their society, and their government. There is also evidence from Herberle (1945) that the Nazis obtained considerable support among peasants, who, like the lower-middle class, found the economic dislocations of the postwar period frustrating and the democratic government unable to relieve their problems. Hitler's attraction to the insecure and alienated in German society clearly exceeded the fascist appeal found in other European countries at the time. The full proportions of the institutionalized paranoia he advocated was not fully acted out until the massive slaughter of Jews gained momentum and the conversion of the state into a weapon of total destruction became clear in the mid-30s. The ceremonial submersion of the individual, the hysterical glorification of leadership, the elaborate rationalizations for unprecedented brutality became the manifestations of a society gripped in an authoritarian syndrome.

In some respects, the Nazi ideology is too dramatic an illustration of the affective appeal because the behavior that followed so closely fulfilled the appeal of the ideology. The parallel between individual insecurity and societal dislocation, their interaction to produce an entire array of institutional devices to act out paranoid fantasies, and the final spiral confirming the wish for self-destruction involve a degree of emotional intensity that ideologies have rarely generated. The experience was almost too appropriate for the application of neo-Freudian theory, much of which sought to extend the range of application of Freudian principles (Hall and Lindzey, 1957) beyond early, if not largely infantile, sexual conflict in personality. For example, several psychoanalytic studies were conducted of parent-child relationships and the subsequent effects of unsuccessful sexual identification in the early socialization of the child. Perhaps the most influential work was the research of Adorno (et al., 1950) on perception of society and interpersonal relations among highly ethnocentric individuals in the United States. Concentrating on the perceptual distortion of individuals displaying severe prejudice, the operation of emotional insecurity in society under less severe conditions than those prevailing in Germany under Hitler was for the first time systematically studied.

Although the research design and the methodology of the Adorno study have been criticized (Christic and Jahoda, 1954), it provided the point of departure for a wider range of inquiry into the relationship of emotional insecurity to perception, learning, and interpersonal relations since the war. The particular value of the Adorno study in the present framework is that it suggests numerous ways that an affective appeal can be used to attract the support of individuals with authoritarian personality characteristics. Whether or not the existence of prejudice can be successfully explained through psychoanalytic theory is a much broader question, but the study shows clearly how the need for direction and desire for definitive orientation to politics is derived from one basic manifestation of emotional insecurity. Much like the Nazi, the highly ethnocentric individual tended to feel that social problems were extraneous to the American way of life, often introduced by a foreign influence or a subversive element in society (Adorno et al., 1950: 153-157). Conflict and differences of viewpoint were rejected. There were little information and little interest in experimentation to find ways of improving society or political life. The prejudiced tended to idealize leadership and, while envying those with power, tended to accept the fact that status and power were on the whole denied to them. These feelings of resignation and submission to authority were attached to very high values on upward social mobility, the acquisition of rewards as now structured in society, and acceptance of material benefits as sufficient justification for human endeavor. Among the prejudiced, maturity was often equated with conformity. Individual imagination and self-conscious excursion into uncertainty were considered unprofitable, if not somewhat dangerous.

The latter section of the book deals in more detail with the political and social implications of the study and their relation to ideology. The Adorno group finds two underlying characteristics of the ethnocentric in their perception of ideological principles. The first is the great functional value of stereotypes to the prejudiced individual. The authoritarian personality does not want to sift information, weigh evidence, or select alternatives. He tends to be suspicious of attempts to reformulate experience and to test conventional wisdom, preferring either the uncritical acceptance of vague generalization or the refuge of very specific, concrete causes. The emotionally insecure, very briefly, prefer simple explanations of society. The second predominant characteristic is the frequency of personalization of ideology and its references to society and politics, again a projection of the insecure of their own preference for submission and dominance as the major dimensions in both interpersonal and more remote forms of social action. Again the tendency is to avoid dealing with the many levels of human experience and the many forces that operate in society. Combined with this form of withdrawal is the similarly rigid adherence to the notion that individuals to whom so much is attributed are inaccessible, remote, and superior. The attitudes of the prejudiced are, then, structured to accept—indeed, to welcome—the symbolic and simplified solutions of the emotional, ideological appeal.

Out of the authoritarian personality studies came a number of ideas that helped link psychoanalytic theory to social psychology. The symbolically derived similarities among withdrawal, projection, and other Freudian concepts and the large-scale manifestation of these problems in society could not be easily studied within the context of the early sexual development of the child. While men clearly displayed in society many of the symptomatic qualities of neurosis and psychosis, many psychoanalysts, such as Fromm (1965), Sullivan (1953), Kardiner (1939), and others, wanted to extend their theory to deal with interpersonal behavior and col-· lective activity. A major step in this direction was the notion of intolerance of ambiguity, developed by Else Frenkel-Brunswik (1949) in the authoritarian personality studies. The uncertainty and suspicion that overcome highly insecure individuals do not always lead to severe personality disorders, but may be manifested in more subtle ways in responding to the human and physical realities of life. The concept is particularly important in the development of psychological theory for it underlies later work of Festinger (1957), Rokeach (1960), McClelland (1961), and others who developed important new concepts in social psychology on the ways individuals deal with conflicting information from their environment, the ways they organize their beliefs about more distant and less emotionally charged problems, and the ways they decide to adjust to less dramatic, but no less real, problems of everyday life.

The importance of this step in our understanding of the role of ideology should not be underestimated. Where the person introjects the tension and frustration of poor adaptation, the behavioral consequences may often be so severe that self-injury or serious injury to others follows. The behavioral consequences of the more subtle forms of externalizing insecurity are not nearly as well understood, even though Hitler's Germany demonstrated how skillful affective manipulation could trigger extremely bizarre behavior on a very large scale. But to deal with the larger-scale problems of existence, both psychoanalysts and psychologists needed concepts that did not depend so directly on sexual dislocations in early life, and their efforts to broaden the scope of their theory brought their interests much closer to the kinds of behavior normally thought to be influenced by ideology. In addition, emphasis was shifted from questions of intensity and direction to problems of diversity, choice, and expectation. The organizational qualities of the individual's perception begins to raise the issue of cognition, which will be dealt with in relation to ideology in Chapter IV.

EMOTIONAL DEPENDENCE AND COLONIAL RULE

The severe intensity of ideological communication in developing countries raises the question of how far one might apply Freudian theory to gain insight into, if not to explain, political and social behavior. In both Freudian and neo-Freudian analysis, the growth of the personality is heavily, perhaps definitively, shaped in infancy by inescapable dependencies and in early childhood by the equally compelling problem of arriving at a sexual identity consistent with one's feelings toward his parents. Where this critical stage in personality development, the Oedipal crisis, generates unresolved anxieties, the individual finds it difficult to adapt to his or her biologically determined sexual role, and a wide variety of mechanisms may be called upon to suppress, to minimize, or to reject the profound sense of inadequacy that follows. Many neo-Freudian thinkers express reservations on the great significance attributed to the Oedipal crisis, but it remains one of the most critical periods of personality development and a time of potentially unbearable and irreconcilable conflict.

The colonized and the colonizer are in many respects in a relationship comparable to the child and parent. Despite the pitfalls of social analysis by analogy, a number of interpretations of the colonial relationship and much of the widely recognized behavior of both parties suggest that the extreme dependency inherent in colonial rule can easily produce anxieties so severe that neither party can accurately perceive the other's behavior and that each regards the other with fear of such alarming proportions that many of the familiar Freudian defense mechanisms appear. Similarities through analogy should not be equated with causal relationships even though perception and behavior regarding sex was often enormously distorted in the colonial relationship. In other words, it would be a gross misapplication of the theory and factually quite incorrect to conclude that the sexual behavior of the colonized or the colonizer was determined by exposure to the colonial setting. Freudian theory itself has difficulty making causal statements and easy reductions must be avoided. But the theory and considerable evidence do indicate the behavior of both parties was often much influenced by the inescapable and rigid form of dependence fostered in the colonial setting. It is possible that individuals with severe sexual anxieties might be attracted to colonial roles, which Fanon (1963) and others have suggested, and it may also be possible that adaptation to colonial roles might resurrect or reinforce otherwise manageable psychological conflict.

A great deal of commonplace knowledge substantiates the conclusion that colonial dependency generates emotional insecurities that can be destructive on a scale approaching German society under Hitler. Nearly everything done by the colonial administrator was overlaid with actions to assert his superiority and the subject's inferiority. The British colonial servant going off to the bush with dozens of pack animals laden with overstuffed furniture; the elaborate, sometimes genuinely serious, efforts to recover the glorious past of the fallen civilization; the socially enforced behavior—sometimes simply waiting for hours in order to air a minor grievance, or not allowing someone to ride a horse in order to remind him of his inferior status; the generation of convenient stereotypes about the native's listlessness and dishonesty, often unreconciled with equally numerous fears about his irrational powers and constant threat to law and order; the frequent glorification of the "l' homme brave," the most primitive and backward of the colonized, as opposed to the often brutal and inhumane attitudes toward those who painfully begin to adapt to urban life and industrial employment; these are only a few of the manifestations throughout the entire fabric of colonial life to reassure the colonizer of his superiority and to remind the colonized of his inadequacy.

To imply that all colonizers or all subjects were overcome with the emotional insecurity reflected in these behaviors would be incorrect, but no one could enter into a colonial relationship without acknowledging them. Colonialism became one of the major forms of institutionalized racism, though even the most bitter nationalists will concede that not all colonial officials were racists. Nor was the relationship by any means confined to officials. Coleman's (1958: 91) quote from missionary records, "when I carry my torch into the caves of Africa I meet only filthy birds of darkness," reflects the ubiquity of the colonial attitude, and it contains more than a passing hint of the profound psychic anxiety experienced by all parties. The colonial official, after all, did provide some obvious services such as cleaning up malaria and other endemic diseases, opening up new lands and irrigation, and providing better transport and communication. The improvements did not escape the perception of the native. There are reasons to argue that missionaries might have generated even more intense feelings of subjection than did the political and economic exploitation. The missionary used his good works—often badly needed schools, clinics, and the like—to extract and to justify a much more overt, even ritualized, form of conversion to foreign ideas than did the officials and bankers. In time of threat, it also became apparent that the church was as prepared as the colonist to use coercion and manipulation. The Berber decree in Morocco in 1930, for example, is often pointed to as the basic stimulus for Moroccan nationalism. With comparable policies across North Africa at the time, it was apparent that the Catholic Church was collaborating with French rule to spread Christianity among the tribal peoples at the expense of more resistant Muslims in urban centers.

The dependency relationship permeates all forms of exchange between the colonized and the colonizer. In retrospect, it is often difficult for Westerners to recognize the pervasiveness of their influence, and, it should also be noted, it may well be equally difficult for the liberated to realize that their earlier anxieties are now being acted out in a new framework. For example, it is interesting that Coleman (1958: 54, 100) criticizes the "undermining of parental authority, the weakening of traditional sanctions, the general alienation of Christian elements from the balance of the community, and the inculcation of disrespect for traditional African cultures" by missionaries, but elsewhere finds the "minuteness of British control and the ease with which traditional authorities could be removed" in the interest of good government. The effectiveness of British administration may well have brought benefits to many Nigerians, as it did to millions of Indians, Sudanese, and East Africans, but the psychological debilitation just as surely underscored native weakness and inferiority as did that of the missionary and the merchant. Again, it should be cautioned that these observations are not detractions from the serious work of many administrators, least of all from the reputations of the Lyauteys and Lugards, who ceasely and sensitively worked within the colonial framework to improve the opportunities and the well-being of colonial populations. Much was accomplished, but unfortunately it was done in a context of mutually destructive forces.

An instructive aspect of the dependency argument is the comparison of how different colonial policies and practices shaped the final conflict leading to independence. Was the British *raj,* the Dutch East Indies Company, or *la mission civilisatrice* of France more damaging to the self-confidence and resolve of colonized countries? British and French dominance of colonial peoples seems to differ basically in the extent to which British rule was individualized and French rule was collectivized. The Englishman abroad in service of the Empire was quite literally a man on horseback, alone for the most part and a member of the carefully selected elite of British society (Woodruff, 1953). Even British preference for indirect rule could be construed as a desire to underscore the

aloofness and paternalism of the colonial regime. The Frenchman abroad was no less conscious of the superiority of his
civilization, but he more explicitly made the extension of
French culture part of the rationalization of his dominance
and generally preferred the collective security of a large
French colony. The Frenchman abroad was more equalitarian, even though persuaded of his cultural superiority, but
assimilation was wholly on French terms (Betts, 1961).
French colonial rule was more inextricable from the subject
societies than British because it demanded greater psychological concessions. The English Speaking Union abroad held
stuffy tea parties, but the Alliance Francaise controlled the
educational system.

The manner of foreign instrusion and withdrawal are also
important clues to the indelible effects of the colonial experience. The Dutch East Indies bastion was the work of an
adventurer remodelled as a commercial enterprise. Indonesia
became the last symbol of Dutch international power, and
for five years the Dutch schemed, plotted and fought by
every means imaginable to upset the new nation (Benda,
1958). The British Empire was conceived by a brilliant Conservative politician, Disraeli, whose eye was as much on his
party's fortunes in parliament and his own good standing
with the Queen as it was on compensating for English shortcomings or relieving English problems. The British developed
a detached view of their colonies and the privileges and
benefits of imperial rule went largely to the elite of Britain.
While the British people generally received some sentimental
pleasures from the Empire, the elite structure of the society
made withdrawal easier, almost abrupt as in the case of India.
With the exception of Napoleon's fascinating romance with
Egypt, the French conquest was largely stimulated by the
Third Republic, whose instability added to the attraction of
more easily won victories abroad (Murphy, 1948). As resistance to colonial rule grew, the collective image of the empire
was clothed in the form of a Union, the early nationalists
were welcomed into the French Assembly and the French

Academy, and, in the case of Algeria, some territory was even legally constituted part of France. The French dependence on their Empire reflected the bourgeois character of their society and thousands of middle-class French settled in colonies to seek rewards they were unable to find at home. The decline of colonial rule was acutely painful for France, starting from the bloody suppression of Arab nationalism in Syria and ending with eight years of disastrous war in Algeria.

The history of colonial experience highlights another important aspect of the dependency relationship: the ruler tends to need his feeling of superiority in the same way as the ruled eventually comes to cherish the security of total submission. The destructiveness of the colonial relationship is reciprocal and therein lies the key to much of intensity of ideological development both prior to and following independence. As Mannoni (1964: 84) points out, the dependency becomes so severe that "every increase in equality becomes intolerable," not just for the colonizer but also for the colonized. The same effect is noted by Waelder (1963: 9) in his essay on the decline of imperial rule when he notes that as inequalities become less, they become more significant. The threat of isolation, either in a superior role deprived of automatic confirmation of one's superiority or in a subordinate role without constant assurance that direction and gratification can be effortlessly obtained, is unbearable. Once the colonial society begins to be differentiated, as inevitably it must as economic, social, and political roles are diversified, the "total confrontation" noted by Worsley (1964: 49) cannot endure. In a society of diverse skills, interests, and activities, a society that gives the individual choice, there are no longer totally reliable formulas to define superior and subordinates. The rigid embrace of the colonial dependence hierarchy is useless in a society where individual worth and dignity are recognized.

Institutionalized forms of racism are, of course, not limited to colonial relationships. The dependence of ruler and ruled has been manifested in prejudice as it appears in every society, not the least important being discrimination and slavery in American society. Recent research of Jordan (1969) adds to the accumulating evidence that white Americans have perceived black society in peculiar ways since the earliest settlement and introduction of slavery. The American colonialists had a much more difficult time resolving their relationship to blacks than that to Indians. Some even advocated intermarriage as acceptable with Indians, but not acceptable with blacks. The American settlers were no doubt exhilarated by their superiority and jealous of their hard-won equality, much like white settlers in Algeria and Kenya years later. Though much of the dogmatism about race came from Europe, colonial leaders were active participants in the discussions and had great difficulty recognizing that the slaves might well be their equal. They reacted with alarm to the slave rebellions in 1741 and again in 1804 worried about introducing politically aware refugees from Haiti. Their views on sex and family among blacks are virtually identical with the racist view of today. Obviously, these attitudes contradicted much of the revolutionary doctrine, and colonial leaders felt compelled to engage in apologetics. As Jordan (1969) points out, however, the even greater paradox is that, after the revolution, immense social injustice was ignored. Whipping, branding, and maiming continued, and public discussion turned increasingly to the threat of freeing black people. The importing of slaves was forbidden by the federal government in 1808, but that was only two years before the first law forbidding the freeing of slaves was passed in Virginia and began to spread. Like the colonial rulers of the nineteenth century, the white settlers found the idea of a free black minority unbearable.

The transition to independence, then, can be looked upon as a very delicate reallocation of emotional energy that in many cases has been repressed for years by the colonial dependency. The nationalist ideologies are in part a function of a very deep emotional metamorphosis, and their intensity reflects the painful emotional adjustment that must be rapidly made. The immense wrench of this transformation can be explosive, even brutal, for all parties immersed in colonial dependence. Although we live in an era of unusual violence, it is the transformation from colonial to independent rule that has generated the indiscriminate, virtually self-indulgent, bloodshed once associated with fascism. The violence used throughout the transition is consistent with the dependence hypothesis. In Madagascar, Syria, Kenya, and Indonesia, the colonizer wiped out hundreds of thousands of persons, often using the same weapons that liberated Europe from Hitler and Mussolini. Many thousands more died in the revolutionary movements in Indochina, Algeria, Cuba, and Malaysia. Nor does the inhumanity cease with the retreat of the colonizer, for the same feelings are readily renewed. Perhaps almost with relief, after generations of subordination, the liberated turn against each other with almost suicidal frenzy: millions of lives were taken in the Hindu-Islamic migration in India; unknown thousands died in the Congo; perhaps a quarter of a million perished in the Indonesian bloodbath in 1967; and still uncounted thousands, possibly millions, were killed in the Biafran war. The contributing factors in all these tragedies are many, and it would be overburdening an already controversial theory to imply that the dissolution of the dependency relationship can fully explain these misfortunes. Nonetheless, these are situations where a rigid pattern of authority, most often a paternal one, was either abruptly dissolved or violently defended by a vanishing power.

Characteristic of the dependency relationship is the inability of either party to establish independent measures of the other's performance and to find the initial striving of the oppressed incredible. Numerous examples could be cited from colonial policy to demonstrate the inaccurate perception of the political environment in developing countries. Benda (1958: 95) notes that it was "Islamic, rather than nationalist opposition that the colonial government was seemingly endeavoring to placate in the closing period of the

Dutch rule." The belated efforts of the French to buttress their power in Morocco by permitting King Mohammed V to travel to Tangier in 1947 became the occasion for the first large display of public support for the nationalists, and the violent abduction and exile of the monarch in 1953 made him the hero of the still poorly integrated nation. It is understandable that before World War I British officials failed to anticipate the implications of the Bombay textile workers' general strike or the water rate protests in Lagos, but as late as 1948 it appears that the British government still did not anticipate an independent Nigeria for many years (Coleman, 1958: 321). The blunders, miscalculations, and frenzy of the colonial rulers are perhaps no greater than the errors made in London or Paris. The home governments, it must be recalled, justified their power by claiming to know more about their subjects than the subjects knew of themselves. Their power rested on benevolence and brutality. The destruction of this myth was the first step toward independence and begins when the colonizer's self-delusion so seriously impairs his perception that even the subdued protest evokes violent suppression.

As nationalist pressure, the nascent form of political self-awareness, increases, the contradictions of the colonial role are revealed. The typical argument of the colonial power in the interwar years, when many young nationalists were forming their ideas, was that self-determination must wait until the colony is economically prepared or until the ethnic and tribal differences in the colony were reduced to manageable form. Although there is some weight to be attached to these arguments, they also contain an element of wishful thinking and defensive hypocrisy. The economies of the colonies had been built to depend on the mother country and to support the colonizers. One of the keenest observers of colonial rule in Southeast Asia, Furnival (1956: 304-309) noted that economic development had meant 200 years of forced labor for the Japanese, the proliferation of a rigid, racially determined division of labor throughout the region, and the multiplication of antiquated technology, such as the rickshaw, which the European would instantly reject at home. Most important, the development argument exposed the hypocrisy of the colonizer because differential wages, monopolistic investment practices, trade quotas, and exorbitant interest rates became irrefutable evidence that dependence would only shift its emphasis with economic growth. Only in the closing years of colonialism did the foreign powers think of economic development in terms of the entire population, and by this time colonies had acquired a compliant local elite, whose greed often exceeded and made unmistakable the exploitation of the colonial economic structure.

The colonizer's claim that he would resolve the ethnic, religious, and tribal disputes of the emerging society now appears almost ridiculous and suggests the inflated self-confidence and false wisdom of a person blinded by his own power. What passed for local reform in the closing years of colonialism was most often a crude effort to isolate the rural population, where unquestioning compliance could still be more easily elicited. Many of the projects for rural development were sincerely intended to improve the lot of the neglected mass in the countryside, and some of the accomplishments were significant, but the timing and form of these efforts reflect the uneasiness of an insecure authority making a final bid for power. Only in the closing years of Dutch rule in Indonesia was *adat* or customary law revived as part of official policy, not as part of genuine hope of invigorating traditional institutions to share power, but as a bulwark against Islamic and nationalist forces in the cities and towns. For all the years that the French romanticized the tribal *jemaa* or council in North Africa, nothing was done to make it an effective unit of government until the nationalists had permeated the cities. Mohammed V was exiled precisely because he refused to condone new laws to isolate rural society in Morocco. Even in the historic, non-European empires, it was the rejection of fractionalized power, such as the decline of the *millett* or self-governed community in Ottoman rule that was the prelude to building a viable nation (Lewis, 1961: 85-97). But the attempts to organize the peasant in the context of colonial dependence failed, in part because they were too late and in part because the colonizer was unable to recognize the full implications of the strategy without destroying his own role. Dependency is in fact an attempt to oversimplify human relationships and the timid efforts to politicize the countryside implied much too complex a society to conform to the colonial model.

The psychological nature of the colonial experience has been explored at some length because its deep effects on the perception and feelings of the colonized are less visible than on those of the colonizer. The subject peoples did not have a press, an intelligentsia, and a bureaucracy to record their reactions to subjection in nearly the detail found in colonial histories. But the dependency relationship requires two parties and generates deep emotional needs in both. The purposelessness of colonial dominance has its parallel in profound sense of futility and inefficacy that overcomes the subjected party. The totality of the relationship blinds the powerholder to the shortcomings and capriciousness of his rule just as the totally overpowered party comes to accept excessive demands and irrational behavior as part of his reality. The colonizer must live with deep fears of revenge and released hostility. The oppressed takes refuge in the imaginary pleasures of an only partially understood past and in the whimsical benevolence of his master, but he is unable either to restore the past or to build for the future. Out of this basically authoritarian relationship is produced the intensity of conviction and purpose so dramatically expressed in much of the ideological rhetoric of the developing country. By understanding the insecurity that was shared by colonized and colonizer through generations of foreign rule, the full emotional content of many contemporary ideologies is better appreciated. As will be argued more extensively in Chapters IV ·and V, in this way, one also acquires insight into the potentially inhibiting effects the colonial experience may have had on its victims as they struggle to recover control of their environments and their destinies.

REVOLUTION AND
EMOTIONAL METAMORPHOSIS

The violent revolutions in Africa, Asia, and, in a rather different context, Latin America, reflect the anguish and frustration of people made aware of how fundamentally they have been violated by colonial history. The colonial masters move on, and often the best of them have the maturity and honest devotion to assist in the transition to independence. But the colonized people cannot move on nor are the problems of adjusting to a society with open and flexible political relationships easy. The colonizer romanticizes the society he left, but his frequent expressions of impatience and superiority regarding his home country reflects the uneasy feelings of once again living and competing as an equal among men. In many cases, the officials, businessmen, and missionaries who were once romantically portrayed in European publications become public charges at home. Many find it impossible to accept life in a more intricate society and become voluntary exiles. The emotional tension of falling from a precarious position of absolute power can be dispelled by finding a new refuge, but the tension of suddenly having power is less readily avoided.

The behavior associated with these changes is most vividly exposed in the major revolutions that have taken place since the war in Algeria—Vietnam and China. Not all revolutionary situations, of course, take place at the national level. There are a number of cases where colonial rule inadvertently brought about radical change in status of subjected tribes or groups only to have these changes erupt in bloody violence. There were no doubt a number of contributing factors, but it is worth recalling that, in Kenya the British subdued the warlike Masai and favored the more passive Kikuyu as agricultural workers, servants, and the like. The Masai tended to retreat into the past, but the recognition of subordination was unendurable for the Kikuyu (Rosberg and Nottingham, 1966). Stimulated by a partially developed nationalist ideology merged with tribal ritual, they embarked on a ruthless slaughter of the European settler. The same relationship is described by Mason (1962: 88) in Rhodesia. British rule relieved the Mashona of the oppression suffered at the hands of the Matebele raiders, but the Mashona were not properly grateful, and few colonialists could understand that the Mashona "preferred the more uncertain threat of the Matabele to the constant presence of the new white masters." Colonial history is filled with sporadic, violent outbursts against the foreigner and in most of these cases careful inquiry will indicate how a people were reacting to a dramatic, sometimes sudden change in their role, destroying the reassurance of the past (Cohn, 1962), but not providing guidance for the future.

Of the major colonial revolutions, the Algerian is perhaps best documented in the context of the psychological strain on the newly liberated man. A black psychiatrist, Fanon gained the confidence of the revolutionaries and eventually fled to join in their struggle. He acknowledged that the tensions of decolonization may be as destructive as the colonial relationship itself, but also believed that violence alone would allow so fully repressed a nation as Algeria to regain its destiny. He wrote, "the development of violence among the colonized people will be proportionate to the violence exercised by the threatened colonial regime" (Fanon, 1963: 69). The bitterness of French resistance, even to the point of self-destruction, can only be explained by the endless failures of a proud and talented people. In a way that is not too dissimilar from American involvement in Vietnam, France found her political and economic life increasingly influenced by the destructive forces generated at all levels of French life. Terrorism spread to French towns, and the bitter disputes over the future of Algeria polarized the National Assembly and corrupted French leadership. While many Frenchmen, such as Jules Roy (1962), saw through the guilt and fear that came to dominate relations between the French settlers and the Algerians, the brutality and ruthlessness of the military, political, and economic organization brought to bear on the revolutionaries borders on the Nazi machinery of hatred. In the closing years of the revolution, the self-destructive drive of the French Algerian regime was fully exposed. The army joined in plots to destroy parliamentary government in France. French terrorists concentrated more and more heavily on their own countrymen. Finally, Salan and a group of French conspirators went underground to subvert De Gaulle's decision to liberate Algeria.

The despair and hate felt by the French settlers, many of whom had lived in Algeria for generations, was reciprocated by the F.L.N. and is suggested in the emotional intensity embodied in Algerian ideology. Though Fanon did not live to see Algerian independence, his essentially Freudian interpretation revealed to him the explosiveness of suddenly terminating the oppressive dependency relationship. He foresaw that nationalist parties, the middle class, and the new proprietors of the land were likely to have been so molded to the French model and French attitudes that their usefulness in rebuilding the society was limited. Lacking the imagination and the will to build a new society, the national bourgeoisie may turn to the same racist views that permeated French thinking, "ingrafting and stiffening [the] racism which was characteristic of the colonial era (Fanon, 1963: 68). He feared the political party that "puffed up in a most dangerous way," forgot the masses, depended on urban cliques and failed to bring basic change to the society. His apprehension was even extended to the army and "drawing-room generals," who turn the military into an autonomous political force in their search for a new role of the intellectuals, who "terrified by the void, the degradation and the savagery" of the transition, become the apologists for a new kind of colonialism in the guise of freedom (Fanon, 1963: 177).

Fanon's views on revolution were strongly influenced by the ambivalence and uncertainty that his psychoanalytic framework underscored. The colonial regime had disfigured Algeria, leaving the people with the fear that in the removal of French dominance the people would return to "barbarism, degradation and bestiality" of a falsely portrayed history.

The escape from dependency stimulates strong feelings of estrangement and loneliness which can turn upon the individual himself and produce the same sense of inferiority and futility used by the colonial regime. Fanon is not entirely clear on how a liberated nation escapes this dilemma and recognized the paradox of an intensified nationalism to neutralize the lingering doubts of a people bewildered by their own liberation. Rebuilding the nation meant finding a new national culture and a new national consciousness. Fanon expected this struggle to be just as painful and difficult as the initial realization and rejection of colonial dependency. The "most elementary, most savage and the most indifferentiated nationalism is the most fervent and efficient means of defending national culture" (Fanon, 1963: 196).

The pitfalls of this transition are many, and perhaps national reconstruction in the developing countries will not be able to avoid the racist interpretations that Arendt has suggested were stimulated by the nation in Europe. Fanon (1963: 112) saw clearly that hatred would not provide the revolutionaries with a program and acknowledged that the "instability inherent in the native is a frightening experience for the leaders of the rebellion." In addition, he saw that the "total brutality" unleashed in the struggle for independence might easily turn against nationalist leadership and destroy the nationalist movement. "There exists a brutality of thought and a mistrust of subtlety which is typical of revolutions; but there also exists another kind of brutality which is astonishingly like the first and which is typically anti-revolutionary, hazardous and anarchist" (Fanon, 1963: 117). There is no way of knowing how Fanon would have responded to Ben Bella's seizure of power in 1962, the subsequent plotting among military leaders, Boumedienne's coup in 1964, and the gradual restoration of central control in Algeria. Much of this was no doubt unavoidable if the new nation was to survive, but much could also be seen in light of Fanon's apprehension that independence would yield to personal feelings of insecurity and the partially suppressed desire to restore the colonial relationship.

The subjected nation can recover its identity more easily than a racially subjected minority, but both labor under similar strains, and there are distinct parallels between the ideologies of revolutionary movements abroad and black nationalism in the United States. In many respects, the plight of the black American is more desperate because slavery wiped out his past completely, and a century of more subtle enslavement has perpetuated, in less easily perceived form, the dependency relationship. Grier and Cobbs (1968: 20) observe, "The culture of slavery was never undone for either master or slave. The civilization that tolerated slavery dropped its slaveholding cloak but the inner feelings remained." After centuries of deprivation and humiliation, the Civil War only served to make socially acceptable the exploitation and destruction of the blacks. The Northern United States adjusted to the potential threat of the blacks by economic, educational, and political subterfuges no less vicious and inhumane than the openly bestial practices of Southern planter. Indeed, racial hatred in the South has been considered preferable to the extent that it made discrimination a visible, predictable barrier.

One need only review the dimensions of racism in America to see the parallels with the colonial relationship. Black women find themselves in a "society [that says] to be attractive is to be white" and where their maternal instincts must be entirely channeled to reward the survival, rather than the growth, of their children (Grier and Cobbs, 1962: 21, 143). The black man devotes his energies to concealing those feelings and actions that would arouse suspicion in his white master and weeps without feeling in psychiatric interviews, "held back by some inner command not to excel, not to achieve, not to become outstanding, not to draw attention to himself" (Grier and Cobbs, 1962: 61). The rejection of femininity and the emphasis on masculine sexual prowess are only two of the more obvious manifestations of a people who, feeling totally rejected and inferior in white society, turn their destructive urges against themselves. Few colonial societies achieved the sophistication of white American society in the systematic subjection of racial groups. To recover his destiny, the black man needed an ideology, and Malcolm X—more than any other individual—filled this need.

Like many of the historic leaders, Malcolm X lived the conflict he sought to resolve. His own development from petty criminal to ascetic and devoted leader symbolizes the transformation of an aimless, fearful people acquiring the direction and the will to assert their destiny. The revelation for Malcolm X came in Norfolk Prison Colony from the reading of Elijah Muhammed and a number of scholars on the origins and achievements of black people. The accuracy of these accounts is less relevant to his development or to the freeing of black men than is having a past, a whole life, and a meaningful history, on which to build. Malcolm X articulated a black viewpoint for the first time: the question was not how so much violence, but how had such merciless violence been endured from white men for generations without rebellion. By accepting dependence on white men, the black man confirmed, even welcomed, his subjection. There could be no integration until blacks had learned to stand alone and had joined American society on their terms, demanding the recognition of their culture and their institutions. The black power movement set out to build these psychological and social preconditions for self-respect that have been denied to black people in the United States, unlike the treatment of every other minority of foreign origin. There is some historic truth in Malcolm X's (1966) accusation that it was the white man who, in Europe and later in America, made race into a difference generating guilt and fear. His candid advocacy of a social order that accepts race by acknowledging it has yet to be fully comprehended. Nor was Malcolm X blind to the violence that the resurrection of the black people might unleash; he expressed concern for the self-destructive energy among youthful blacks on the edge of rioting in Harlem.

The need for affection and the individual's apprehension over domination by affection are basic themes of human existence; their frequent appearance in ideology is, therefore, to be expected. Social behavior constantly reflects man's search for direction and his apprehension about possible helplessness by his acceptance of that direction. The revolutionary cases of Algeria, Cuba, and a few others display this fundamental ambivalence elevated to the level of the political system and reinforced by subtle, if unconscious, patterns of behavior. In such situations, it is to be expected that the demand for a totally new orientation in political relationships would be most clearly expressed in the ideology. Moreover, it also follows that, where the institutional buttressing of a uniform pattern of subordination across all relationships in the society has been coercively enforced by alien power and endlessly prolifereated in a complex social structure, the sudden release will be explosive. Ideology that may easily appear excessively emotional or irrational to the observer in a stable, open society may in fact fill a vital need for individuals and institutions liberated into a world that has previously shown nothing but hostility and distrust for a subjugated people. The colonial relationship is surely one of the most merciless and dehumanizing social patterns devised by man, in many ways equalled only by the institution of slavery and, as much of history has shown, quite capable of accommodating slavery to glorify the superiority of the industrial state.

The experience of America's post-Civil-War development and the continued subjugation of black society in the United States is ample proof that the removal of the most objectionable and obvious features of subjugation does not necessarily bring about institutional and cultural change. One might even argue that the noticeable absence of ideological conviction in the Civil War was a clue that the white man did not intend, or possibly was not able to perceive, that the humiliation of an entire race would not be undone simply by allowing them to fall within the formalities of a political doctrine, however laudable, that was designed by and for the ruling group. The termination of dependence in those colonies where there was immense resistance by the colonial power is comparable. The resentment of continued dependence on the European and American economies among the revolutionary elites of the newly liberated country must be acute. It may even be one reason why revolutionary leaders find the nation-building process intolerable and often turn to ambitious plans for changing the structure of international relations. Nkrumah's devotion to pan-African unity, Nasser's entanglement in the Israeli conflict, possibly even Nehru's fascination with neutrality, are all forms of expressing the continued feeling of subordination in a world of large powers beyond the reach of the new nation, but critically important in its economic growth and political security.

The major revolutionary conflicts since the war most dramatically reveal the intensity of the individual and, in time, the organization aware of the injustice of relentless subjugation, but ideology has also been influenced by internal situations in the search for direction. Many of these situations are, as one might anticipate, racial, and as their intensity is elevated, the problems of the developing country defy easy solution. The persecution of the Chinese in Indonesia and many other Southeast Asian nations is typical, but racial or religious minorities around the world might be cited as scapegoats of an inflamed ideology. In some instances, such minorities were the innocent victims of an occupational specialization that was at one time sorely needed in the developing country, but which, with the evolution of the society become rigid barriers to the spread of skills and even the economic growth of the country. Not by accident, these occupations are frequently involved with commercial and banking activities. The Lebonese in Equador, the Indians in East Africa, and the Chinese in Southeast Asia at one time provided vital technical skills, and only by themselves assimilating into the growing society did their identification with the colonial power and foreign oppression become clear.

The racial minorities are in many ways the most pitiful remnant of the viciously structured dependence relationship. With independence, they are not particularly welcome in their home countries, as Pakistanis and Indians from East Africa find on taking refuge in England, nor are they spared the wrath of the liberated people. Their role deprives them of the respect of both the superior and the subordinate in the colonial situation. Forster (1924) has dramatically recorded the anguish of the Anglo-Indian, another variant of the irremediable distortion of society generated by the colonial occupation. The quarter of a million or more Euroasians isolated in Indonesia were threatened with decimation and were painfully repatriated to their unfamiliar homeland. The search for equality by an oppressed people paradoxically commits the same injuries that the colonial power once directed at the population. One can read endless tributes to human freedom and tolerance in the manifestos of nationalist movements and in the constitutions of the new nations, but the elemental force of insecurity, the need to dominate, and the gratification of unlimited power can as easily be expressed within the new nation as in the memoirs of a colonial servant.

HARNESSING EMOTIONAL INSECURITY

The anxieties generated by the transition from colonial to independent rule clearly combine with a number of additional factors in a well-developed ideology, and, as has been suggested, the direction and release of the high emotional content of many ideologies in developing countries may indeed assist in focusing a people's attention on the new nation and the monumental tasks it faces. Psychologists and others have recognized, however, that severe emotional insecurity can be generated in a number of social situations less historic than the liberation of an entire society. In Algeria, Cuba, and perhaps even in the United States, the disparities between values and behavior have become so great that ideology must necessarily be directed at the level of the culture. Where emotionally rooted tension is not so profound or pervasive, the implications may be less apocalyptic. Emotion is an integral part of focusing attention on and eliciting a response to institutional and individual change. Every culture has its folklore and corresponding evidence to show how the deprived member of the society might direct his emotional frustration into new activity to recover his self-respect and maybe to change society to fit his own image.

In societies spared the most acute forms of dislocation, ideology may support new leaders and innovations that bring about important change. In some instances, the new ideas may be introduced by exogenous elements, and in others by groups within the society. Perhaps the most dramatic illustration of the latter situation has been the use of ideology by the leaders of Communist China. China has never been the monolith portrayed in much conventional knowledge and China scholars seem agreed that, as Schurmann (1968: 551) puts it, the "revolution against authority has deep roots in China." Confucianism declined from the nineteenth century onward; the gentry were discredited under Chiang Kai-shek and finally eradicated by Communist agrarian reform; paternal authority had steadily deteriorated, to be given a final blow by marriage reform in Communist society. Though often coerced by foreign powers, China escaped massive suppression by other countries, and the emotional tensions of her transformation were dispersed, not without violence, toward many traditional structures. Humiliation under the Japanese was the ultimate exposure of the weakness and provided Mao with the Yenan interlude to develop and test the ideas that were to restore China as a world power.

The use of ideology by the Chinese elite was clearly to bring about widespread institutional change after the dismantling process was complete. Schurmann (1969) sees this process unfolding in what he has termed the formation of a "practical ideology." The Chinese approach to ideology was influenced, if not determined, by Mao's own theory of contradictions or notion that thought and behavior should be imagined as polar and then fused in a new, "correct" idea of how to use ideas. The influence of Marxian dialictic is obvious, but Mao added to this his own insight into the necessity of recognizing social, economic, and political conditions. His views on revolutionary warfare are typical of the kind of ideological accommodation he felt essential to arriving at the most appropriate institutional and organizational solutions. Clearly, the theoretical premises from which one embarks on this process are critical. Mao's preference for revolutionary solutions, mass involvement, and direct communication was basic to many of the techniques and goals used in the reconstruction of China (Tsou, 1969).

The choice of the party as the major institution for rebuilding China would seem obvious were it not that the army would be much more in keeping with trends among developing countries and was no doubt the most prestigious force in China when the Chiang Kai-shek was driven from the mainland. The underlying concept forged by Mao and Liu Shaoch'i was to form a party cadre that would be "red and expert." The phrase summarizes the contradictions on which practical ideology is formed, the devoted party militant is to carry out the organizational struggle to rebuild China. Mao's wisdom suspected the existing military elite, and, in the early years of Communist rule, the new party cadre fulfilled his notion of a highly visionary core of workers to bring the ideology directly into contact with the society. Most of the early campaigns were to do exactly this, combining the constant communication of slogans, speeches, and exhortation of ideology with work to be done. In the early 1950s, building the party cadre was the major aim of the government, and it was perhaps the only way that China's remarkable progress could have been achieved. To train the cadre, the process of "thought reform" was devised, a kind of ideological self-help procedure that overcame the huge inadequacies of education and communication in the countryside. As the party cadre grew and became increasingly involved in every facet of national development, the notion of the Great Leap Forward or total participation in social and economic change was a logical consequence. The Cultural Revolution represents another turning point in devising a practical ideology once the party elite itself became dominant and Mao felt it necessary to reassert both ideology and popular will.

The underlying phenomenon in the redirection of emotional energy in China, however, is skillful in that, at least until the Cultural Revolution, this energy was directly focused on institutional and organizational problems of the society. Although the importance of "thought reform" may have been exaggerated, the process of "thought reform" at the level of individual experience indicates how China has utilized what Mao once called the "emotional stage in cognition" (Schurman, 1969: 47). The aim of thought reform was not simply to test loyalty or to propagate the ideology, but to directly utilize emotional energy in order to perform the urgent tasks of the new government. The effects can be traumatic, as Lifton (1963: 379) has described, and play heavily on converting resentment of traditionally rooted subjugation, familial and social, into devotion to the party: "Hate your past—but not too much; hate your father—but remain filial." The process involves the public recital of every facet of the individual's life, which is then subjected to intensely hostile commentary and probing by the group. As the subject approaches the point of annihilation, the group directs him toward "correct" solutions and takes a more sympathetic attitude toward his "errors" of the past. The final stage is demonstrating one's redemption by going out to the people and behaving correctly.

The emphasis on the behavioral consequences of conversion are by no means unique to ideological purification in Communist China, but seldom has an induced state of anxiety been used on such a large scale. Nor is the process limited to the lower ranks of society. Public confession is a standard procedure among the Chinese elite as policy and ideology shift. Self-exposure, of course, is also used in other political systems to restore trust and to demonstrate equality, as many an American politician knows. The important difference between the exploitation of personal tension in China and earlier examples in this chapter should be noted. In Germany, inferiority was channeled toward the destruction of a minority, the world, and eventually Germany herself. In revolutions, outrage is generally converted directly into organized warfare and terrorism. In exploiting centuries of subjugation and oppressive rule in China, the Communists have added behavioral and organizational themes whose significance goes beyond providing an emotional outlet and which will be further explored in Chapter IV.

Although limited to the interpretation of behavioral change at the level of the individual, the most ambitious effort to relate anxiety to structured change in society has been Hagen's (1962) work. A number of developmental economists have concluded that innovation and technological change are basic to the growth of the developing countries, and also that the behavioral links implied in these changes are not well explained by economic growth theory. To change behavior, one must go beyond traditional ways and begin to question the environment. Both colonial society and traditional cultures direct psychological as well as social and political forces to see that change does not occur. The authoritarian relationship that prevails in most traditional societies is not necessarily destructive given the formidable odds against survival and the utter necessity of near perfect integration into the community. It is not irrational to live in ways that help one accept the uncertainties and violence of climate, sickness, and death, but these become less dominating features in societies that have the productivity to support more rewarding lives.

Hagen argues that status withdrawal, which may take place in a variety of forms, is the key to understanding how the crust of tradition, the essentially authoritarian structure, is dissolved. When the individual finds that his father, his superior in the old order, or his government are unmistakably inadequate, he is thrown into a quandary not unlike that of the victim of more brutal forms of racial and social subjugation. The capricious and severe punishment and the *rites de passage* to subdue childish outrage forever are no longer effective. Quite literally, the father can no longer answer the child's questions and is no longer a model to be imitated. The distribution, timing, and intensity of this experience vary greatly from society to society, but there is substantial historical evidence to buttress the argument. The occupation of Southeast Asia by the Japanese, the humiliation of the Ottomans in European power politics, and sheer coercive superiority of the European in Africa clearly set in motion doubts and anxieties that played heavily in bringing down rigid social orders.

The extent to which the reaction to status withdrawal is rooted in the Oedipal conflict described by Hagen has not been clearly demonstrated, although there are numerous studies of child-rearing in traditional societies that confirm his interpretation of the deadening effects of highly arbitrary socialization in early life. Most pertinent from the perspective of ideology is his discussion of the innovational personality, the critical mechanism in social adaptation and reorganization. Emotional tension may most certainly drive an individual to question the traditional structure that appears to be crumbling around him, but ambivalence and apprehension do not stop when he disconnects himself from the conformity of the past. In every historical case, the diffusion of innovative skill and the emergence of an experimental attitude toward the environment has taken a generation, often several generations. Throughout this period, individuals and groups need reassurance that their departures will contribute to a better society. There is a continuing strain in noting "relationships where others had not thought to find them" (Hagen, 1962: 68) and in soberly reflecting on the inconsistency and confusion of a society subjected to overpowering external threat. To be "unafraid of the unconscious" does not preclude the reflection of stress in new institutions or even the reassertion at some later point of the anxiety that for a time was worked out by adaptive measures.

The similarity of the underlying psychological mechanism does not assure similarity of institutional and social response. Hagen's own case studies indicate that the appearance of innovation varies greatly with the timing of the threat to traditional status structure, the historical and social patterns of traditional society, and the intensity of the threat itself. A number of factors of this kind contributed, for example, to China's stubborn resistance to change in the nineteenth century, while Japan's response was relatively rapid. Moreover, as discontent grew, the Japanese were able to transform parts of the old society while rebellion in China succeeded largely in removing old elites without building new institutions until the very recent recovery under the Communists. The emergence of a working ideology in the transition appears to be a highly salient feature in translating the initial individual tension into social structures and new institutions. Japan restored the Emperor as a symbol in the Meiji Restoration, kept a group of highly traditional advisers, the *genro,* close to the center of power, and imposed on the modernization process a status structure that bears many similarities to Tokugawa and earlier periods of Japan. The working ideology that was developed in Japan did much to legitimate the new society, but it also drew on many traditional symbols of Japanese society and restored many traditional patterns of behavior. The vulnerability of the new society to military leaders in the 1930s and its eventual total collapse into fascism suggests that the experiment was not an unqualified success.

The shortcomings of Hagen's highly imaginative effort are worth outlining because they bear directly on how emotional insecurity is converted into new kinds of behavior (Moore, 1963). First, the intensity of the Oedipal conflict varies greatly and may be moderated in a number of family relationships. While Freudian analysis alerts us to the many social repercussions of severe anxiety, it was mainly directed at exposing anxiety's pathological consequences for the person. However one may choose to evaluate these theories, they underscore the simple fact that reaction to threat may be so severe as to paralyze the individual or to damage his perception permanently. Total withdrawal remains an alternative change to constructively focused, innovative change. Second, the projection of anxiety on to the society can vary widely with the kind of scapegoats offered in the society and with the distribution of anxiety in the old class structure. The Japanese *samurai* and *ronin* were clearly disenchanted men, but their historical position in the society no doubt helped prepare them to play significant roles in a changing society. Moreover, their discontent permeated Japan over several hundred years prior to the major changes of the nineteenth century. The feudal chiefs or *daimyo* provided an intermediate target for their outrage, and one that had no key role to play in modernizing the society. The third possibility has been described in earlier sections of the chapter. The sense of inferiority and hatred may be so overpowering that the effects are socially destructive, leaving the potential innovator bewildered and adrift. Even worse, the uniformity and intensity of response may trigger brutality and violence that is just as inhumane as the repression of the old order.

THE EMOTIONAL DIMENSION
OF IDEOLOGY

In the context of a working ideology, emotional responses influence personalities, social and political systems, and culture. To say that hatred, fear, and uncertainty are seldom absent from human behavior is not to extol them as the central features of human existence, nor is it to deny the corresponding virtues of trust, affection, and security. But there is an unavoidable polarity of emotions which may be manifested in an endless number of ways toward every object or person we encounter. The exploitation of emotional insecurity in society and the denial of deep emotional needs can often be traced to many of the excesses of political and social systems. The modern totalitarian state tried to reject human emotion and affection by equating very basic fears and guilt with rationality and social order. The Marxists have also produced several of the most highly totalitarian societies known to man in the name of a still unachieved society where human feelings and desires would be unrestrained. The elliptical nature of the emotional response, especially in ideology, should be obvious: dichotomization of feelings and behavior elevated to the level of general principles of society or policy has always ended in disaster.

Ideology did not create this dilemma and is only one formulation of how men deal with it. The difficulties of attaching feeling to life have been most eloquently expressed in literature. Achebe's (1958) tormented schoolteacher, unable to accept his old village and destroyed by the "freedom" of the city, symbolizes the elementary and vital truths of emotional stress. Some writers, like Camus (1953), have been transfixed by the dilemma, unable to bear "slave camps under the flag of freedom," and acutely aware that Marx's oversimplifications took the lives of five million *Kulaks.* Men must both prove their innocence and unburden their guilt, and much of this is acted out in political history. The language of the social psychologist may seem far removed from the despair that enveloped Camus' life, but the destructiveness of either unbridled aggression or total withdrawal represent the same polarities in behavioral terms. Neither the autonomic nor the paranoid make good companions.

In his examination of the relation of emotion to ideology, Camus' disenchantment strikes a note that social scientists have begun to take more seriously, though without the preoccupation with the extremes of emotional stress that characterizes Camus' views. For Camus, all forms of rebellion, all attempts to adjust thought to action, eventually ended in defeat. The metaphysical rebel is most like the political revolutionary, where rebellion becomes "a demand for clarity and unity . . . an aspiration to order." The romantic rebel is perhaps more familiar to university life. "Compelled to astonish . . . spurred by provocation," he is the intellectual dandy of our age. The nihilist rebel is "compelled to do evil so as to be coherent" and is "consumed with pity and incapable of love." He closely resembles the paranoid in his compulsive and untempered hostility. All these figures could be identified among the ideological spokesmen of real life, and they all represent the destructive repercussions of compulsive responses to reconciling thought and action, hopes and reality, vision and practicality.

The thematic quality of the emotional content of ideology has made it difficult to measure and to relate to other political and social activities, but it is also the reason for its ubiquity as a form of expression. Politics, perhaps more than any other aspect of society, deals with superior-subordinate relationships. The political system has been defined as the procedures for the "authoritative allocation of values" (Easton, 1953). Symbols and themes are the building blocks for authority and legitimacy in political life. As Apter (1964: 22) puts it, ideology "promotes authority." As suggested in the context of the working ideology, emotional content provides direction and intensity to behavior at the individual, institutional, and cultural levels of action. Clearly, these are not the only functions of ideology in the political system, but they are functions that might easily be considered prerequisite to the cognitive and evaluative implications of ideology to be outlined in Chapters IV and V. The political system depends on being able to elicit some degree of uniformity of response from its members. This cannot be accomplished unless the people have a positive emotional orientation to the system, which means both an awareness of the direction that authority flows in the political system and a readiness to accept some degree of behavioral control from higher levels in the system.

The emotional dimensions of a working ideology provide important contributions to the social and political system. As previous examples indicate, these may be most easily observed among individuals, where the symbols and themes of the doctrine may have therapeutic effects, may direct attention to new goals of the system, and cultivate the minimal loyalty needed to establish a government. For the institutions of the society, both developing and developed, the ideology provides a medium for the dispersal of new norms. The institutionalizing effects are multiple: the new norms must, first, be communicated, new members must be attracted to the institutions, and they must be prepared to accept those standardized behaviors consistent with the achievement of its purposes. Normative change in highly industrial societies is generally not advanced by explicit, intensive use of ideology, but the juxtaposition of norms is constantly taking place and often does strike highly sensitive themes. The poverty program and racial integration in the United States are examples, though the latter problem may well merge with cultural change where differences are acute. Many developing countries have used ideology to promote new institutions such as the land reform in Mexico in 1910, or, more recently, the Algerian *autogestion* or self-management methods. Indeed, given the strong influence of ideology on the institutional development of a number of developing countries, it is curious that the democratic countries have on the whole been reluctant to examine their own ideological advantages more carefully in assisting development in the third world. Even in foreign policy, it seems apparent that American fears about Communism have excluded from our perception the primarily organizational role of ideology in China.

The relationship of emotion to ideology is difficult to trace, in part because cultures change very slowly and the cumulative effects of cultural values on social and political institutions are not easily differentiated from more immediate causes. Moreover, only the most foolhardy leader would, even if he could, indiscriminately attack the most fundamental and widely shared values of his society. Ataturk comes to mind as a nationalist leader who set out systematically to secularize religion in Turkey by removing the Sultan, supplanting Islamic law and closing centers for Islamic teaching. But forty years later, religious feelings persisted and were often highly influential (Rustow, 1965, 1957). Ataturk knew that deeply rooted cultural values had to change if Turkey were to modernize, but the attack on Islam was modulated by the relatively primitive state of communications, the lack of organization, and heightened loyalties he stimulated, making the tension of Islamic reform more bearable. There are some reasons to think, particularly from the Chinese experience, that intensive exploitation of the culture through mass communications and large organizations can cause severe dislocations. The relative advantages and disadvantages of directing ideology toward cultural values are no more easily calculated by social scientists than by politicians. It remains one of the more fascinating unanswered questions in the analysis of ideology and political change.

The exploitation of emotion in ideology is familiar in the West, and may even reflect a Western suspicion of emotion. In the individual's perception of his environment, there is ample psychological evidence that emotional intensity tends to increase rigidity and inflexibility. Most of these experiments have been done under clinical conditions (Postman, 1951) and remain generally unnoticed in our efforts to understand the relationship of ideology to broader forms of change. Under stress, individuals learn less efficiently, tend to exaggerate differences, and reject contradictory evidence. If these findings are indeed reflected in the process of social and political change in developing countries, developmental programs and projects could be seriously handicapped. The work on dogmatism and much related research in social psychology suggests that the use of traditional symbols to reinforce authority, as suggested by Huntington (1968), might well have substantial costs if the new citizens, in turn, become less innovative and less critical of their efforts to remodel the society. Similar disadvantages might well appear where ideology directs strong emotional appeals toward new norms.

The strong resistance to reorganization among the Algerian farms and factories under *autogestion* is one example. The initial transformation of the productive resources of the country was strongly supported by the ideology, but such intense feelings were involved that subsequent efforts to improve marketing, cultivation methods, and credit facilities were not easily understood by the participants.

A working ideology, of course, means more than the particular doctrine of the regime, and it is instructive to note how cultural values and institutional norms interact with the politically justified doctrine. The status of women in the society is often a revealing example, and one that Fanon gives special attention to. Independence movements in both traditionally oriented societies like Morocco and more secular settings like Tunisia played heavily on the subordination of women in their resistance to colonial rule, and the major parties in both countries and large feminist branches. But the feminist values advocated in the ideology of both countries interacted with very different cultural values and institutional patterns. Following independence, the advance of women in the society in Morocco became more or less a fashionable charity, and the feminist organization dwindled away, while, in Tunisia, feminist reforms, though certainly not without a certain vogue, continued to be highlighted by Bourguiba and were supported in educational programs. The full explanation of the different sequences of change can only be found by considering the entire fabric of the society, not just the political predispositions of the Moroccan monarch and the Tunisian president. The important point in the evolution of the respective ideological structures, however, is that individual beliefs and institutional norms about women varied widely in Morocco, and the emotional energies that were generated were easily dissipated with independence. Until we are better able to judge the intensity of feeling at various levels of the society, it will remain a difficult task to anticipate the differential impact of emotionally laden themes and symbols in political ideology.

While Apter's (1963) views on the "political religion" are phrased for the most part in terms of individual roles, the sharp distinction he makes between the use of emotional appeal in mobilization and reconciliation regimes may be misleading. It does not appear that more heterogeneous societies are immune to emotional appeals and emotionally justified behavior, but only that intensity of feeling may be directed into other channels.

But excessive dependence on emotion in politics has all too often ended in tragic and useless violence. It is an error, perhaps compounded by the failure to take into account the nature of structural differences, to suggest that ideology's emotional implications are more easily misdirected if centrally focused than if dispersed in subnational groupings of tribes, provinces, or communities. A stronger sense of national identity might have helped avert the Biafran disaster and the Bengali riots. The cultural and institutional setting into which the emotional appeal is introduced must be explicitly allowed for if the effects of emotional stress are to be appreciated.

Historical circumstances are such that leaders seldom need to make the rough estimates of how emotions will be stimulated, changed, and redirected by emotional themes and symbols in their doctrine. At worst, governments are reduced to a survival strategy that eliminates interest in how an emotional appeal might affect change in any systematic way. At best, they operate in hectic political settings with severe constraints and prefer to avoid the uncertainties and risks of emotional forms of communication. Lest this appear too cynical, there may be good reason for hesitating to exploit intense emotions and to encourage rigid commitment. Strong emotions are unstable, and the uniformity of behavior they stimulate can be damaging. The working ideology must also help articulate the more specific goals of the society and outline change in ways that can be adapted and judged by the citizens. Motivation and evaluation qualify emotional responses and will provide the focus for the next two chapters.

The overall framework of value change is not sufficiently

developed by dealing only with the emotional aspects of a country's ideological structure. However, the choices that are made, often implicitly, can be outlined. An appeal to emotion falls along a range of possibilities for individuals and for an almost endless number of collectivities. Individuals can be extremely rigid and fixed personalities, the authoritarian type described above, or open and experientially oriented persons. Institutional norms can be defensive and intransigent or flexible and adaptive. Likewise, the emotional orientation of newly introduced political values can appeal to historic and cultural fears, or open the way for more experimental and adaptive views of national development. Social science does not have tested ways of judging how either the individual's emotional vulnerability or the group's shared sensitivities will interact with new norms and political values. A first step toward improving our knowledge of how beliefs, attitudes, and norms are linked in political life is to recognize the affective dimension of all ideologies, including those often assumed to be highly rational and instrumental. Indeed, the present crisis of liberal, pluralist ideologies may be deepened by the ease with which Western nations have selectively ignored their own irrational behavior.

REFERENCES

ADORNO, T. V. et al. (1950) The Authoritarian Personality. New York: Harper.

APTER, D. E. [ed.] (1964) "Introduction: ideology and discontent," in Ideology and Discontent. New York: Free Press.

––– (1963) "Political religion in the new states," pp. 57-104 in C. Geertz [ed.] Old Societies and New States. New York: Free Press.

ACHEBE, C. (1958) Things Fall Apart. London: Heinemann.

BELL, D. (1965) The End of Ideology: On the Exhaustion of Political Ideas in the Fifties. New York: Free Press.

BENDA, H. J. (1958) The Crescent and the Rising Sun: Indonesian Islam under the Japanese Occupation 1942-1945. New York: Institute of Pacific Relations.

BENDIX, R. (1953) "Social stratification and political power," in R. Bendix and S. M. Lipset [eds.] Class, Status and Power. New York: Free Press.

BETTS, R. F. (1961) Assimilation and Association in French Colonial Theory. New York: Columbia Univ. Press.

CAMUS, A. (1953) The Rebel. London: Hamilton.

CHRISTIE, R. and M. JAHODA [eds.] (1954) Studies in the Scope and Method of the "Authoritarian Personality." New York: Free Press.

COHN, N. (1962) The Pursuit of the Millenium. London: Mercury.

COLEMAN, J. S. (1958) Nigeria: Background to Nationalism. Berkeley and Los Angeles: Univ. of California Press.

EASTON, D. (1953) The Political System. New York: Alfred A. Knopf.

FANON, F. (1963) The Wretched of the Earth. New York: Grove.

FESTINGER, L. (1957) A Theory of Cognitive Dissonance. Stanford: Stanford Univ. Press.

FORSTER, E. M. (1924) A Passage to India. London: Edward Arnold.

FRENKEL-BRUNSWIK, E. (1949) "Intolerance of ambiquity as an emotional and perceptual personality variable." J. of Personality 18: 108-143.

FROMM, E. (1965) Escape From Freedom. New York: Avon.

FRYE, R. N. [ed.] (1957) Islam and the West. The Hague: Mouton.

FURNIVALL, J. S. (1956) Colonial Policy and Practice. New York: New York Univ. Press.

GRIER, W. H. and P. M. COBBS (1968) Black Rage. New York: Bantam.

HAGEN, E. (1962) On the Theory of Social Change. Homewood, Ill.: Dorsey.

HALL, C. S. and G. LINDZEY (1957) Theories of Personality. New York: John Wiley.

HERBERLE, A. (1945) From Democracy to Nazism. Baton Rouge: Louisiana State Univ. Press.

HITLER, A. (1943) Mein Kampf (R. Manheim, trans.). Boston: Houghton Mifflin.

HUNTINGTON, S. P. (1968) Political Order in Changing Societies. New Haven, Conn.: Yale Univ. Press.

JORDAN, W. D. (1969) White over Black: American Attitudes Toward the Negro, 1550-1812. Baltimore: Penguin.

KARDINER, A. (1939) The Individual and His Society: The Psychodynamics of Primitive Social Organization. New York: Columbia Univ. Press.

LASSWELL, H. (1960) Psychopathology and Politics. New York: Viking.

LEWIS, B. (1961) The Emergence of Modern Turkey. New York: Oxford Univ. Press.

LIFTON, J. (1963) Thought Reform and the Psychology of Totalism. New York: W. W. Norton.

McCLELLAND, D. C. (1961) The Achieving Society. Princeton: D. Von Nostrand.

MANNONI, O. (1964) Prospero and Caliban: The Psychology of Colonization. New York: Frederick A. Praeger.

MASON, P. (1962) Prosper's Magic: Some Thoughts on Race and Class. London: Oxford Univ. Press.

MOORE, C. H. (1963) "Politics in a Tunisian village." Middle East J. 17 (Autumn): 527-540.

MURPHY, A. (1948) The Ideology of French Imperialism 1871-1881. Washington, D.C.: American.

POSTMAN, L. (1951) "Toward a general theory of cognition," pp. 242-272 in I. H. Rohrer and H. Sherif [eds.] Social Psychology at the Crossroads. New York: Harper.

ROHRER, J. H. and H. SHERIF [eds.] (1951) Social Psychology at the Crossroads. New York: Harper.

ROKEACH, M. (1960) The Open and Closed Mind. New York: Basic Books.

ROSBERG, C. G. and J. NOTTINGHAM (1966) The Myth of the Mau Mau: Nationalism in Kenya. New York: Frederick A. Praeger.

ROY, J. (1962) The War in Algeria. New York: Grove.

RUSTOW, D. A. (1965) "Turkey: the modernity of tradition," in L. Pye and S. Verba [eds.] Political Culture and Political Development. Princeton: Princeton Univ. Press.

——— (1957) "Politics and Islam in Turkey, 1920-1955," pp. 169-207 in R. Frye [ed.] Islam and the West. The Hague: Mouton.

SCHURMAN, F. (1968) "The attack of the Cultural Revolution on ideology and organization," in J. Ho and T. Tsou [eds.] China in Crisis: China's Heritage and the Communist Political System. Chicago: Univ. of Chicago Press.

——— (1969) Ideology and Organization in Communist China. Berkeley and Los Angeles: Univ. of California Press.

SULLIVAN, H. S. (1953) The Interpersonal Theory of Psychiatry. New York: W. W. Norton.

TALMON, J. L. (1955) The Origins of Totalitarian Democracy. London: Secker & Warburg.

TSOU, T. (1969) "The Cultural Revolution and the Chinese political system." China Q. 38: 63-91.

WAELDER, R. (1963) "Protest and revolution against Western societies," in M. Kaplan [ed.] Revolution in World Politics. New York: Free Press.

WINTHROP, J. D. (1969) White over Black. Baltimore: Penguin.

WOODRUFF, P. (1953) The Men Who Ruled India. London: Johnathan Cape.

WORSLEY, P. (1964) The Third World. London: Weidenfeld & Nicolson.

X, MALCOLM (1966) Autobiography of Malcolm X. New York: Grove.

Chapter IV

ADAPTIVE IDEOLOGY AND INDIVIDUAL COGNITION

Confining the discussion of ideology to the realm of emotional insecurity and anxiety reduction limits analysis to those relatively clear-cut cases where emotional stress becomes unbearable. The affective element of an ideology can never be excluded simply because it touches such primordial characteristics of men, but it is equally clear that societies do not constantly operate under such intense circumstances. The psychoanalytic model of man bears many resemblances to the classical economic model of man. The underlying psychic forces are defined in terms that escape demonstration and that are manifested in opposed forms of behavior. For many years, economists operated under similar assumptions, using an economic model of man that led to the conclusion that acting in one's immediate self-interest produced the most favorable economic results. The assumptions of the perfect market were needed to make this result appear, and much economic research has been devoted to showing that these assumptions seldom obtain. In some ways, Freudian and neo-Freudian thinkers were more modest. Starting from similarly embracing assumptions of human drives and needs, they realized that deep forms of emotional stress were limited in their application to normal societies, though social and political systems may sometimes act in pathological ways. A good deal of psychological theorizing since Freud has been directed toward easing this limitation.

The psychoanalytic model of man has severe constraints. It explains behavior most reliably under conditions of most severe stress, a state in which men fortunately do not always find themselves. Sullivan, Erikson, and other contemporary psychoanalysts have tried to devise theories to allow for the unfolding of personality through an individual's life span. Erikson (1963) has suggested that anxiety may be introduced into the individual's life at many stages. Important as early childhood and infantile experiences may be, one may success-fully adapt to the crisis of youth only to encounter new fears and obstacles in adulthood and old age. In some instances, they may be produced by the surfacing of very early frustra-tions and failures, and in other cases the individual may find adjustment to age and circumstances unbearable after a pre-viously successful and happy life. What Erikson suggests to improve our understanding of the temporal dimension of personality, Sullivan relates to the spatial dimension of per-sonality. Men must cope with a wide range of problems, many of them very remote and seldom recurring. The person-ality exists in a field of other persons, objects, and problems. While the immediate pressures of sexual adjustment persist, the person can be equally distressed by anxiety caused by more distant conditions.

The common quality of both these views that is funda-mental to this chapter is the concern for the environment of man and how he relates himself to it. The psychotic may be so unhappy that he will be unable to exist in any environ-ment, but for most people emotional conflict is less direct and less intense. As children, we may see important similarities between our fathers and political authorities (Easton and Hess, 1962), but as adults our relationship to authority has become, in most cases, much more complex. The political system is not just the parental relationship, happy or unhappy, extended to the entire society (Greenstein, 1965). To feel as intensely about political relationships as one does about sexual identity is rare. To respond to the hierarchical aspects of politics in the same manner as one might respond to parents, either as a child or as an adult, is unworkable in a complex society. Though used in a number of ways, the concept of motive describes our responses to objects in their environment in less emotional form. The advantages of this notion over psychoanalytic concepts in analyzing societies should be clearly understood (Berger and Lambert, 1968).

Motive enables us, first, to pose a much more diverse, and therefore much more accurate, representation of the environment in studying behavior. In addition to reacting to their basic drives, men also respond to a variety of problems about their work, their community, and their society. Though not necessarily inconsistent with psychoanalytic concepts, these more remote problems take diverse form and are difficult to generalize without the concept of motive. Second, motive permits us to pose the problems of individual choice in more remote settings and in a much more realistic manner (Deutsch and Kraus, 1965: 77-125). Men generally do not see each choice they make as central to their identity or closely bound to their basic needs. In a complex society, choices are made among numerous alternatives and objects, many of which are in fact interchangeable. Many of our goals are not absolute and essential, but relative and interdependent. Fundamental needs pose direct and inescapable choices, but there are numerous infinitely different ways to fill less immediate needs. The diversity of political life itself indicates the many ways men may find to achieve some minimal order in their lives. Third, motive makes it possible to talk much more explicitly about the behavioral consequences of perception. Important as it is to understand the individual psyche under stress, we also need to know how less emotional choices will affect society and institutions. Modern organizations and industrial social structures are only comprehensible to individuals by utilizing motives to thread our way through the overlapping, interchangeable mosiac of goals.

MOTIVE AND
IDEOLOGICAL STRUCTURE

An understanding of the importance of motive in ideological structures requires that some attention be given to the concept as it has been developed in social psychology. Very early in the emergence of the discipline, the experiments of Pavlov, Watson, and Thorndike focused attention on the learning process. From their early research can be traced the debates over theory that have predominated in social psychology to the present. The basic mechanism is the stimulus-response synapse by which secondary learning takes place in the form of habit. There are two prevailing theories of secondary learning, although either is consistent with the interpretation of motive for the general study of society and ideology (Hall and Lindzey, 1957: 421 ff.). Reinforcement theory advanced by Hull remained closer to the behavioral origins of social psychology, while Guthrie's associational theory was less concerned with the biological foundations of behavior and focused more heavily on cognition. Motivational or learning psychology did not so much reject psychoanalytic thought as take it for granted. Learning occurs by a stimulus, which, in the preponderance of experiments, is derived from basic needs for relief from hunger, pain, or sexual deprivation. The controversies in social psychology occur more at the next level of the theory in interpreting acquired drives, such as shame, anxiety, or conformity.

While the controversies among social psychologists cannot be resolved here, it is important to underscore the secondary response as a link between the personality and the environment. In the reinforcement framework, the reward becomes potentially generalizable, can be shared in society, and can become the common focus for behavior. All the social sciences dealing with more complex behavior, politics, economics, and sociology make critical assumptions about the proliferation of secondary responses in the form of rewarded behavior in society. In the associational framework, much the same step is made, but in the form of generalizations about communication and the learning of shared expectations, meanings, and attitudes. The early psychological theorists did not deny an interest in social behavior, although experimental and clinical research prevailed as the basic assumptions were tested. In either case, the psychologist seeks to discover the characteristics of individual responses of a higher order than the primary drives and, where possible, in terms that can be observed and measured independent of the actor himself. For example, a society that contains numerous ways of saving wealth for later consumption can quite predictably be interpreted as having a number of situations to develop the secondary response of thrift.

Without the concept of motive, it would be virtually impossible to link psychology to social behavior. For most human situations, it has great advantages over Freudian principles and theory. When we see a man driving a post into the ground, we do not reflect on his childhood experience and speculate about Oedipal rage, but we consider how he is protecting his property and look for the shape of the plot or the object he wishes to protect. Protecting one's property is a strongly reinforced habit in our society. One that may be overdone, even to the point of suggesting neurotic behavior, but also a kind of action that is generalized in the values, institutions, and norms of every community and nation. Without reasonably reliable guidelines about the behavior of those around us, we could not live in complex social systems any more than we could live in a society given over to unrestrained hostility.

Considering the large amount of rigorous research on learning and reinforcement, there is relatively little confirmed theory. The theoretical frameworks of social psychology are as rich and diverse as the findings. Deutsch and Krauss (1965: 545-546) were able to write that, despite the careful accumulation of findings, psychologists were still uncertain if rewards are necessary to learning. Likewise, Hall and Lindzey (1957: 538-557) reflected on the continuing difficulties of psychology in considering interpersonal behavior in complex environments and raised, as many other theorists have done, the continuing need for research that will somehow acknowledge the multiplicity of motives involved in normal behavior.

The political scientist has, on the whole, tended to oversimplify the concept of motive in his work, although political research must make many of the same assumptions about the interdependence of motives that have troubled numerous psychologists. On the other hand, it is only fair to note that the bulk of the psychological research on interpersonal perception and social learning is not easily transferable to the impersonal setting of politics, nor are the precise controls desired by psychologists easy to achieve in political research.

The underlying proposition that seems most helpful in relating motivational studies to social learning on the grand scale of ideology is perhaps the statement of Dollard and Miller (1941: 10) in one of the classic theoretical studies: "Individuals must be trained, in many situations, so that they will be comfortable when they are doing what others are doing and miserable when they are not." From this interest in how people extract commonalities from their interaction, it is only a short step to role theory and the organization of individual behavior around shared goals or rewards. Though not of central interest in much of the earlier psychological research on motivation and learning, the formulation of the desired rewards and goals is clearly a key aspect of ideology. Indeed, it will be argued that a working ideology may well be more important as a device to communicate and to describe motives than as leverage for affective loyalty to the regime.

The organizational implications of ideology will be referred to as its cognitive orientation (Symposium, 1957). More recently, psychologists have attempted to differentiate among levels of motivation or, more commonly, among attitudes. The distinction between a motive and an attitude is that the latter refers to the individual's orientation to a class of objects as opposed to the more limited scope generally attached to motive (Scott, 1968). Attitude is the notion of motive generalized to categories of responses and, as such, is a powerful concept enabling social scientists to refer to behavior in much broader terms. It should also be noted that the distinction is particularly useful where cognitive and affective distinctions are involved. It is less applicable to interpretations of behavior under emotional stress where feelings are projected, often uncritically, onto more general goals of the society. An emotional drive—intolerance, for example—may operate in an individual's immediate field of choice among occupation, friends, and the like, and also in his larger field of perception about government and education. Emotional intensity produces views that are undifferentiated in order to displace feelings of insecurity or fear. Thus, a person who hates black people does not want to learn about blacks, has no need for information about blacks, and resists cognitive distinctions in considering problems of race.

Because political scientists move much more freely than psychologists in considering motives and feelings in politics, politics has given little attention to the distinction between affective and cognitive responses. Indeed, one might consider the work of a generation of psychologists brought together by Hovland (1953) at Yale as dedicated to clarifying this distinction in interpersonal terms. For present purposes, the distinction may be sufficiently clear in the suggestions of several cognitive psychologists that we should differentiate between attitudes related to the individual's need to externalize his feelings and to reduce anxiety as opposed to those related to social adjustment or to perform specific functions, often of a routine nature. Bruner et al., (1957) point out that, in his terms, affective "categories" are not amenable to ready description in terms of the properties of the objects comprising them, while functional categories are because they "fulfill a concrete and specific task requirement." He also continues to distinguish "formal categories" or evaluative aspects of attitudes.

By facilitating the study of differentiated problems of interpersonal relationships and reward patterns in society motives, and its more general formulation in attitudes, the concept of motive becomes a powerful research tool. The affective dimension only enables us to make statements in the form of nominal variables—e.g., "I feel more strongly about my family than about my nation." Nominal ordering is, of course, extremely useful in empirical research, and, some would argue, often neglected or only partially exploited in political research. However, the experience of psychology suggests that finer distinctions are needed if we are to explore many of the more routine actions of individuals as well as collective behavior. The concept of motive adds an element of specificity by making it possible for the analyst to compare cognitively oriented behavior both in terms of the individual's overall pattern of motivation and in terms of the collective significance of the reward or object. There is no way to equate hatred or frustration, nor does it help much in social analysis to know that a person or group hates black men more than yellow men. What is needed to discuss collective behavior, as well as the more complex patterns of interpersonal behavior, is a way of translating feeling into more specific characteristics of the individual and the group. Motivation makes the critical additional step by posing statements in the form, "I hate black men because they threaten my job, my property values, and so on."

By talking about motives and attitudes, we can arrive at a more direct and detailed statement of the arrangement of goals and rewards in the society. Obviously, if all objects are intensely attached to some highly emotional response, the refinements of motivational studies are not very useful or necessary. We know how the severely prejudiced person will act in all his roles, and we are thrown back into the authoritarian syndrome outlined in Chapter III. The nominal quality of observations made in this framework allows us to make statements about direction, as previously noted, but it does not contribute greatly to understanding shades of difference and degrees of commitment. A man may love his country, but he may not love it enough to support an unjust war, as the Vietnam conflict so clearly demonstrated. In this case, a number of other incentives, such as solving urban problems and overcoming internal racial crises, are more important than the war. People value a number of other goals in their society which qualify national loyalty, though these complications may not be readily apparent at the very remote level of national opinion. Motives and attitudes permit us to make relatively specific formulations concerning the interdependence of national and group objectives.

Clearly, the entire fabric of goals, rewards, and sanctions that represent the diverse motives in a society are not easily contained in a single research design. Much less is it desirable to include them all in a study of a political system. On the other hand, so long as ideology is conceived as only an expression of positive or negative feelings about authority, government, or the state, very few useful conclusions can be drawn. In our conventional knowledge, we often speak of the United States as too materialistic or of England as too class-conscious. Such crude statements are in fact assertions about the mosaic of motives operating in the society and how they relate to the environment. Whether or not they are to be included in the framework of ideology is an arbitrary choice in the sense that ideology or any other social phenomenon can be defined as an important factor. The more important consideration, however, is how such a definition helps solve important problems and clarify theory. There are a number of reasons why motive and attitude should be included in ideological analysis.

An ideology extended in meaning from a simple doctrine to the motivational pattern of a society is much closer to the way in which political values are indeed communicated and applied in society. In early childhood, citizens are in fact conditioned in a way that closely approximates the laboratory study of motives. School children are taught not only to love their country and to respect the President, but also to accept certain kinds of action and goals as necessary to the political system and as relevant to their obtaining valued rewards in society. Moreover, a working ideology conveys important notions about participation in politics, the responsibility of office and the duties of citizens. These are all derived from commonly accepted goals in the society which may be stated in only the most general form in ideological statements. The county, the state, and the nation are not simply objects of affection, but centers for a number of activities that people in varying degrees learn about, find useful in their lives, and, in turn, decide to support through taxes, fees, and the like, under pain of commonly supported sanctions. Given the very easy way in which one might speak of the political system as a particular kind of reward and punishment relationship, it appears curious that political science has not more effectively incorporated motivational research in its studies.

The reasons for this shortcoming are worth examining. First, under normal circumstances, the existence of sanctions and their form is seldom questioned in politics. In most nations, specific actions involving individual punishment are carefully isolated within the judicial system. Second, most modern political systems are quite permissive in the exercise of individual choice outside socially approved sanctions for directly threatening political order. In only a few democracies is voting obligatory. Very seldom are the choices among issues of public policy crystal clear for the analyst or the participant. Third, there are difficult problems of stating the institutional differences that shape goals in different political systems. Rewards and inducements are very differently structured in a more highly bureaucratic France than in a federal system such as the United States. Motivation in politics will clearly differ radically between a less-developed country and an industrial country with a more diverse and more affluent society.

Nevertheless, our habitual responses to politics are fundamental to the working of a political system and closely linked
to ideology. Indeed, a working ideology might be measured
in terms of the range of choice or variety of rewards related
to the political system, the kinds of behaviors it sanctions in
order to affect these choices, and its usefulness in helping
citizens order politics in more specific terms. The cognitive
dimension of an ideology is how it helps citizens, groups, and
institutions differentiate their environment and attach shared
values to numerous specific alternatives. This seems to be a
more important question for developing countries than for
more developed countries, where many of these choices are
in fact passed on to more specialized and more competent
groups whose actions may or may not be subject to review.
The proliferation may become so great that it is actually
difficult to keep the mosaic of rewards and punishments
under scrutiny. This is a very different problem from that of
the less-developed country which, as Bendix (1964: 230)
noted in India, may lack an "ideological rationale." By this,
he does not appear to mean that Indians do not love their
country or revere their leaders, but that the ideology fails to
underscore the tasks to be done.

LINKING MOTIVES
TO IDEOLOGY

The problem of linking ideology to motives can perhaps be
most easily conceived by thinking first of the general question of how the members of a society relate an immense
range of social differences to the political system. The society
represents a variety of choices, goals, and rewards to which
its members are oriented, in many cases conditioned to from
early childhood. Broadly speaking, the industrial societies
pose a more specialized set of goals—i.e., have a greater
division of labor—and individuals are organized more inten-
sively around the production process. Goals are more diverse
and social behavior more specialized. In the less-developed

countries, goals are less diverse and there is less division of labor. The organization of society has a direct bearing on the interdependence of ideology and motives. The goals toward which industrially organized men are oriented require fine distinctions and pose quite specific, concrete alternatives to the individual.

The developing country has a very different problem in linking motives to social action. After the initial hurdle of establishing loyalty to the government, there remain difficult choices of how to articulate and diversify motives at the national level. Some ideologies strongly resist such articulation, as seen in Gandhi's preference for village industries and peasant resistance to modern forms of credit, marketing, and the like. In many ways, articulating the motivational field to encourage social change in the developing country is a more delicate task than generating authority and loyalty in the early stages of development. Ideological doctrine almost always talks of motives in an indirect fashion, exhorting the populace to make greater sacrifices, organizing national loans and subscriptions for development, and associating centrally determined restrictions with loyalty. For the initial step toward generating a more articulate and more specific range of motives in the society, these tactics are probably necessary, but they do not convert emotionally stated goals into a form that can be learned and widely applied by citizens. Only in a very crude sense do the initial efforts utilize reinforcement theory, nor is this easy when the rewards and benefits of government are limited by the overall level of social and economic development.

The first step toward evolving a working ideology is establishing those national goals and rewards considered central to growth. There are several stages in this process, the first being to acquire enough confidence to express publicly more specific ideas about the future. Simple as this may sound, most developing countries remain hesitant to articulate their goals in sufficiently specific form to promote learning about the newly emerging society (Ashford, 1965). The limited resources, the fear of excessive expectations, and the uncertainties of political decision-making all contribute to this reluctance to use values to begin to establish new behavior. The leaders are usually acutely aware of the very low level of specialization of labor and the strength of tribal, communal, and religious values that often conflict with change. The result is that the first motives to be articulated through ideology are often diffuse and not well suited to changing behavior. The more specific goals to emerge are generally vague statements about the necessity to industrialize, to maintain defenses, and to pay taxes. New governments tend to describe means of support before they turn to problems linking individual and group view of the nation to growth. They fail to realize that the two processes—more effective government for change and more productive social behavior—are interdependent.

The problems of relating motives to ideology will certainly vary in complexity with the size of the society, its overall level of development, and its resources and capacities. Thus, a very small country with fairly limited opportunities for growth may well have a much simpler task of demonstrating the ways in which individual motives and group norms link to change than will a highly diverse country. These are problems of scale which complicate every form of social analysis but are particularly difficult in understanding political systems. In a large society, the problems of both political control and selection of developmental opportunities must operate with large numbers of persons and over greater distances. The entire organizational setting for channeling goods and services is complex, as are broader problems of distributing rewards and sanctions in society. For these reasons, the best illustration of the necessity for ideological change is a large society, such as China, which has encountered enormous organizational problems in a relatively short time. The revolution in China could not be propelled into an indefinite future by the emotional energy aroused by liberation, nor could any group of leaders manage the vast array of problems facing China in 1949 without some reasonably specific notions of how individual actions might most appropriately fulfill the highly abstract goals of the struggle.

Tsou (1969a: 289) has noted that the ideology of traditional and Communist China has changed radically in content but not in form. He sees substantial historical continuity in the emphasis on correct leadership, the role of the bureaucracy, and the use of power in China. These similarities facilitated the transfer of power, which is why the remnants of the traditional power structure come under such fierce attack. But the new society, as Tsou notes, had to cope with immense environmental changes, such as industrialization, land reform, collectivization, and defense, all of which were essential to the success of the new government. An Ivory Coast or a Thailand might set out gradually to adjust ideas to the tasks at hand, and might to some extent succeed in keeping its political and socioeconomic problems distinct. However, the changes in content necessary to China's recovery and growth in 1949 had to be ordered in a more explicit way not only to harmonize with doctrine, but also to focus change on specific, concrete actions required on a vast scale in order to rebuild China.

There were a number of predisposing factors that make the motivational transformation of Chinese ideology more obvious than it may be in most other countries. Ever since his retreat in the 1930s, Mao's thought had focused on how best to unite ideology, policy, and social practice (Lewis, 1963: 10). Perhaps Mao's distinctive contribution to Communist theory has been his conviction that the struggle for success is finally resolved by effectively linking the mass to government through change. The purpose of ideological controversy is to find the correct practice, the most appropriate policy, and the most effective motivational form to bring about social and economic change. The Yenan exile was itself a learning process and an experiment in motivating peasants. Experience and ideology led Mao to place great emphasis on the peasant and worker as the basic agents of change. To a degree that was never achieved in Russia and other Communist countries, the new society was to have a mass base for implementing policy and for directly bringing about change. The larger implications of this tension within Chinese ideology has been the shifting between mass-based and party-based tactics, the competing efforts to mobilize population and to bureaucratize behavior, and the intensive application of communication techniques to overcome the immense distances between citizens and leaders. The Cultural Revolution (Tsou, 1969b: 80) can be viewed as one sequel in numerous campaigns to bring people into close contact with leadership and policy.

Another strand of Mao's thought that placed emphasis on motivational ties to the ideology is his constant awareness that expertise and administration may corrupt or arrest the continuing struggle to rebuild the country. His concern for the dilution of revolutionary effort goes far beyond the usual revolutionary dilemma of how to institutionalize progress. Lewis (1963: 18) has noted Mao's attack on "localism," "opportunism," and "careerism" in the party can be traced back to 1928. The same thought continues in Mao's 1967 statement during the Cultural Revolution, "Let the masses liberate themselves and educate themselves." The rivalry between Mao and Liu Shao-ch'i was essentially a controversy over how best to link the massive change needed in Chinese behavior to the ideology. Mao might be looked upon as an extreme example of a national leader who considers ideology as a learning device and who, in turn, felt it essential to keep direct lines of ideological communication open to the very roots of society. This, of course, does not resolve the problem of how to assure sufficient coordination of new behavior to accomplish new tasks successfully. The Great Leap Forward, with its communal steel factories and mass-directed enterprise might be considered the most daring experiment among contemporary developing countries to eliminate the constraints of directors, managers, and planners as the intermediaries in conveying policy to individual citizens. Its failure demonstrated that some kind of sorting out or ordering of motives was essential to a complex social structure.

A distinguishing characteristic of ideologically inspired change in China has been not only that individuals must act differently, which after all could be accomplished by coercion alone, but also that individuals should acknowledge that they are acting differently and publicly express the reasons why their behavior has changed. These experiences are, of course, heavily larded with symbolic forms of ideology, but they could hardly have been performed on such a large scale without mechanisms to convert pure ideological statements into a form that enables individuals to identify specific goals and to interpret their choices. The device used in China has been the rectification campaign, which Lewis (1963: 169-175) considers the hallmark of Communist Chinese thought. In effect, the rectification campaigns serve as correcting mechanisms for motives set in action by earlier policy decisions. Many developing countries have relied on more institutional forms of central control—the army or the bureaucracy—to adjust motivation. China is distinguished by the extent to which this function has been channeled directly to the people. Though obviously not uniformly successful, the magnitude of change in China in twenty years should caution one against an easy dismissal of the role of ideology in transforming a society.

The importance of attaching ideas to action in China has been analyzed in great detail by Shurmann (1968: 22), who developed the distinction between pure and practical ideology to underscore Mao's stress on ideology as a "rational instrument for action." Rectification was to serve as the mediating device in bringing about change. As contradictions or failures appeared, the masses engaged in the self-criticism and self-examination needed to find a new course of action. In a specialized economy, this can lead to extraordinary problems in determining the best kind of organization or the most appropriate form of management. For example, the "three-unification movement" during the Great Leap Forward was to remove the distinctions among party cadres, workers, and technicians. The solution was not simply one of finding a justification for the three roles, but actually of having one person act in all three roles. More simply, the ideal Chinese was to learn about three kinds of behavior and himself reconcile the motives that might lead to each kind of activity by in fact performing each activity. Clearly, the pressures placed on individuals in such a society are immense. But the awareness generated of the necessity for change and the understanding disseminated in a relatively brief period of time of the actual behaviors needed to reconstruct a disorganized and depressed society has no parallel among contemporary developing countries.

The campaign technique is, of course, basic to the entire process of linking motives to ideology in China. Only the organization of the army might have equalled the capacity of the party to mobilize millions of citizens, but it could have been more difficult to adjust to new goals using military power. Even the party has undergone massive transformations as the necessity to adjust policy and to revise methods has arisen. Shurmann notes that, in 1958, the Great Leap Forward nearly destroyed the bureaucracy. Potential vested interests—i.e., those who might devise distinct motives (such as the intellectuals) are under constant surveillance. The effects of this procession of change on the individual are curiously like those of Protestant thought in the early stages of capitalism. Thus, knowledge is "participation in social practice" (Lewis, 1963: 42), energies are furiously applied to reshaping the environment, and accomplishment is the final proof of individual virtue. One must not just believe; he must also do something. Like predestination, participation in the class struggle still does not guarantee salvation because the activity selected may itself fail.

The crucial institution in relating massive behavioral change to ideology has been the party, though the party itself has undergone substantial change in the past twenty years, and the tactic of direct mass action has taken its toll in party purges. Mao and his colleagues set out to organize a party that would in fact be the communicator of new behavior, not just new values, to the society. There is a "party line" for everything: how to raise hogs, how to start a credit cooperative, how to build a house, and countless additional detailed instructions. The training of party cadres and the preparation of party members obviously become the most critical and central features of political life. Intensive education, obligatory discussion, endless memorization, and detailed plans for individual advancement are the key to conditioning the mass to ideology and motivational goals. But the cadres are not performing a task ritually or under constant personal threat. Their training is to prepare them to find the practices that fulfill the ideology, to study information and results critically, and to undertake reviews and evaluations of progress. The party has enabled China to make amazing economic and social advances, although there remain unsolved problems of selecting leaders and keeping open the direct link between mass and elite.

The Chinese experience illustrates a fundamental problem in using the concept of motive in political analysis. Both Schurmann's (1968) discussion of practical ideology and Johnson's (1966) insight into the use of values as explanations omit an important distinction in relating motives to political ideas. The massive application of ideology in a highly applied form—that is, directly to problems of the environment—neglects the tendency to conceal how to generalize motivational attachments as behavior becomes more complex. Each degree of success threatens to become grounds for resisting future change and the basis of power for a group standing between the leaders and the mass. Mao's application of direct, individual conditioning, largely directed into productive behavior, dramatically reveals the use of ideology in working situations, but the technique itself minimizes the extent to which individuals and groups attribute independent meaning to their successful acts. China was prepared to use ideology in a practical way, but the entire scheme of rectification and continued self-examination places a very rigid limitation on future learning and how motivation can adapt to unforeseen conditions. As Johnson observes (1966: 35), "value sharing" expands collective capacity beyond that possible through coercive cooperation. Precisely for this reason, growing nations must begin to interpret their ideologies in motivational form. But each increase in refinement of a working ideology brings new complications and new capacities for choice. The Chinese want to use ideology to create more complex kinds of productive behavior, but are most reluctant to see the effects of such motives examined except in terms of their concrete, material results.

WORKING IDEOLOGY
AND STRUCTURAL CHANGE

The Chinese example has indicated the cumulative effects of aligning motives with ideology may be resisted by the same leaders who first took a more experimental view toward the use of ideology. China is not alone in this experience. The emotional stimulus of ideology appears attractive to an elite and seems more easily manipulated than the organizational and institutional norms evolved as goals are manifested. There is a difficult analytical problem in moving from individual motivation, which the social psychologist has studied in great detail, to the social effects of shared motives (Teune, 1970). Much the same problem exists for the national leader and the policy maker in the developing country. The analyst who generalizes too readily from individual data to statements about the society may commit an ecological fallacy; the leader who does this is engaging in wishful thinking and may make serious errors.

Aggregate measures of links between political behavior and national ideology are most difficult because of the immense structural variations among societies. The difference in the levels of development of villages (Jacob, 1971), contrasting views on the future of tradition, and the varying degrees of exposure to government officials and to political parties all influence motives. In developing countries, most of the social research on this kind of problem has been done with broad measures of social mobilization, which, in turn, permit only vague generalizations about the degree of uniformity of individual motivation. Thus, the early work of Deutsch (1961) and Lerner (1958) on socioeconomic and communications correlates of development provide rough indicators of how motivational forces begin to penetrate a society. At best, they tell us that a minimal level of literacy, followed by increments in urbanization and political participation, is a general pattern by which new behavior permeates the society and takes shape as new normative habits. Important as these findings are in helping us understand the broad forces at work in the development process, they tell us very little about the structural obstacles and inhibitions affecting the organization of norms, much less how the thousands of people acquiring new skills and expectations begin to restructure their emotional ties to ideology. The aggregate figures represent increased social differentiation, reflected in higher productivity and wealth, but do not describe how the mobilized individual attaches new organizational and cognitive meaning to these achievements.

Until more detailed research is done on the linkage between motivation and political values, only the most tentative statements can be made. Thus, it seems reasonable to hypothesize that persons moving into cities are politically less content with the system and tend to be prone to more violent forms of political expression. A secondary analysis of the Almond-Verba data on Mexico indicates, for that country at least, that the converse appears to be the case (Cornelius, 1969). Recent immigrants into the larger towns and cities included in their survey tended to be less activist politically than did long-term residents. Their motives for moving into urban environments appeared to have less relation to political protest and dissatisfaction than an easy assumption about frustration and emotional insecurity might suggest. For the Mexican—and very likely for many others attracted by urban life in developing countries—the goals being south in the city seem to be distinguished from political motives and expectations. Moving into the city places the individual in a situation where he can more easily express his political preferences, but it also presents him with a much more diverse range of goals and needs, requiring a more specialized and complex view of his role in society.

PUTTING MOTIVES
TO WORK

The descriptive and historical materials on the earlier modernizing nations are perhaps the best illustration of the slow, often hazardous process by which individual and group goals become linked to national ideology. The upheavals of late nineteenth-century Japan and early twentieth-century Turkey and Mexico can be looked upon as the first step in a long and tortuous process of increasing politial awareness and redistributing incentives in the society. Hopefully, this transpires in a way that permits the population to lead more productive and more rewarding lives. The process of generating goals, that can be shared while also increasing specialization in the society, can be more easily viewed over the two or three generations that have passed while the early modernizers rebuilt their countries. Their experience is also instructive because it suggests how the emotional energy released by the revolution can be channeled into new kinds of behavior and reshaped to meet cognitive needs. These intense shocks early in the reconstruction of the society not only forced old elites to revise their thinking, but also set in motion forces that provided a more articulate ideology.

The Mexican revolution and its consequences are a particularly good illustration. It is possible to make a persuasive argument that the highly manipulated and centrally controlled process of change under Diaz and earlier strong men before 1910 was an effective and even preferable way of transforming the society (Scott, 1964: 102-109). Nor did the decade of violence following the revolution put an end to the government of *caudillos,* or strong men. But there is also evidence to indicate that diverse social changes unleashed by the revolution enabled Mexico to take control of her development, most definitely since the nationalization of oil in 1938. The PNR *(Partido Nacional Revolucionario)* became an accepted mechanism for the transfer of power and was explicitly based on interest groups. Like Japan and Turkey, the prerevolutionary, intellectual ferment raised profound questions about the ordering of Mexican society. As early as 1889, there was a conference to explore how to promote nationalist sentiment in Mexico. There was increasing awareness that the caudillo regime not only confined a sense of nationality to the privileged few, but also severely limited the ways that peasants and workers could articulate their interests in the political system.

The forces that generated irrepressible pressure for change were multiple in Mexico, as in most developing countries. The long history of foreign intervention, the growing discontent among strategic groups such as teachers, and the linguistic and ethnic homogeneity of the people facilitated change at the level of the entire social and political system. The provisions of the 1917 Constitution for agrarian reform, educational opportunity, legal rights for women and illegitimate children, and the recognition of trade unions and reasonable working standards indicate the extent to which the revolution incorporated a range of relatively specific goals. The redirection and linkage of individual motives in this transition defies easy description, but the participation of peasant groups in the revolution became the foundation for land reform, the recognition of workers' rights opened the way for union organization, and the efforts of the Catholic Church to reassert its influence were brought to an end. Though the costs in bloodshed and disruption were high, it is difficult to conceive how so thorough a restructuring of the society could otherwise have been achieved. Out of the revolution came a new set of goals for the society, in part enshrined in the constitution, which were to serve as standards for subsequent governments and, more importantly, which became the concrete aims by which Mexicans could attach their interests to the national political system.

The way in which the motives embodied in the revolution were eventually attached to the political system is especially instructive in the Mexican case, for it may well provide an example for similar problems of linkage for African and Asian countries now undergoing rapid socioeconomic change. Out of the diverse interests associated with the revolution, a nationalist party emerged with a functionally based organization. Seldom has a political organization so directly reflected the motives of political groups. From 1945, the PRI *(Partido Revolucionario Institucional),* successor to the PRN, was built on sections for workers, peasants, and popular groups. Within each of these categories, a number of organizations exist, and there has from time to time been jockeying for power among these groups, but the PRI has managed to amalgamate the interests of these three well-defined sectors of the society into a continuing party structure. The party institutionalized the motives linking various interests to the political system and, by doing so, transformed the revolutionary ideology (Needler, 1961).

The problems of aligning psychological forces with developmental change are formidable, but reorienting individual motives to a national pattern of beliefs must be accomplished. The full dimensions of the restructuring of goals at both the individual and collective levels can only be seen in the panorama of events preceding the more successful attempts to transform societies. The reforms of Mahmud II in the early nineteenth-century Ottoman Empire and the mid-century struggle over the Tanzimat created a long period of agitation and self-doubt that did much to prepare Turkey for more radical change. The reaction against these early reformers suggests how profound a threat they posed.

The old safeguards, the old balances provided by law, custom, and established interests had been abrogated or eliminated. The limiting power of the Janissaries . . . had been destroyed; the Holy Law itself had been disregarded or violated, and replaced by a caricature of Western laws which . . . left the sovereign power free from any check at all (Lewis, 1961: 167).

The disillusionment with the Tokugawa regime was perhaps less forcefully voiced, though the same pattern of criticism, doubt, and imitation can be found. While "the final assault on the shogunate, made in the name of the emperor and national interest, did not destroy the social hierarchy (Hall, 1964: 40), the way was opened for those determined to change Japan. The Meiji Constitution of 1889 represents a partial restoration of oligarchic rule in Japan, but it also put Japan on the course of rapid change and dramatically transformed leadership in the society. The important quality of the transformation of national values espoused in Japan, Mexico, and Turkey was precisely that they survived on the affective level of perception—i.e., they sustained loyalty and affection for the country—while also adding a cognitive dimension—i.e., providing alternatives for individuals and groups to learn about their environment, to change social organizations, and to experiment with ways of influencing society.

The motive as conceived in social psychology does not answer questions about ideological transformation because it remains basically a model of individual behavior and gives little direction toward understanding the cumulative effects of motives that are justified and ordered by more remote values. A typical example might be Pakistan, where substantial economic progress was made in the past decade by launching new entrepreneurs and even turning over some public activities to private ownership. Ayub's rationale for this policy, which was not derived from the general aims of the society, was pragmatic. Pakistan lacked managerial skill, the public bureaucracy had not fostered growth, and industrial growth had to be given precedence over infrastructure. The effect was to elicit more new behavior motivated by material gain, which did indeed contribute substantially to growth. But the new entrepreneurs pursued their goals so assiduously that they were increasingly detached from the more general aims and conflicts of the society, became objects of resentment, and were easily exploited for short-run political interests. Pakistan achieved considerable growth under Ayub, but it was not as readily evident that she made comparable progress toward fashioning a working ideology that could assure citizens that change helped manifest the overall aims of the society.

Although the difficulties of structuring newly motivated behavior are substantial, the importance of generating new motives as an impetus for social change and economic growth has been strongly advocated. The most elaborate case has been made by McClelland (1961), whose work has made the "achievement motive" part of the common parlance of development. Like Hagen, McClelland arrives at his inquiry by examining the inadequacy of several economic and historical explanations of how growth starts. McClelland reasoned that the capacity to reconstruct one's environment must have motivational origins. Weber and others suggested that ethical change in Western societies predisposed Europeans toward changing conditions and enabled them to derive satisfaction and rewards from making such changes. From this position, it is only a short step to considering whether or not persons may develop a "need" to perform well, although McClelland and his colleagues have limited their inquiry thus far to the performance of productive forms of behavior.

Many experiments and studies have been conducted to demonstrate the association between economic growth and the need for achievement. Using school books, popular literature, and the press, McClelland and his group were able to demonstrate that the motive favoring achievement appeared in a number of societies before periods of substantial economic growth. Clinical studies identified the motive among children. Historical studies suggested comparable associations in ancient Greece, medieval Spain, eighteenth-century England, and nineteenth-century America. The research also explored the influence of institutional change in the family, the political system, and communications. Though the findings are subject to some qualification, the link to ideology is suggested in McClelland's (1961: 193) conclusion that "the more successful societies are those which have prevented . . . disorder by switching loyalties most effectively from tradition to organized public opinion as represented by the mass media." Combined with other indications that societies that use peer group support for leaders rather than authoritarian measures have often been better achievers, there are indications that achievement motivation is related to structural changes and to more general beliefs in the society.

Nevertheless, the achievement motive is largely concerned with productive behavior and gives less attention to the structural problems of how individuals discriminate among new roles, seek to change their initial state, and act in the more remote environment of the political system. The more general values of the society affect the structuring of motivation for change by communicating and describing the range of opportunity for the achiever. Subsequent research added to the McClelland model the individual's expectation of success from previous experience and the degree of satisfaction anticipated in a successful act (Crockett, 1964). How the desire to achieve may well be channelled in different kinds of behavior given the individual's family background, social status, and the variety of social opportunities to change one's status. The work on achievement underscores the extent to which the pattern of development, thought of in terms of increasing differention and production, is constantly generating new values and attitudes in the society that may or may not have a bearing on national political values. To take the extreme case, it is conceivable that, in the reconstruction of the country, the subordinate goals established to motivate individuals and groups to engage in new behavior might be totally disconnected from the affectively stated bases for national identity and loyalty. Because economic growth often plays a predominant part in establishing programs and priorities for change in developing countries, they run a high risk of demonstrating that the highly laudable purposes for creating the new state are unrelated to the actual changes in the society.

The possibility of successfully disengaging the ideology from the values that indeed motivate change in the society may well be greater in early stages of development. If resources are scarce and those privileged to have access to them are reluctant to confront global issues of political change, growth may serve both to concentrate power and to undermine loyalty to the system. Rigid class lines, restricted access to opportunity, and arbitrary limitations on the flow of information enhance such disparities. The more severe these disparities become, the more difficult will be any subsequent effort to expand participation. The political system is probably the most important device for ensuring some reconciliation between motives and ideology, but this is difficult in early stages of socioeconomic change when the first innovators are indeed being asked to take large risks and depart from traditionally reinforced, widely approved patterns of behavior. Direct checks on the formation of influential interests, which may easily incorporate the new entrepreneurs, may be counter-productive by actually slowing growth and placing more emphasis on income distribution than appears economically feasible. As the total wealth of the society increases and as more and more people find that their motives can contribute to advancing both personal and social goals, the possibilities of major disparities decrease.

MOTIVE AS AN
OBSTACLE TO CHANGE

Countries undergoing rapid socioeconomic change encounter particularly difficult problems of constructing motivational linkages to national ideology. But it must also be recognized that change on the scale required to generate new wealth will in the early stages of development have to call on individual and group motives. This appears to be valid for a number of capitalist-oriented societies, such as Taiwan and South Korea, as well as socialist societies, such as China or Yugoslavia. Individuals cannot be brought into more effective organizations and be given more productive skills without becoming more aware of their increased contribution to national prosperity and growth. Especially in the first attempts to increase productivity, the new government is dependent on the educated segment of the society, who, often quite regardless of doctrinal justification for change, may take a shortsighted view of national reconstruction. The result is not so much a crisis of production, because these problems can be reasonably well supervised and planned, but a crisis of ideology as the unavoidable disparities in rewards become obvious and acute.

Such a crisis of ideology may not only diminish affective ties to the nation, but may distort the more delicate task of continuously devising the organizational and institutional norms needed to bring new behavior into some broadly understood relationship with the explicit doctrine of the developing country. As differentiation takes place and privileged interests appear, the simple reassertion of popular national symbols—i.e., the renewed use of affectively stimulated loyalty, can be at best only a stopgap and may increase conflict for individuals trying to adjust to new roles. Thus, Menderes' appeal to the Turkish peasants in the 1950s had its economic costs in supporting less efficient farmers, but it also had great importance in persuading the still remote rural segment of Turkish society that it too had a stake in Turkey's future. Nationalism was not being used to unify a nation in the manner of Ataturk, but to facilitate a redistribution of national wealth and effort. Despite the excesses of the Menderes regime, the isolated population began to see that their activities as well as their feelings were joined in supporting the political system. There are no clear guidelines to suggest the best organization and timing for such changes, but they appear crucial to the elaboration of an ideology in more effective, working form.

Another way of stating this problem is the assumption in much of Western thinking that self-perception—i.e., motives—and roles are easily integrated. Through a number of fortunate historical circumstances, this may be correct when speaking of the United States or Britain, but it is equally apparent that the effective relationship between one's self-image and the tasks he performs has not been a simple transformation even in many Western societies. There is a good deal of evidence that French citizens find the gap between their political and social roles and their self-perception difficult to reconcile (Converse and Depeux, 1962). Violence is, of course, the most easily observed indication of such disparities. But the dislocation between motive and role appears in many more subtle forms, such as the difficulty many Frenchmen have in identifying their party affiliation. Further evidence is found in the Almond and Verba (1965) study which reveals the large disparities between affective attachment to the French political system and their confidence that it can indeed fulfill their goals and respond to their needs. Thus, it is probably correct to argue that emotional ties to France have been reinforced or intensified relative to the expectation that the system will work well even at times when the society was materially improving (Greenstein and Tarrow, 1969). The Frenchman takes refuge in the glory of France because he does not identify more specific relationships between himself and the system. The subsequent problems of achieving a viable political order and an effective economic change are well known.

A working ideology depends on generating consistent links between the affective attachment to values and the activities of the society itself. The motivational model of man asserts that the appropriate allocation of rewards in society will bring about behavioral change. While this may be correct, it does not assure that the newly created roles will be effectively internalized or well distributed. Hence, the assumption behind a good deal of developmental effort that an increasingly productive society will be accompanied with increased loyalty to the political system and satisfaction with the society may be seriously misleading. The inducements to enter into new roles may conceivably even be working quite well—i.e., productivity may be increasing, while the individual finds his new role unrewarding. To minimize this risk, the ideology, which at an earlier point in development may have been able to meet the emotional demands of a people, must begin to devise cognitive linkage with the new roles. The individual entering into a new role must himself perceive the relationship between what he is doing and transformation of the society. The Chinese have perhaps gone to an extreme by making the manifestation of ideology an immediate, individual task for each citizen, which has, of course, also created immense organizational problems, but the meaning of the role in terms of the national system of values and beliefs may be communicated by less draconian measures.

The dissociation of self and role is not, of course, always centered around new performance roles, and such cases pose even more difficult obstacles in the application of motivational devices than in social inequality. Many societies have achieved a harmonious relationship between self and role over centuries of cultural and historical adjustment while also operating at relatively high performance levels. These appear to be countries with relatively homogenous cultures, many of them in Asia. One of the most fascinating examples is Thailand, where motivation has come to focus on hierarchical status, while status has been substantially divorced from performance (Siffin, 1966). The Thai appears to have achieved reconciliation of self and role by an acute awareness of position, but status is not ascriptively preserved for individuals of specific social class or by a hereditary aristocracy. The paradoxical result is that there can be significant mobility within Thai society; i.e., many citizens have access to rewards and social approval, but relatively little change takes place. Wilson and Phillips, (1958) calls this the "necessary and just unity of virtue and power." Hierarchical position is a key value in structuring Thai society, but it is hard to use it to change the society.

The psychological dimensions of this relationship have been carefully studies by Mosel (1963), who comes to the conclusion that the stress on status combined with the very modern trait of depersonalizing status has resulted in an open social system, but also one that is unable to use status to assess achievement. His research uncovers a remarkable harmony between the individual's estimate of his position in life and his ideal self. Individual change does not require rejection of earlier self-images, but involves "becoming more of what one already is." Mosel (1957) concludes that this permits the administrator, the most important of Thai social positions, "to act in modern ways and still keep the self intact by detaching it from these actions." The relationship of superior to subordinate is widely understood and accepted in the society. The system leads to a high degree of social consensus and self-acceptance, but there are few ways to change the content of roles or to make the content a measure of any new allocation of status.

The result is a social system which is remarkably stable and even adaptive without much individual awareness of the links between hierarchical values and the acts being performed. Within the status system Thais can be motivated to change, even in the direction of increased productivity, but these changes are kept distinct in the perception of the society and are not permitted to affect the hierarchical order. Thus, in 1959, a Budget Office was created to improve financial management, but projects continue to be introduced through political channels. Although entry to the civil service is conducted by examination, its purpose is more to assess the alteration of a person's status than his qualifications for a more demanding job. Siffin (1966: 175-196) considers hierarchical status the prevailing norm in allocating resources, assigning official proprieties to routine affairs, and determining the preference for vertical communication over lateral, face-to-face relationships. A Civil Service Commission was established in 1933, but its activities are carefully circumscribed to insulate the bureaucracy against external—i.e., nonhierarchical—interference. Neither of these control agencies would probably have endured were they not eventually attached to the Prime Minister's office and thereby integrated with the basic pattern of power in the society.

Many of these organizational problems are by no means unique to Thailand, but the distinguishing feature is the extent to which issues of differentiation, function, and effectiveness are isolated from how power is used. The mutual assurance individuals derive from such a system is apparent in Mosel's study of how superiors and subordinates perceive one another. Superiors report that they spend less than ten percent of their time supervising subordinates. A majority felt that giving too much information to subordinates was a source of trouble, and a large majority considered how a subordinate felt about his work was very important. Subordinates felt they were kept uninformed, but also maintained that their superiors would consider their ideas. Very few thought their boss hard to talk to and nearly all expressed a high degree of approval of him. Simultaneously, they also considered him quite correctly oriented to those above himself and considered themselves closely supervised and well understood. These characteristics lead Mosel (1965) to conclude that the Thai official has only superficially internalized the values that prescribe his role even while performing adequately. "The administrator seems to be a spectator unto himself, to be witnessing his own behavior as an audience would; he seems to be consciously concerned with image management."

The motivational realignment of perception in a developing country encounters a number of obstacles. Some of these have been acknowledged directly by the psychologists in refining their generalizations. New motives cannot escape the structural constraints of their setting so that family, custom, social class, age, and so on inhibit and channel newly stimulated efforts to change the environment. Where societies have devised extremely effective ways of divorcing status and performance, there may be socioeconomic change without modification of old status systems. The change in patterns of differentiation may in this way be detached from a well-reinforced status system which continues to control change. The Westerner may regard this phenomenon as a kind of fantasy, but a self-contained status system places severe constraints on how new motivational forces can relate to ideology. In time, the complexities of socioeconomic change will conflict with the insular symbols of status in political life, and there will be even less institutional preparation for such a shock than in the developing country struggling to keep class or group differences in popularly acceptable form. Disruptive as the continual demonstrations, conflict, and turmoil may be in many developing countries, it is the expression of newly generated motives demanding recognition in the existing hierarchical order of society. Only by recognizing and absorbing such pressure can the ideology hope to extend national values to the myriad of new activities that constitute development.

The examination of motivational links to a national ideology leads into a discussion of hierarchy, and individual needs for consistency are changed as society becomes more complex. The analysis of motives has concentrated on how persons change their environment to increase wealth and to achieve growth. It is by no means belittling the problems of socioeconomic change to suggest that differentiation and specialization affect hierarchy. For reasons that have little to do with development, the psychological study of motives has concentrated on stimulating change of a more readily measurable kind—i.e., directly observable changes in behavior. The concept of motive is surely applicable to examining superior-subordinate relationships, but hierarchical change is once removed from the concrete toals essential to defining motives in the strict sense. Important as it is for developing peoples to acquire goal-oriented behavior and to respond instrumentally to their environments, they also confront equally demanding problems of hierarchical restructuring of which we know much less (Kessel, 1965).

ORGANIZATIONAL
FUNCTIONS OF IDEOLOGY

The functional notion of how ideology operates in society is derived in part from the psychologists' interest in more general attitudes and beliefs. While subject to dispute, perception has been frequently described along three dimensions: affective, cognitive, and evaluative. The affective and cognitive elements of perception must be reconciled, and how this is done appears to differ among cultures and also among political systems. Many of the disparities between affect and cognition in political life are described in the Almond and Verba (1963) study, and there have been determined efforts since to build more ambitious models of how men assess their progress, handle the huge flow of information bearing on their values and motives, and arrive at conclusions about the "reality" of their political system. The interrelationship of affect and cognition may be viewed as a constraint on beliefs and attitudes, creating a functional dependence of the desired and the possible.

The task of designing a more general model of beliefs is an ambitious undertaking, but it does not depart as sharply from more conventional notions about ideology, as may appear on first glance. The sharing of basic values in society cannot be fully explained using motivational and emotional influences on perception. Nor do such influences provide wholly satisfactory explanations of shared expectations in the more general contexts of state and society. The notions of ideology advanced from psychoanalytic and motivational assumptions makes little sense in explaining more abstract and remote problems of politics. Very little anxiety of the kind described by most theories of personal insecurity seems to be released at the level of the nation, and where this has indeed become the underlying rationale of an ideology, the results have often been terrifying. Nor is there much common sense to the view that ideologies are fundamentally a way of maximizing individual goals, important as ideology may be in the learning process in developing countries. Concern with ideology has always been with the quality it contributes to common endeavor, not just the personal significance of such pursuits or the efficiency with which goals are achieved. Despite the highly analytical character of ideology conceived as the interdependence of values, attitudes, and opinions, it focuses attention on an important set of problems, many of which are familiar from earlier, more philosophical inquiry. In the state, citizens must have some device for reconciling their opinions, which may differ greatly in substance and intensity.

The functional theories of personality stress the individual's—and, indirectly, society's—need for some minimal degree of consistency and order. As Lane (1962: 30) suggests in his remarkable study of Eastport citizens, "at some partially unconscious level for all the men, and manifestly for a few, there is a grave struggle against confusion, disorder, disorientation." It should be noted that this approach is consistent with the models of man suggested above, but places more stress on interpersonal relations and resolution of role conflict, especially in modern society. An individual subjected to a totally random environment begins to strike out blindly, may become violent, or may withdraw (Cantril, 1965). In highly unpredictable circumstances, the personal threat may be sufficient to cause neurotic and even psychotic behavior. Similarly, in a social environment where the person finds that he cannot rely on support from associates or where social organization provides no means for identifying worthwhile endeavor, the motivational concept is inapplicable.

Individuals cannot form attitudes about events or begin to learn how to control their environments without generalizations about experience.

The organizational approach departs from the psychoanalytic and motivational interpretations of man in placing stress on how conflict, differences, and uncertainties are resolved. It is not as much concerned with personal insecurity or with defining social rewards as with describing the contextual, qualitative characteristics of perception. Men not only need to externalize feelings and achieve some degree of social adjustment, but also have problems of object appraisal or "reality testing." Attitudes perform evaluative functions, enabling us to establish relevance and coherence to our behavior. This is not to imply that, by a given standard, one form of appraisal is more rational than another, but it recognizes that without diverse outcomes political systems would be paralyzed. Men require different degrees of "rationality" for different situations (Smith et al., 1956). The pattern of reconciliation we use for one set of problems—say, our relationships to our family and friends—will have only a partial relationship to how we organize our thoughts about more remote, more abstract problems, such as politics.

In relating a value to the political system, an individual must make a number of complex judgments. He must acquire a time perspective to justify sustained activity. He must discover ways of sorting out and storing information about problems so that it can be recalled as needed in relevant and convenient form. Above all, he must devise a way of attaching salience to political life, and how to attach priorities to political problems. This has also been described as the "centrality" problem in political perception or how to reduce the ambiguity of politics. The centrality problem has been differentiated most sharply from affective and cognitive problems by Katz (1960). In every political system, the members might be differentiated according to how they see issues, problems, and events related to the values affirmed by the system. This is not the same as how strongly they feel about any given issue, nor is it the same as how well they consider that any particular motive helps govern specific behavior. There will be, of course, some correspondence among emotions, motives, and evaluation, but the latter seeks to identify the quality of an individual's perceptual framework rather than some specific or substantive dimension of it (Rosenberg, 1960).

The illustration used by Sarnoff and Katz in explaining their approach to attitudinal structure is prejudice against blacks. The individual may first attribute inferiority to blacks because of deeply hostile impulses having psychoanalytic explanations. Second, he may discriminate because he finds a pattern of rewards and punishment reflected in society that is both convenient and useful to his interests—a motivational explanation. A third possibility may simply be that he does not attach importance to the position of the black in American society, if you like, the case of the disinterested individual. But one would choose very different methods to change the attitudes of three such persons. The first requires a strongly authoritative voice to overcome his insecurity and to play on authoritarian attitudes; the second would be likely to respond to a changed environment where he saw social disapproval removed from association with blacks; and the third faces a very different problem of being persuaded that the priority attached to the question of discrimination in America must be changed. All these explanations may be to some extent correct about American life, but the latter suggests a very different course of action to change behavior than do the former two.

There have been a number of approaches suggested by psychologists in order to study how individuals generalize about situations. An inquiry begun by Harvey (et al., 1961) places emphasis on relativistic as opposed to stereotyped perception. In their view, flexible concepts provide "a system of ordering by means of which the environment is broken down and organized, is differentiated and integrated, into its many relevant psychological facets" and the means by which

the individual tends to be "more categorical and absolu-
tistic . . . to conceptualize in bifurcation, in black and white
or at the most in minimum alternatives." The concepts that
people use are described along four dimensions: clarity-
ambiguity, compartmentalization-interrelatedness, centrality-
peripherality, and openness-closeness. The individual whose
concepts are well defined and interlocked will behave less
compulsively, will be less stereotyped in his thinking, and will
tend "to call into play in an orchestrated way his concepts
singly or in totality" (Harvey et al., 1961: 79). There will be
less dependence on externally derived approval, less constraint from fear of rejection, and less rejection of conflicting
or contradictory information. Harvey and his associates are
not describing any single dimension of perception, but are
trying to underscore the way in which individuals establish
interdependence in their thinking and find links between the
principles they apply to problems (Kogan and Wallach,
1964).

Perhaps the most elaborate attempt to provide a general
model of belief has been made by Rokeach (1966, 1960) and
his collaborators. Their assumptions are important in helping
us understand why the earlier psychological models, and the
possible derivations from them for the analysis of ideology,
are misleading. Rokeach argues that Freudian and, to a lesser
extent, motivational assumptions work from closed models
of thinking. As suggested in earlier chapters, these models are
useful in understanding how individuals deal with certain
constraints, some of them internally induced by emotional
tension and others externally produced by social pressures
and sanctions. Ideology is shaped by these ways of influencing personalities and behavior, but interpretations of
ideology based on these models tend to incorporate the same
limitations as the models of man from which the psychological theory came. The emphasis is placed on substantive,
concrete reactions with relatively little opportunity to compare responses in diverse areas of activity. As Rokeach
suggests, "it is not so much *what* you believe that counts, but

how you believe." We should look not only at how individuals exclude or distort stimuli, but at how the pattern of exclusion or distortion is reproduced in dealing with diverse situations.

Another important assumption is that understanding the closed portions of an individual's perception—his fears, prejudice, or submissive qualities—is an incomplete version of a person's thinking. Earlier analysis was in a sense biased toward constraint and, as Rokeach suggests, placed emphasis on how we resist change. By examining the belief system as a whole, one should take into account views on ideology, social relationships, and authority that are open to change. Hence, Rokeach argues that, for every set of beliefs, an individual also has a set of disbeliefs. Dogmatism can be differentiated from prejudice and other authoritarian attitudes by the extent to which belief and disbelief patterns are similarly structured. For example, the prejudiced person who holds discriminatory opinions about blacks might or might not hold similar opinions about whites. To be prejudiced in one's perception of both dimensions of blacks is very different from similarly structured values and attitudes for any question of race. A dogmatic individual is rigid in thinking about all dimensions of race—both his positive and negative reactions reflect intolerance—while a prejudiced person is biased on only one aspect of his belief-disbelief system.

A person's belief-disbelief system is more than ideologically rooted opinions and attitudes, which Rokeach considers the institutionally derived elements of the belief-disbelief system. The entire belief system "is conceived to represent all the beliefs, sets, expectancies, or hypotheses, conscious or unconscious, that a person at a given time accepts as true of the world he lives in" (Rokeach, 1960: 33-35). The systems of belief and disbelief are characterized by the extent that they are isolated from one another in a logical sense and that each is differentiated and articulated in varying degrees. Thus, persons differ in associating authoritarianism of the left and right, and in articulating the characteristics attached to each set of beliefs. Systems of belief also differ in the degree of interdependence of central and peripheral views—i.e., the important of primordial values and in the attachment of time perspective to each dimension.

Like other psychologists of the functionalist school (Bruner et al., 1957), Rokeach sees the relationship of beliefs and disbeliefs existing in a state of tension and embracing both emotional stress and cognitive needs. The systems serve "two powerful and conflicting sets of motives at the same time: the need for a cognitive framework to know and to understand and the need to ward off threatening aspects of reality" (Rokeach, 1960: 57). Open belief systems result where the need to know predominates; closed belief systems, where threat and anxiety predominate. Subjectively speaking, the closed mind and the open mind provide individuals with understanding and assurance to the extent that each is demanded by the personality as a whole. Excessive dependence on a single ideology, authority, or social relationship is a function of the entire pattern of an individual's feelings of isolation, adequacy, and guilt. The tightly closed belief system is similar to the impenetrable, rigid system of defenses described in psychoanalytic theory.

OPEN AND CLOSED
DIMENSIONS OF IDEOLOGIES

Perhaps the best evidence of the extremely heterogeneous character of a citizen's perception of government is found in studies of how people use information and communicate. Men differ in how they weigh evidence, attribute reliability to it, and weigh experience in making political judgments. The constraints and inhibitions they feel do not occur in any uniform pattern, nor do emotional rewards come from achieving the same objectives. The extreme variability in communicating political information and the diversity of individual decision-making processes can be accommodated by the functionalist view of attitudes and values. It is not the specific emotion or the particular goal that helps us understand the working ideology or general system of beliefs so much as how the various elements of making a political choice are pieced together by individuals. Lane and Sears (1964) have tried to incorporate these interlocking parts of perception in their explanation of rationality. A decision involves how a person seeks information, how he weighs it, how he relates choice to his own feelings or inhibitions, and how he blends choice with his own motives. The resulting configuration of factors in political perception is much harder to put into operational form than more specifically goal-oriented relationships established by motives or insecurity.

One of the earliest attempts to analyze the complexity of belief systems was made by Eysenck (1954). He argued that the most general political values were built from less general predispositions to behave in certain ways, much like the accepted concept of attitude. Attitudes, in turn, were derived from regularities in individuals' opinions of a more stable, specific kind, which he called "habits," and from more detailed, discrete views on particular issues and events, which he called "opinion." Eysenck's theory, given in Figure 1, remains fundamental to nearly all functionalist interpretations of value and idelogy. The diagram conveys the hierarchical nature of belief systems by which more general principles and values are related to information, habitual views, and opinions. It also suggests the complex interlocking of opinion, custom, attitude, and value in a working system of beliefs.

Eysenck noticed that statements reflecting attitudes and opinions did not neatly correspond to ideological viewpoints for any given population. Using a conservative-radical dimension for ideology, it was apparent that some conservatives shared attitudes and opinions with radicals, and vice versa. Though there was less concern with the consistency theory than was shown by later investigators, it also appeared that, a

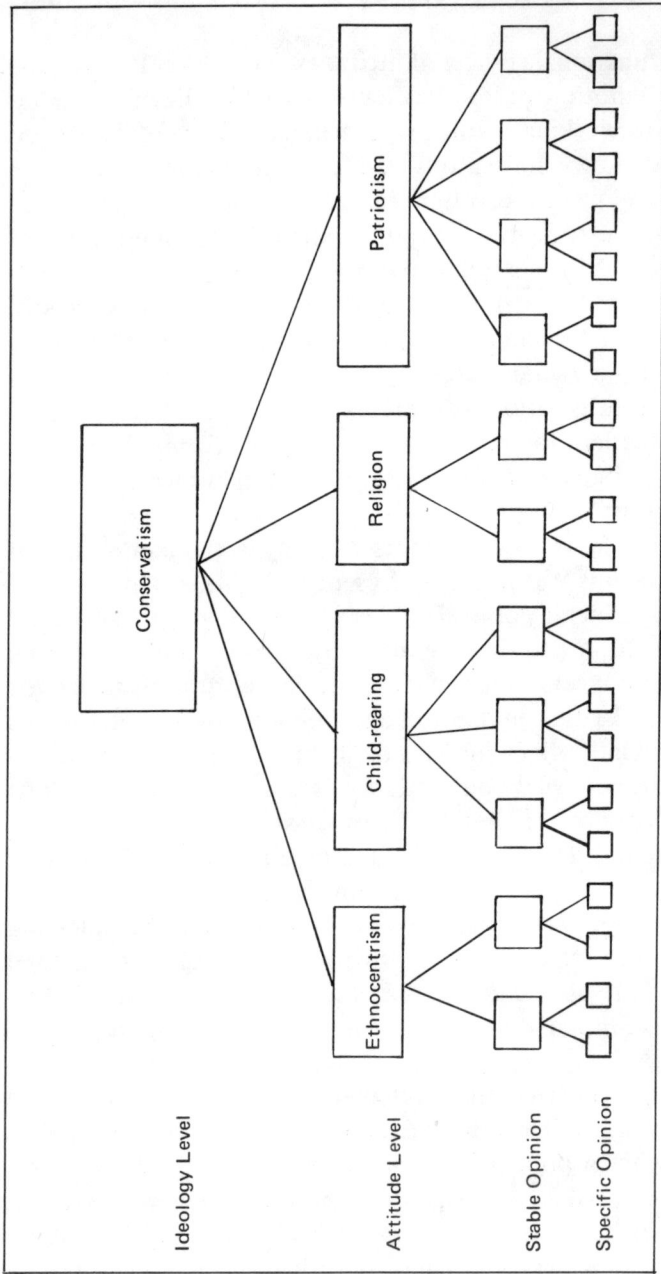

Figure 1: ELEMENTS OF A BELIEF SYSTEM

Ideology Level

Conservatism

Ethnocentrism   Child-rearing   Religion   Patriotism

Attitude Level

Stable Opinion

Specific Opinion

knowledge of the views of some conservatives—as well as some radicals—on a single problem (such as the importance of religion) would also predict with remarkable reliability their other views. But the emphasis was less on attitudinal and value change than on how the degree of interdependence related to broad, ideologically described positions. The inspiration for much of this inquiry came from Frenkel-Brunswick's earlier work on the intolerance of ambiguity as a critical dimension of ethnocentric attitudes. These early findings on how the elements of belief systems indicate that prejudice, concreteness or compulsive specificity, and rigidity in perception were closely correlated. Like much of the early inquiry into belief systems, the emphasis was on how beliefs are limited in their complexity.

Eysenck hypothesized that the ideological dimension—conservatism-radicalism—involved another dimension, which he labeled "tough-mindedness" and "tender-mindedness" after a distinction made by William James. Some attitudes and opinions, such as views on nationalization and private property, very reliably separated radicals and conservatives along a single dimension. Other issues, such as divorce, pacifism, harsh punishments and birth-control, were not neatly distributed along an ideological dimension. Eysenck designed a study to see how these and other opinions and attitudes cluster around conservative-radical and tender-tough distinctions. He found that a number of opinions and attitudes—such as the need to return to religion, making birth-control illegal, abolishing the death penalty, anti-Semitism, and compulsory religious education—composed another dimension, which he felt was explained by introvert-extrovert tendencies at each ideological extreme. Thus, the orthodox conservative is oriented to power, an extrovert trait, but some acquire introverted values and attitudes and become idealistic in their thinking. The orthodox radical tends to reflect introverted traits, but some have acquired tough-minded characteristics of thinking more concretely and pragmatically.

The articulation and organization of political values is of particular interest in Great Britain because of Tory working-class habits. Roughly a third of the British workers vote for the Conservative Party, and they provide approximately half the Conservatives' electoral strength (Abrams, 1964). Some predominantly industrial cities of England—Birmingham, for one—have been consistently Tory in both local and national elections. This curious division of loyalties has its historical roots in Conservative awareness that they could not survive in a parliamentary regime without labor support (McKenzie and Silver, 1967). A number of the nineteenth-century reforms benefiting workers originated with Disraeli. At the turn of the century, Joseph Chamberlain, whose constituency was Birmingham, directly exploited conservative preferences among workers, so much so that many of his tactics bordered on totalitarian practices. But the reluctance of many workers to join the Labour Party and support its candidates as historical fact is not the same as uncovering the underlying values and attitudes differentiating pro-Conservative workers from pro-Labour workers, nor does it tell us much about how, if at all, the two groups' perceptions of the democratic process may be differently structured.

An analysis of Conservative preferences among workers by Nordlinger (1967) helps us examine in more detail the values and opinions of the Tory worker. His study is not designed around an attitudinal model, but does uncover some strikingly different outlooks compared to workers voting Labour. The Tory worker, for example, expresses much higher preferences for a peer's son as a political leader, and also for an Etonian over a grammar school product. In stating reasons for accepting upper-class leadership, two-thirds of the Tory workers stressed ambiguous qualities such as "upbringing," "having been taught to lead," and "correct social atmosphere." Their reasons for selecting an Etonian were also heavily influenced by the prestige of the school, while Labour-oriented workers made such choices because they felt Eton provided a better education. The evidence is clearly less than conclusive, but it suggests that the Tory worker organizes his political thoughts around the ascribed characteristics of upper-class British leadership.

A very different image of the worker who votes Labour emerges. Although it is interesting that neither Tory- nor Labour-oriented workers felt that class conflict was a basic problem of British society, the Labour voting worker attached much more significance to class in discriminating among political problems. Nearly all the sentiment that Labour helps the working class was located among workers with Labour preferences, even though this did not figure heavily in their perception of authority. The Labour voting workers also revealed that they felt inordinately powerful groups were working against majority interests, identifying the "rich" more frequently than they mentioned other groups. Though the differences are not always large, the workers supporting Labour seem to organize their views about the political system around the ideas of class and wealth. Given the fact that the Tory workers tended to have smaller incomes, one cannot help but wonder if the pageantry and glamor associated with social position might not serve as a substitute for more substantial claims on the system.

Both groups expressed overwhelming confidence in the operation of the British political system, even to the point of accepting a parliamentary majority's right to act against the express wish of their supporters. This distinctly Burkean principle, though clearly imbedded in the thinking of all kinds of British workers, elicited different kinds of reservations at the prospect of a party they opposed taking such privileges. The Tory voter quite commonly expressed doubt about the abilities of Labour leadership. In the analysis of partisan attitudes among Tory voting workers, Nordlinger concludes that they simply regard Labour leaders as "untrustworthy." These results are particularly interesting with relation to the functionalist theory of attitudes, because they indicate that the Tory worker does indeed hold similar priorities—namely, the importance of leadership, whether referring to the virtues of Conservatives or to the hazards of Labourites. The Tory worker displays a consistency between his reasons for favoring Conservative rule and his fears over the conduct of a Labour government. The same coherence in the Labour-oriented worker could be found, but in this case it was organized around the potential neglect of the working class under Conservative rule.

Though concentrating on demographic and ecological factors rather than on attitudinal factors, the work of Allardt (1964) and others among Finnish Communists suggests another kind of ideological structuring of beliefs. In Finland and in some other countries with both peasant and urban Communist strength, it has been noticed that political behavior among the rural segments of the party differs greatly from Communist voting industrial workers. Allardt (1962) analyzed the differences between what he called "backwoods" and "industrial" Communism. The rural Communists were mostly lumbermen, living isolated lives, having precarious employment, and enjoying very little social interaction with other groups. The industrial workers who voted Communist, on the other hand, were better assimilated into modern society, revealed more specific grievances about such things as housing conditions and generally adhered to the procedures of the parliamentary system. They had a variety of friends and contacts, tended to read and discuss a number of interests in politics, and displayed much less alienation from society than did their rural numbers.

While the nature of Allardt's analysis precludes easy interpretation of the two groups' opinions and attitudes, it does appear that they differed significantly in their social activities and feelings of solidarity with the society. Communism for the lumberman was basically a protest and a way of expressing concrete but inclusive objections to Finnish politics. In the cities, the Communist workers had a more articulated version of Communism, yielding demands on specific issues and pressure for defined benefits. Their version of Communism indicates a more open formula in applying Communist values and a more experimental attitude in arriving at policy demands. The more rigid, inclusive form of Communism in rural Finland suggested to Allardt that it had some similarities to totalitarian ideological expression, rather like the compartmentalized perception of the dogmatic personality.

The distinctions made by psychologists interested in the organization of thinking and the use of concepts in learning are not easy to apply to political perception, but their ideas help us make critically important distinction. Highly general, abstract ideas are important, not only to sort out emotionally gratifying symbols and instrumentally useful guidelines, but also as ways of dealing with the complexities of political life, making the issues and problems to which we attach priority meaningful in the context of the entire political system, and, in turn, providing us with a broad framework for weighing evidence, testing our effectiveness and appraising our success. Political experience for citizens of advanced societies is disconnected, fragmented, and discontinuous, very likely even more so than in less-developed countries where authority may enter forcefully and uncontrollably into the lives of ordinary people. The level of material achievement of the industrial society makes citizens less dependent on power, and, by virtue of the decreased dependence, they find it more difficult to uncover easy solutions to political affairs and ready-made formulas to give coherence to the system. The marginality of political life in democratic countries may be a rationalization of apathy in some instances (DiPalma, 1970), but it is also a condition that requires the individual to build his own political reality, to search out the degree of consistency appropriate to his personality, and to engage himself directly in politics on his own terms.

REFERENCES

ABRAMS, M. (1964) "Party politics after the end of ideology," pp. 56-64 in E. Allardt and A. Littunen [eds.] Cleavages, Ideologies and Party Systems. Helsinki: Transactions of the Westermarck Society.

ALLARDT, E. (1964) "Patterns of class, conflict, and working class consciousness in Finnish politics," pp. 97-131 in E. Allardt and A. Littunen [eds.] Cleavages, Ideologies and Party System. Helsinki: Transactions of the Westermarck Society.

——— (1962) "Community activity, leisure use and social structure." Acta Sociologica 6, 1-2: 67-82.

ALMOND, G. and S. VERBA (1963) The Civic Culture. Princeton: Princeton Univ. Press.

ASHFORD, D. E. (1965) Politics and Planning in Morocco and Tunisia. Syracuse: Syracuse Univ. Press.

BERGER, S. M. and W. W. LAMBERT (1968) "Stimulus-response theory in contemporary social psychology," pp. 81-178 in G. Lindzey [ed.] Handbook of Social Psychology. Reading, Mass.: Addison-Wesley.

BENDIX, R. (1964) Nation-Building and Citizenship. New York: John Wiley.

BRUNER, J. S., J. J. GOODNOW, and G. A. AUSTIN (1957) A Study of Thinking. New York: John Wiley.

CANTRIL, H. (1965) The Pattern of Human Concerns. New Brunswick, N.J.: Rutgers Univ. Press.

CONVERSE, P. E. and G. Depeux (1962) "Politicization of the electorate in France and the United States." Public Opinion Q. 26 (Spring): 1-23.

CORNELIUS, W. J. (1969) "Urbanization as an agent in Latin American political instability." Amer. Pol. Sci. Rev. 58 (September): 833-857.

CROCKETT, H. J. Jr. (1964) "Psychology origins of mobility," pp. 280-309 in L. Smelser and S. Lipset [eds.] Social Structure and Mobility in Economic Development. Chicago: Aldine.

DEUTSCH, K. (1961) "Social mobilization and political development." Amer. Pol. Sci. Rev. 55 (September): 493-514.

DEUTSCH, M. and R. M. KRAUSS (1965) Theories in Social Psychology. New York: Basic Books.

DiPALMA, G. (1970) Apathy and Participation: Mass Politics in Western Societies. New York: Free Press.

DOLLARD, J. and N. E. MILLER (1941) Social Learning and Imitation. New Haven, Conn.: Yale Univ. Press.

EASTON, D. and R. D. HESS (1962) "Youth and the political system," pp. 295-315 in S. Lipset and R. Lowenthal [eds.] Culture and Social Character: The Work of David Riesman Reviewed. Garden City, N.Y.: Doubleday.

ERIKSON, E. (1963) Childhood and Society. New York: W. W. Norton.

EYSENCK, H. J. (1954) The Psychology of Politics. London: Routledge & Kegan Paul.

GREENSTEIN, F. J. (1965) Children and Politics. New Haven, Conn.: Yale Univ. Press.

——— and S. J. TARROW (1969) "The study of French political socialization." World Politics 22 (October): 95-137.

HALL, C. S. and G. LINDZEY (1957) Theories of Personality. New York: John Wiley.

HALL, J. W. (1968) "A monarch for modern Japan," pp. 11-64 in R. E. Ward [ed.] Political Development in Modern Japan. Princeton: Princeton Univ. Press.

——— (1964) "The nature of traditional society: Japan," pp. 14-41 in R. E. Ward and D. A. Rustow [eds.] Political Modernization in Japan and Turkey. Princeton: Princeton Univ. Press.

HARVEY, O. J., D. E. HUNT, and H. M. SCHRODER (1961) Conceptual Systems and Personality Organization. New York: John Wiley.

HOVLAND, C. I. (1953) Communication and Persuasion. New Haven, Conn.: Yale Univ. Press.

JACOB, P. (1971) Values and the Active Community: A Cross-National Study of the Influence of Local Leadership. New York: Free Press.

JOHNSON, C. (1966) Revolutionary Change. Boston: Little, Brown.

KATZ, M. (1960) "The functional approach to the study of attitudes." Public Opinion Q. 24 (Summer): 163-204.

KESSEL, J. H. (1965) "Cognitive dimensions and political activity." Public Opinion Q. 29 (Fall): 377-389.

KOGAN, N. and M. A. WALLACH (1964) Risk-Taking: A Study in Cognitive and Personality. New York: Holt, Rinehart & Winston.

LANE, R. E. (1962) Political Ideology. New York: Free Press.

——— and D. O. SEARS (1964) Public Opinion. Englewood Cliffs, N.J.: Prentice-Hall.

LERNER, D. (1958) The Passing of Traditional Society. New York: Free Press.

LEWIS, B. (1961) The Emergence of Modern Turkey. London: Oxford Univ. Press.

LEWIS, J. W. (1963) Leadership in Communist China. Ithaca: Cornell Univ. Press.

McCLELLAND, D. C. (1961) The Achieving Society. Princeton: D. Van Nostrand.

McKENZIE, R. T. and A. SILVER (1967) "The delicate experiment: industrialism, conservatism, and the working-class Tories in England," pp. 115-125 in S. Lipset and S. Rokkan [eds.] Party Systems and Voter Alignments. New York: Free Press.

MOSEL, J. (1965) "Some notes on self-role, and role behavior of Thai administrators." (mimeo).

——— (1963) "Communication patterns and political socialization in transitional Thailand," pp. 184-228 in L. Pye [ed.] Communications and Political Development. Princeton: Princeton Univ. Press.

——— (1957) "Thai administrative behavior," pp. 278-331 in W. Siffin [ed.] Toward the Comparative Study of Public Administration. Bloomington: Indiana Univ. Press.

NEEDLER, M. C. (1961) "The political development of Mexico." Amer. Pol. Sci. Rev. 55, 2: 308-312.

NORDLINGER, E. (1967) The Working Class Tories: Authority, Deference and Stable Democracy. London: MacGibbon & Kee.

ROKEACH, M. (1966) "Attitude change and behavioral change." Public Opinion Q. 30 (Winter): 529-550.

——— (1960) The Open and Closed Mind. Boston: Basic Books.

ROSENBERG, M. J. (1960) Attitude Organization and Change: An Analysis of Consistency among Attitude Components. New Haven, Conn.: Yale Univ. Press.

SCHURMANN, F. (1968) Ideology and Organization in Communist China. Berkeley: Univ. of California Press.

SCOTT, R. (1964) Mexican Government in Transition. Urbana: Univ. of Illinois Press.

SCOTT, W. A. (1968) "Attitude measurement," pp. 204-273 in G. Lindzey [ed.] Handbook of Social Psychology. Reading, Mass.: Addison-Wesley.

SIFFIN, W. (1966) The Thai Bureaucracy: Institutional Change and Development. Honolulu: East-West Center Press.

SMITH, B. V., J. S. BRUNER, and R. W. WHITE (1956) Opinions and Personality. New York: John Wiley.

SYMPOSIUM (1957) Contemporary Approaches to Cognition. Cambridge, Mass.: Harvard Univ. Press.

TEUNE, H. (1970) The Logic of Comparative Social Inquiry. New York: John Wiley.

TSOU, T. (1969a) "Revolution, reintegration, and crisis in Communist China," in P. Ho and T. Tsou [eds.] China in Crisis. Chicago: Univ. of Chicago Press.

——— (1969b) "The Cultural Revolution and the Chinese political system." China Q. (April-June): 63-91.

TURNER, F. C. (1968) Dynamic of Mexican Nationalism. Chapel Hill: Univ. of North Carolina Press.

WILSON, D. A. and H. PHILLIPS (1958) "Elections and parties in Thailand." Asian Survey 23.

Chapter V

VARIATION AMONG INSTITUTIONAL NORMS

In the two preceding chapters, my discussion has been in terms of the individual, his attitudes, and beliefs about the political system he lives in, and the ways in which he links ideology to the political system. These concerns are represented by the top row of the tabulation in Chapter II, describing variations in individual need for consistency. The basic notion was that persons vary immensely in the emotional and cognitive meaning they attribute to political values. The Almond-Verba (1963) study was an attempt to look at these meanings cross-sectionally. The validity of the emotive or cognitive expression elicited in the survey was assumed in relation to the system; i.e., each was treated as a separate factor, and the differences among countries were examined in aggregate form. Whether empirical research can go beyond these simplifying assumptions in examining how individuals perceive politics is a methodological question, but we should nonetheless be aware of the limitations of the analysis (Verba, 1969).

The fact that no two people are alike, however, does not necessarily lead to the paralyzing conclusion that no two people are alike in their perception of political norms and values. In stable political systems, some minimal degree of variation is also possible in the interpretation of these norms and values in political life. People do not have to be identical in their preferences in order to participate in collective endeavor. If this were the case, political, social, and economic institutions would be impossible. A working ideology can be examined, then, both in terms of the kinds of stress it creates for individual citizens trying to make the ideology meaningful in their own lives, and in terms of the variations permitted in combining citizens in collective endeavor. At any time, we can examine in behavioral terms how much the norms of political institutions can vary, just as we can study in psychological terms how much citizens vary in their individual expressions with reference to the primary values of the system. Thus, in this chapter, I will be most concerned with the second row of the tabulation in Chapter II.

As societies evolve, higher levels of differentiation and specialization activities are increasingly organized around institutions, and the shared expectations of the members of institutions are manifested in norms. In many ways, a working ideology operates in more concrete and specific ways in observing institutionalized behavior than in observing individual expressions. Institutions perform specific tasks in society: providing wealth, education, and numerous other services that can be effectively organized by grouping individuals with special skills and talents. Because more traditional societies do not achieve as high a level of differentiation, there is less institutionalized behavior at the level of national politics and probably in other realms of behavior, too. Indeed, institutions are barely distinguishable from the culture generally in primitive societies. However, the general problem of status determination within institutions and of relating norms among institutions raise comparable issues about superior-subordinate relationships for every political system. In order to devise institutions, some fundamental questions must be answered, directly or indirectly, about the general nature of status relationships in society. In the Western case, answers to these questions were gradually derived from the Protestant ethic, whose influence on the initial choices for institutional development in Western society has been widely studied (Weber, 1930; Tawney, 1949).

The issue is perhaps more clearly drawn in the developing countries, where the temporal sequence of defining status has not followed the Western pattern outlined so well by Marshall (1950). European institutions associated with the nation can be described in a sequence of events beginning with a religious upheaval, the Reformation, followed by periods of redefining legal relationships and, finally, by a concern for the distribution of social and economic benefits. The fundamental institutional choices of developing countries are more limited, though the constraints of time and resources have been unduly exaggerated. The elite of the developing country in many ways has more influence in determining the new nation's institutional development than the unhappy Stuart and Bourbon monarchs. The pressures to concentrate on rapidly increasing wealth are, of course, immense, and most developing countries have in fact placed emphasis on building economic institutions. How these institutions relate to more general political values ordering status in society remains largely undetermined. The traditional cultures are not easily converted into guidelines for status determination in the nation, and the meaning given to political culture in most cases must emerge from the doctrine of the new national leaders themselves.

The stress on ideological doctrine in developing countries can be interpreted as an attempt to deal with the two basic institutional problems of a polity, the definition of broad guidelines for hierarchical relationships in society and the development of more explicit agreement on how institutional norms interrelate. Countries such as Tanzania, Guinea, Cuba,

and India have tried to give preference to the first problem—
i.e., formulating the "rules of combination" in political life as
well as in other key areas of social activity. Other countries
have opted for the more pragmatic approach of building new
institutions for more specific needs, often determined by
economic forces, and gradually evolving a better-defined
working ideology from their experience. The Ivory Coast,
Senegal, Pakistan, and the Philippines would be examples. In
these cases, a working ideology has been derived from conventional liberal economic principles interlaced with careful,
sometimes cautious, experimentation with representative
political institutions. It would be foolhardy to speculate on
the relative success of these two strategies in developing a
working ideology, but it is also apparent that the second is ·
much closer to the Western experience and provides greater
opportunity for economic development along capitalist lines.
The Western nations have clearly found the second strategy
more compatible with their own experience and have often
found it easier to extract international support from countries following the more pragmatic path.

Where the more pragmatic view prevails, the nation inescapably depends more heavily on the experience of industrial
nations, with its consequent emphasis of industrial development and economic growth. On the whole, there is less
concern with how institutional norms mesh with one another
or relate to individual views. Large disparities may appear
between the norms governing economic development, for
example, and the norms advanced for religious or educational
activities. The priority is given to increasing role differentiation in the society combined in many cases with the
Westerner's optimism that the multiplication of institutions
themselves will resolve problems of normative conflict. Where
the capitalist model is more literally applied, the outcome
often means simply giving way to the requirements of economic institutions and making a direct, if somewhat precarious, transfer of liberal values to the working ideology.
The Philippines is perhaps the most clear-cut example of free

enterprise unhampered by other institutional requirements of the society or by more generally applicable values governing status relationships in the society (Abueva, 1964; Douglas, 1968).

In the development of institutional norms, there may be considerable variation. A society may espouse democratic values and succeed in building a number of institutions in which democratic values prevail, but there may remain, perhaps must remain, a number of institutions where rigid heirarchical values persist. The problem is in part terminological because the sociological usage of "institutions" tends to treat as a continuum activities with very low levels of specialization and relatively fixed status structure, such as the family, and activities of more complex and specialized institutions, such as industry. In the context of a working ideology, more diffuse institutions, while they clearly have normative implications, do not impinge directly on the political system (Dawson and Prewitt, 1968; Adler and Harrington, 1970). The problem is a critical methodological problem because, in relation to the full range of social activity, the family is a much more important institution in a traditional society than in a more advanced society. In the course of industrialization, the European family was forced to comply with new norms (Smelser, 1959). Families exist in Tikopia and Trenton, but political values and behavior in Polynesia are directly linked to the family and kinship. The emergence of specialized institutions changes the significance of norms with relation to the entire society. Despite the popular arguments of the uniformity of values and behavior in industrial society, the development of complex institutions also permits more variation in how values are related to society. The contradictions and conflicts among institutional norms are then more explicit and visible. A country cannot be heavily committed to political and social change without encountering such problems and, implicitly and explicitly, articulating a working ideology.

DIFFERENTIATION,
STATUS, AND NORMS

Every society must deal with problems of hierarchy and differentiation. A working ideology provides general guidelines for collective behavior by defining status in political institutions and by developing institutional norms. These guidelines must to some degree be consistent with the citizen's interpretation of the society's political values. Rules for the regulation of conflict and reconciliation of individual and institutional differences are by no means independent of the level of socioeconomic development a society has achieved. Well before the functionalists drew attention to the problem of social equilibrium in sociological theory, Durkheim (1964) suggested that, as roles were increasingly differentiated, there would be an accompanying transformation of hierarchical relationships. As behavior was increasingly specialized and social tasks reflected an increasing division of labor, the new lines of individual and institutional interdependence would, in Durkheim's terms, change mechanical solidarity into organic solidarity.

Although the issues raised by the early social theorists remain central to the study of society, the refinement of their ideas and subsequent empirical research have produced a number of qualifications. Combining more effective organization of production, largely contained in the tremendous multiplication of primarily economic institutions, with new patterns of control and participation, produced severe social conflict and stimulated acute political differences. Values and beliefs did not harmoniously change as these new institutions emerged, nor has it been a simple process to resolve conflicts of interest and purpose among institutions. Relatively early in the process of industrialization, legislation appears regulating hierarchical relationships. The British Factory Act of 1833 limited the working day to ten hours, and further legislation of the period tried to terminate the exploitation of women and children in factories. Repeal of the Corn Laws in

1832 helped lower the price of food in the rapidly growing cities and rejected the norms of a rural society that had kept the price of grain high (Halevy, 1950, 1947). Though still far from resolving the upheavals of the industrial revolution, there is ample evidence that, even at this early date, the most advanced industrial state began to restrain the process of differentiation through industrialization and recognized that the norms of production could not be the prime determinant of status in British society.

Structural differentiation refers to the relationship between the increasing differentiation of roles in society and the hierarchical structure of the society. As individual behavior becomes more specialized, there tend to emerge more autonomous and more specialized institutions. The polity has a fundamental part in deciding how great the variance among institutional norms may be and how conflicts among specialized norms will be decided. Just as role relationships can be conceived as basically transitive and relational, so also institutionalized sectors of society pose problems of normative conflict and regulation. These problems can only be resolved by the articulation of political values to determine the status or relative priority of roles and the terms of reciprocity among institutions. Structural differentiation is being used here in a more limited sense than in the sociological literature. The reason is that polities must make decisions about the relative importance of institutions in society. On a number of occasions, countries have foregone the rewards of increased production and wealth that might be derived from some form of increased specialization in order to manifest humanitarian values and achieve justice. For purposes of political analysis, and particularly in articulating the significance of a working ideology among institutions, it is essential to underscore the distinct role of the polity.

Sociological theory often focuses too strongly on the largest unit of interaction, the society, to permit dealing with structural relationships in the polity, almost the reverse of anthropological theory, which has so heavily concentrated on the small community that linkage to the political system may be neglected. In this sense, politics falls somewhere between the macro-level of sociology and the micro-level of anthropology. But the more important difference between political and sociological analysis is the tendency of sociology to concentrate on the independent effects of differentiation. Social class and social stratification link sociology to political problems, but most often only in ways that are defined by the kind of differentiation under consideration. Oddly enough, this seems to be a characteristic of both extreme Marxist and extreme functionalist analysis. The rigid Marxist falls into the trap of arguing that status is wholly determined by class with the final collapse of society coming about when the oppressed realize that all power (wealth) has been allocated to the privileged. The enthusiastic functionalist (Parsons, 1966; Mitchell, 1967) can, of course, also regularly arrive at the rather less alarming conclusion that the effective social system can always dredge up an integrative device to reconcile any change in differentiation with status. These are both oversimplifications, but it is probably correct to note that the stress on role differentiation in both schools of thought makes it difficult to deal with problems of status as a separate problem.

In the study of a working ideology, political analysis requires consideration of how subunits of society ineract, and of how normative priorities and conflicts are dealt with. Whether emotionally or cognitively based, principles and generalizations enter into the political process and are critical to understanding how collective behavior is organized. An illustration might be taken from the contrast frequently made between institutionalized racist behavior in the North and South of the United States. Not only does the Southern white openly manifest his prejudice, but Southern institutions more explicitly reflect the effective exclusion of blacks from social opportunities and the denial of political influence. The result is that the normative conflict is visible in Southern society, while it remains to a large extent concealed in Northern institutions. The norms of Northern schools, communities, and political organizations reject discrimination against blacks to a much greater degree than in the South, but the status and rewards given blacks in the North do not greatly differ. The black power strategy and black militancy generally is a movement to change status first and differentiation second. This is accomplished by revealing the disparity between the ostensible goals and norms of Northern institutions and the behavior that in fact takes place. Though the South may indeed vary more greatly from the norms of the national political culture than does the North, institutionalized racism in the South may be more easily overcome because discriminatory application of norms is more easily identified.

The problem of differentiation and its relationship to a working ideology has a direct bearing on our understanding of the process of political development. Both Lipset (1960) and Deutsch (1953) point out that the level of socioeconomic development is dependent on the structural characteristics of mobilization and communication. Lipset (1959) was most concerned with how various levels of socioeconomic development—i.e., increasing differentiation—provide support for democratic politics. His conceptualization of the problem tends to exclude institutional complexities because dichotomous measures are used, thereby precluding allowance for the norms governing the combination of new behavior in the various states. Lerner (1958) and Deutsch (1961), on the other hand, explicitly recognized in earlier work that there were "thresholds" in the increasing mobilization of the developing country when the factors contributing to mobilization might be combined in very different ways.

The convergence of new skills in organizations and institutions represent major turning points in the history of the developing country, and it is by no means established that the choices made as institutionalized behavior multiplies can be explained by the overall level of development. Indeed, if this were possible, the conflict of expectations and norms would not be a problem. In fact, the new productive capacity of the developing country can be organized in diverse ways, and hardly appears to have reduced political conflict. Material progress appears to be a necessary—but hardly a sufficient—condition for a number of institutional changes. Several writers have pointed out the ethnocentric assumptions and the methodological difficulties of the early efforts to quantify the process of political development (Retzlaff, 1965; Cutwright, 1963; McCrone and Cnudde, 1967). While industrial growth appears to be a prerequisite to transforming traditional agriculture, freeing resources for investment, and expanding the activities of government, there remains a wide variation in how different countries decide to relate these new activities to political values (Olson, 1968). Political institutions have thus far eluded any demonstrable relationship to the level of development.

In short, sociological approaches to political behavior have not resolved many of the key controversies in political analysis. Though social differences may tell us a good deal about the inner workings of parties, cabinets, and voting, the process whereby social differences are transformed into structures affecting the polity are fundamentally decisions about superior-subordinate relationships. The extreme neo-Marxist theory offered by Lenski (1966), for example, does not hold when one examines the composition and the organization of a political pary. Authority is not the arbitrary allocation of wealth, nor is power simply the use of coercion. Political systems permit varying degrees of choice in how behavior will be reconciled and evaluated in the society. As differentiation increases in a society—i.e., as new organizations, agencies, and institutions proliferate in order to take advantage of the division of labor, their relative priority, their internal form, and their relation to the political values of the society must be decided by the participants in the political process.

The way this process takes place is, of course, a central concern of political analysis and, as has been suggested, reveals how norms are related to a working ideology. The prevailing theory of democratic governments has been the pluralist view, which compares the political process to a marketplace wherein groups compete for influence. There is an obvious parallel to the assumptions of a free market in economics, and, of course, the same distortions and obstructions can also be uncovered. The pluralist notion of the interplay of institutionalized norms assumes that the manifestation of individual and group interests accurately reflects the overarching structure of power in a society. Theirs is an essentially pessimistic estimate of citizens which underscores the significance of self-interest in political life and asserts that men will devise "rational" solutions through political interaction. The controversy is not so much about what happens when issues and decisions are made, but over the significance of nondecisions, the options that are not raised, and the issues, which for a variety of reasons, may escape explicit treatment in the political process. The prevailing concept of pluralist through is that collective human behavior is "governed in large part by inertia" (Polsby, 1960; Anton, 1963).

The pluralist theory has come under severe criticism for a number of reasons. First, it is by no means clear that groups represent all the options that might pertain to any given issue. The National Rifle Association powerfully represents those who want to own weapons with no restraint, but those who object are a diverse and scattered group who find it difficult to press their views. Second, there are important disparities in the effectiveness with which group interests are communicated to the power structure. The American Medical Association can collect large sums from its members to forestall action on medical welfare, but those receiving inadequate care have no comparable access and resources. Third, there are the problems of whether the groups that do assert themselves at any given moment do indeed differ in the alternatives they represent. The leaders of various businesses concerned, for example, with war industries may not overlap with other businesses seeking influence, but they may represent essentially the same norms and take similar positions on issues involving political conflict. Fourth, if certain groups acquire sufficient influence, they may effectively prevent other groups from challenging their positions, which seems to have been the case in raising issues about consumer interests and ecological problems. The political arena, to use the somewhat misleading metaphor of the pluralists, can be as distorted as the economic marketplace.

The pluralist dispute raises questions central to the normative articulation of a working ideology. They center on how a society is to control its elite and are at least as old as Michels' (1959) "Iron Law of Oligarchy," based on the reluctance of men to forego power as a central phenomenon of political life. No complex social and political system can endure without leaders, and social analysts from Burke to Dahrendorf agree that modern societies are unimaginable without elites. The assertion that political values should be inferred from increasing differentiation is not sufficient. The most outspoken critic of this view has been Nettl (1967), who argues that the multiplication and diversification of group activity in society may in fact restrict the exercise of authority. A similar argument is made by Bachrach (1967) to refute Kornhauser's contention that increased access to elites through group activity will assure the preservation of democracy. The reason for these doubts is that, from time to time, values and norms themselves must be independently evaluated and judged. Institutional norms—assessed in terms of the basic values of a society—change their meaning as the problems, setting, and capacity of the society itself changes. A context can always be found to justify the norms of an existing group or organization, but the context itself is open to evaluation and is essential to understanding the political system.

In summary, it may be possible to identify three kinds of situations in which a political system's basic values interact with institutional norms. The first, and in some respects the most important, are those embryonic struggles between individuals and the existing norms to engage in new activities and build new kinds of institutions. Among current controversies are disputes over censorship, pollution, abortion, and military service. Institutional innovation may originate in these struggles. A second category is the conflict of norms among existing institutions, which may occur at many levels of social organization. Much political and social analysis of Western countries deals with these problems as questions of economic control, social welfare, and public finance. The third are those crises in political and social life where the norms of all institutions are subject to review and adjusted in light of new evidence. The black power struggle in America certainly falls into this category, and there are numerous examples in the revolutionary changes attempted by developing countries. Nettl (1967: 119) makes the distinction between the second and third forms of normative conflict by suggesting that the first produces political action—i.e., a reallocation of authority among institutions—while the third represents revolution—i.e., a redefinition of the basis of authority in the society. The massive redefinition of status in society brings about a change in the political culture, outlined in Chapter VI, while the regulation of conflict among institutions involves how precedence will be given to norms as they are manifested in the society at that time.

NORMATIVE CHANGE
AMONG LATE MODERNIZERS

The evolution of a working ideology in the developing countries has occurred in two major historical situations. There were, first, the nations that emerged before World War II, often as a consequence of the dissolution of European world hegemony. These states would include a number of the Arab nations, much of Latin America and Eastern Europe, China, Turkey, and Japan. In all these countries, the interplay of ideological doctrine and normative change can be followed over a much longer period than is possible among the multitude of new nations that have emerged in the past twenty years. The late modernizers found themselves in radically different situations. The upheaval of World War II was much broader and more profound than earlier world crises. The conflict ended with an acknowledgement of national aspirations that provided a stimulus to nationalist movements throughout the world. In a number of countries, such as India, Indonesia, and Pakistan, the issues surrounding independence were aired in the late 1930s and nationalist organizations were beginning to take shape. Most important, the postwar development of new ideologies took place in an environment where mass communications and widespread participation were central to achieving independence. In a world often bitterly divided between Communist and free states, the emerging nations were also able to exert leverage in world politics and tended to place more emphasis on economic and social equality than in the past.

In selecting an illustration of how ideological doctrine is blended with institutional development, a good many nations must be rather arbitrarily put aside. In the general sense of ideology, there is, of course, no reason to claim that Morocco's Islamic preoccupations (Waterbury, 1969) are less ideological than Tanzania's doctrines of *uhuru* (freedom). But there are significant differences in shaping a working ideology—i.e., the extent to which institutional change has been guided by national values, particularly in the determination of status in the new societies. Being heavily dependent on the bureaucracy and the army, the Alaouite monarchs have found it difficult to foster participation and have sought to reinforce traditional values. Differences between the nationalist movement, the Istiqlal, and the monarchy tended to crystallize around highly abstract issues like restoring

Mauritania or sensitive religious questions like educational reform (Ashford, 1969, 1967). The result has been that economic and social change in the more traditional society is isolated from ideology, in part because traditional values establish their own priorities and in part because they often do not provide guidance for many of the technological and economic issues raised by development.

A working ideology establishes links between individual and collective endeavors. The more national efforts shift toward economic and social change, the more difficult becomes the problem of articulating links between traditional values and new behavior. Many new institutions to foster growth tend to be divorced from national values and, not infrequently, critical decisions are left to the most influential groups involved. Thus, in Morocco, the monarchy is able to deal almost unilaterally with trade unions in determining wages and benefits, and political parties are relegated to relatively minor roles. As the priority of devising new definitions of status is neglected, whole sectors of the population may be left aside, and questions of social, as well as individual, justice are difficult to raise. The Moroccan rural sector is a typical example, and Moroccan agriculture was seriously mismanaged until the World Bank raised some fundamental questions about its future role in the society. Further improvement of agricultural production in Morocco may require that the peasant be brought more directly into Moroccan politics. Increased differentiation may thus require that political status be fundamentally redefined.

The Tanzanian experience has involved such a reexamination of the fundamental nature of status in the society and a continued effort to reflect this redefinition of status in institutional norms of the society. If Moroccans have not emphasized ideology because Islam provided them with a temporarily workable alternative, it might also be claimed that Tanzania has given precedence to ideology because there were so few alternatives (Bieneu, 1967). The country has a widely dispersed population, much of it located on the peripheral regions of the territory. There are over a hundred tribes and numerous languages, though several tribal group- ings, such as the Chagga and the Sakuma, approach half a million persons. The nationalist movement recently devel- oped, gathering a million members between 1954 and 1960. The responsibilities of government in a very poor land were handed over in December 1961.

Thus, the conditions surrounding Tanzanian independence encouraged the articulation of an ideology in a society which was and which remains more knit together by aspirations and beliefs than by social structure and history. But necessity has not always produced a persuasive body of thought about a nation's future, much less provided the links between values and institutions. Moreover, the necessity for new political values in Tanzania may easily lead one to overestimate their significance in the working relationships of the society. Nyerere's blend of African, Christian, and socialist ideas has no doubt been essential to the survival of the new nation, but it is the process of working out how these ideas would relate to the actual policies and programs of Tanzania that has determined whether or not a working ideology would evolve. This process has gone through two stages, from independence to the 1965 Constitution and from 1965 to the Arusha Declaration. The theme of the first period was *Uhuru na Kazi* (Freedom and Work) and of the second period *Uhuru na Ujmaa* (Freedom and Socialism).

Throughout his life, Nyerere has espoused the values of human dignity, work, and unity. He has remained convinced that only through widespread participation can the principles of equality and development be reconciled and has been prepared to take unpopular stands to defend his values. Another thread running through his speeches, particularly in the immediate postindependence period, has been the uniqueness of the African experience and the necessity for Africans to devise their own form of democracy. The articu- lation of these ideas in the initial phase of Tanzanian inde- pendence was clearly difficult to achieve. One of the first problems was to find a workable relationship between the strong cooperative societies, often codeterminous with the major tribal areas and the new government. Under the British, several regions had developed prosperous cooperative societies for the production and marketing of coffee cotton, and other products. The cooperatives were often closely tied to regional councils. In the early years of independence, the government had serious conflict with cooperatives under the Chagga, the Sukuma (Maguire, 1969), and the Haya (Hyden, 1968). Party activity began to decline, resistance to national policies built up around the strong cooperatives, and differences multiplied between the newly appointed TANU officials of the party and the new government officials. There were increasing signs of crippling dishonesty and opportunism in both the party and government ranks. In the midst of growing disorder and disenchantment, Nyerere decided to resign as prime minister of the new government and spent most of 1962 designing a new strategy to implement his ideology.

Few countries have experienced as self-conscious an attempt to translate basic political and social values into institutional norms. The readiness of Nyerere to confront the full task of eliciting new norms from his doctrine makes Tanzania an unusual case. His retreat in 1962 was no withdrawal for reflection, but an intense effort to overcome the vexing issues of irresponsible party activity, arbitrary administrative behavior, increasing public apathy, and the reassertion of highly divisive factors in Tanzanian society. Many developing countries have confronted these questions in a piecemeal fashion, but in Tanzania they arose at a single time and were treated as an interdependent problem. A number of critical decisions were made in 1962 and 1963. The party asserted its control over TANU district-level officials. Though the government had expressed its readiness to remove recalcitrant chiefs, the first removals did not begin until this time. The colonial local and provincial administrative structure was overhauled. Regional and Area Commissioners replaced the old provincial and district officials with TANU secretaries and civil servants subordinate to them.

Nyerere's preoccupation was clearly to establish a working hierarchy linking citizens to the government, a hierarchy that could not be distorted by the remnants of traditional authority or localized interests (Nyerere, 1967). The political device to assure institutional reconciliation was the one-party state, which was in turn to become the keystone for the 1965 Constitution. The now famous article in *Spearhead* is an explicit statement of how problems of status and hierarchy were to be handled. Nyerere, much like some of the pluralist critics, doubted the viability of "football politics" in the new nation (Glickman, 1967). He objected to party systems that tended to magnify and increase class differences in the society or that exploited conflict for immediate gains. In the developing country, the majority interest could not be defined in parochial terms or isolated from the broad concerns of a people still unfamiliar with exercising their rights. Nyerere faced the logical implications of his assumptions. The possibility of a neutral civil service was doubtful, and he reversed a 1960 decision barring officials from the party. In 1964, officials were required to join the party. providing the higher cadre and a measure of accountability in TANU, and the policy of special preferences for Africans was discontinued. Economic forces in the society had to be brought within his framework, and large-scale nationalization followed.

These measures to construct a coherent and consistent status structure for Tanzania were given priority over developmental needs. Nyerere realized that, if new productive institutions crystallized into a new status structure, the very roots of the society would be affected. His answer was the village settlement scheme and village development committees to bring the "Freedom and Work" slogan to the people. Although the projects proved too ambitious, they are dramatic evidence of Nyerere's determination to communicate the meaning of the nation to the grass roots and to cast developmental activities in a form that would moderate increasing differentiation at higher levels of the society. New projects were to avoid encapsulation by the administrative structure of the state and were to relate to the general mobilization of people. The First Five Year Plan called for some seventy supervised resettlement projects involving half a million people. The people were to leave the dispersed hamlets *(shambas)* of rural Tanzanian society and become members of modernized rural communities stressing cooperative enterprise and self-help under the tutelage of the regional and area committees (Nye, 1963). The productive results of both these experiments were marginal, and the experiments were terminated, but they can only be accurately assessed by taking into account the President's concern in preventing the norms of established interests from dominating the effort to rebuild the country and his determination to give his ideology tangible meaning.

There are no formulas for weighing the productive and financial costs of these experiments against the evidence they provided at a critical moment in national development. As it became clear that the economic burdens were unbearable, Nyerere became more aware of the interdependence of economic and political structures. The second stage of transforming ideological doctrine into new institutions may be dated from the 1967 Arusha Declaration, though the President had been engaged in revising his ideas for some months prior to the declaration. A major inquiry was held into the operation of the cooperatives, and the government decided that more careful management and direction were needed. The 1965 Constitution established the primary concern of the state over the means of production, and the local elections of the party in 1965 were a test of TANU's viability at the community level (Cliffe, 1968). In 1966, the President announced a national service obligation of two years for all students under government scholarships, and high officials followed Nyerere's lead in reducing their salaries and benefits. The aim of these changes is consistent with the earlier thrust of Nyerere's thinking: the privileges and wealth of the new society must not become the justification for a rigid status system based on economic values.

While the early period of articulating Nyerere's doctrine concentrated on directly communicating new patterns of work and the new framework of Tanzanian politics, the Arusha Declaration (Nyerere, 1968) reveals the increasing concern that structural conflict will overtake the effort to devise new institutions. The declaration opens with a strong rejection of monetary evaluations of Tanzanian problems and of the nascent class divisions in the society. Nyerere saw economic development as a subordinate aspect of asserting Tanzanian independence and objected to the growing economic divisions between rural and urban and industrial and agricultural activities. To preclude these divisions from influencing the entire political system, severe changes were needed among both leaders and citizens. The people must accept the essentially agricultural character of the country, and the peasant must not be permitted to become the pawn of urban interests. Leaders must renew their dedication, specifically by giving up investments, positions, and benefits they derive from private sources. Shortly after the declaration, the government nationalized all banks and insurance companies and a number of manufacturing and trading firms.

Nyerere's efforts to articulate a working ideology have been characterized by their thoroughness and consistency. Despite resistance from some TANU leaders, he proceeded to elaborate its application to other sectors of the society. Several months later, his speech called "Education for Self-Reliance" outlined how the educational system should be reoriented to provide for the vast majority of citizens who can receive only primary education and spend their lives on the land. He criticized the country's failure to make Swahili the national language and to relate the practical problems of agriculture to education. Specific modifications included removing the emphasis on examinations and, indirectly, individual achievement; the association of work with education by attaching farms to schools; and fostering community attitudes by improved ways of bringing together students, teachers, and parents in the school system.

In late 1967, the President's speech called "Socialism and Rural Development" traced the outline of a new rural social structure, in part inspired by the traditional self-reliance of the African community and in part by the necessities of development. Recognizing the shortcomings of the early village settlement scheme, Nyerere also rejected becoming "a nation of individual peasant producers" who gradually drift into the system of incentives and attitudes of capitalist societies. In his view, it was none too soon to attack some basic problems of Tanzanian agriculture, which must be recognized as a major opportunity to improve the lives of the vast majority of citizens. He cautioned against the emergence of a rural proletariat as the small proprietors took more advantage of government support and developed better methods for their private advantage. He warned that the large regional marketing cooperatives, though collective in inspiration, could easily become an appendage of a capitalist economic system and the instrument of a privileged minority. Tanzania's rural development should be directed toward extending the meaning of ujmaa in farming communities where work is collectively organized, private land ownership disappears, and rural change can more effectively and more equitably utilize technical and financial assistance from government. The new communities would not have a standard form, nor would they be built in short periods, but government would provide advice and assistance for the staged regrouping of hamlets in collectively organized farm communities.

Relatively few of the ideological justifications advanced in the developing countries have had so consistent and so articulate an advocate as Nyerere, who in fact prefers to be called *Mwalimu* or teacher. Two qualities of his effort to explain the new ideological framework of the society stand out.

First, the process of eliciting consistency between institutional norms and basic political values has preceded the actual emergence of new institutions. Despite failures and bitter internal controversies, such as the 1964 mutiny, each step in development has been accompanied by an evaluation of its consequences and its relation to the nation's guiding values. Nyerere's approach differs because of his candor in acknowledging the gap between aspiration and reality, his skill in translating aspirations into terms that are meaningful to African society, and his determination that Tanzania not permit its ultimate objectives to be submerged by the unanticipated consequences of institutional change.

The second characteristic is that—despite the strong socialist and, hence, economic thread running through his proposals—it remains basically an ideology directed toward building a coherent political system. The norms guiding new institutions, including trade unions, cooperatives, farms, and industry, must not become so inconsistent with underlying values of the society that they in turn justify inequity and injustice in politics. Nyerere wants socioeconomic change, but he does not want it at the price of individual dignity or of national submission to international political forces. Although Tanzania is a dispersed society and has a number of relatively strong, tribally delimited organizations, a working ideology has evolved that underscores the reciprocity of political relationships and the importance of achieving political equality.

NORMATIVE CHANGE
AMONG EARLY MODERNIZERS

The articulation of norms has followed a somewhat different course in work of men who are often referred to as the "early" modernizers, though the differences may be exaggerated. In much of the literature on development, the experience of Turkey and Japan in particular has been examined to uncover how they made such apparently successful transformations of traditional institutions and were able to move with relative speed toward industrialization. A number of events, however, have begun to raise doubts over the "success" of the early modernizers. The military coup in Turkey in 1960 and the subsequent revival of more militant nationalist attitudes suggest that some fundamental problems persist. The military subversion of Japan in the early 1930s (Morley, 1968) and tensions in her political life since World War II cause one to doubt whether the process of recasting a doctrine into a working ideology ever ceases. In both cases, historical evidence can be found to suggest that the critical events leading to the formation of the nation excluded large segments of the population and were heavily influenced by a relatively small, centrally placed elite.

Mustapha Kemal and his army, like the leaders of the Meiji restoration, were able to secularize society and to lay the groundwork for more effective socioeconomic change, but it seems doubtful if these changes constituted a fundamental reexamination of status relationships in the society. Kemal took a number of steps to give Turkey a national identity. The capital was moved from the cosmopolitan setting of Istanbul to Ankara on an austere plain in central Turkey. A sharp break was made from the country's Ottoman history and Islam was disestablished, if not repressed. The Sultanate was abolished, the religious foundations and courts were dissolved, and religious education virtually eliminated. But Islamic values were only dormant, and in the more open political conflict after World War II concessions were made to religious institutions (Frye, 1957). Important as the Kemalist reforms were to the establishment of a viable state, it now seems clear that his nationalistic policies affected a very small portion of the population, and did not revolve underlying differences over church-state relations.

Kemal's solution to the hierarchical problems of the society was essentially an elitist one and it was the bankruptcy of the elitist formula that ushered in a new era of ideological conflict in Turkey. Systematic evidence is now available to indicate that the upper military elite never relinquished effective control of the political system (Frey, 1964). Turkey acquired legitimacy in the eyes of her people, but Kemal's doctrine failed to provide the working principles for periodic adaptation of political values to change and for the evaluation on consistency among institutional norms. Karpat (1968, 1964) has pinpointed the issue in describing the postwar years as the period when the official ideological monopoly of nationalism was disrupted. The accumulation of social and economic changes in the society were sufficient to bring about a serious breakdown of government in 1960. A period of military rule followed until the disparities could be absorbed by new parties and the issues raised by widespread socioeconomic change could be reflected in the democratic process. In Karpat's words, the crisis was caused "on the one hand by the break-down of narrow traditional forms of organization and values, and on the other hand by the pressing need to reorganize the society and its economy into modern, broader social and political units suitable to the requirements of a nation-state."

Turkey's need for a better integrated, working ideology was particularly apparent in two areas touching the lives of all citizens. Kemal's policy of *etatist* development through government agencies and corporations opened the way for the growth of an enlarged, entrepreneurial middle class, but it did not provide a way to weigh their accomplishments against the needs of other Turks. Rapid economic growth after World War II produced powerful interest groups and also provided an irresistible temptation to those in high political office to profit at public expense. Moreover, the policy of state economic control fostered a second problem, the protection of the peasantry and their isolation from the momentous socioeconomic change in the cities.

Under Kemal, the peasants had continued their village existence, where their lives were still ordered by traditional village headmen and local Islamic officials. The efforts to communicate a more secular version of Turkish nationalism to the countryside through the People's Houses failed, and the vast majority of Turkey's people accepted the oligarchy of the family and the village. After the war, the huge increase in communication, the movement of nearly a third of the population to the cities, and the growing dependence of agriculture on the national economy eroded the barriers between urban and rural environments. The concessions made to farmers by the Menderes government for votes became a national burden, while numbers of city intellectuals went to the villages as teachers under the national service scheme and learned of the poverty and exploitation in the villages. In retrospect, one may argue that Kemal's precedent of autocratic rule prevented a working ideology from emerging and gave the Democratic Party under Menderes a framework for political manipulation that ignored the larger issues taking shape in Turkish society.

If the articulation of national values in Turkey were judged solely on the political changes that have occurred, one might well conclude that a working system of beliefs and attitudes had successfully linked the citizen to the political system. In 1950, the Republican Party, Kemal's party, peacefully gave way in elections to the Democratic Party. In the late 1950s the Menderes government found it increasingly difficult to manage dissent as the issues raised by rapid development became more controversial. The army found it more difficult to continue its traditional neutrality as the repression and corruption of the Menderes government became more severe. With the revival of party politics after the 1960 coup, many of the suppressed issues in Turkish politics were manifested in the splintering of parties, although the renewed People's Republican Party, under Ataturk's close friend, Inonu, and the revived Democratic Party, under the mantle of the new Justice Party, continued to dominate Turkish politics. In the 1965 elections (Szyliowicz, 1966; Rustow, 1963), both parties made concessions to socialist elements in their ranks, the Republicans favoring extending the state sector to achieve more equitable distribution of benefits and the Justice Party proposing a more conventional liberal view that appealed to the new middle class.

While it would be impossible to claim that Turkey might have developed more rapidly if her political values had been more successfully articulated at an earlier time, the crisis of 1960 turned on the question of how the diverging, and sometimes contradictory, norms set in motion in the early stages of Turkish nationalism would be reconciled. The early modernizers had an option that the more recently established nations do not have. Nationalism in the interwar period could be used to buttress the country's legitimacy—i.e., to establish popular acceptance and central control, without confronting more complex issues of institutional change. Kemal's autocratic rule acknowledged that institutional proliferation would take place at some later time, but his doctrine was not easily extended to regulate such conflicts and help articulate the changing mosaic of new interests and groups. Part of the test of a successful ideology is whether it can expand its range of concern with response to change outside the realm of formal politics. The early modernizers, especially Turkey and Japan, illustrate the pitfall of confining national values to such a narrow scope and within such restricted political institutions that the political system is unable to make adjustments and to examine new sources of institutional conflict.

Ward and Rustow (1964) have pointed out that, in 1920, Japan arrived at a level of development roughly comparable to Turkey in 1960. Although many important reservations are needed, their analysis suggests that the requirements being placed on the two countries at these times were broadly similar. The implication is that, as societies undergo substantial socioeconomic change and acquire a number of new institutions oriented to industrial life, they experience new problems of resolving institutional conflict and relating new norms to their underlying political values. Though the historical and cultural circumstances of the two countries are very different, it is important to note that the structural problems of the two societies did indeed bear some similarity to each other. The accumulation of problems in Japan, like that in Turkey, followed a dramatic change in the country's political life that was directed by a relatively small number of men who were eager to acquire both the status and the material benefits of being a modern industrial nation.

The evolution of a working ideology in Japan placed even more emphasis on ordering institutional norms than did Turkey. The leaders of the Meiji Restoration in 1868 were heavily influenced by their country's humiliation in the mid-nineteenth century and the disintegration of the Tokugawa regime when confronted with the pressures of modernization. But the transformation of Japan was much less a popular uprising than the Turkish revolution, where the army based its claim on popular support and where its aims were explicitly republican. The Satsuma and Choshu clans that led the rebellion had no desire to dismantle central authority in Japan, nor were their ideological views at variance with the traditional views on authority in Japanese culture. Ward has pointed out that "the appeal was to an institutional complex which was traditional not only in terms of the circumstances of the 1870s but would have been equally so in 1603." The institutions that were to make Japan a world power by the turn of the century brought very little change in the basic concepts of status in Japanese society and politics.

A number of institutions were perpetuated to assure that the hierarchical structure of Japanese society was relatively unimpaired (Norman, 1940; Sansom, 1950). Perhaps most important, the preservation of the political myths *(kokutai)* surrounding the role of the Emperor, whose powers were conceived as divine, unique, and eternal. The Emperor has been described as "the private legitimizer for the Tokugawa shogun" (Ward and Rustow, 1964: 39-40), and the institution continued in much the same capacity in part because the isolation of the Imperial Court at Kyoto enabled it to survive the turbulence of the Tokugawa decline. Hall has pointed out that the resurrection of the imperial sovereignty had significant popular meaning in a period of social upheaval and external threat. By 1871, it had become the ultimate symbol of unity and the keystone for the oligarchic structure assembled to rule the country. With the shift of the imperial court to Tokyo, the new leaders acquired an institution that was both above the turmoil of politics and provided a powerful sanction for their actions.

A second key element in the new hierarchy of Japan was the *genro* or elder statesmen whose stabilizing influence on institutional change until World War I has been frequently noted. The fact that they had no official position and kept no formal records is an important clue to the decision-making process that enabled them to exercise immense influence. Until the introduction of the cabinet system in 1885, they were the link between the official power of the rapidly growing government and political leaders. They remained the senior statesmen of Japan throughout their lifetimes. The genro had all been active in the restoration, were of low or moderate *samurai* origins, and came from the Satsuma-Chóshú alliance (Hackett, 1968). The genro worked through casual meetings in one another's homes, in response to requests from the prime minister or the imperial court, and in occasional formal meetings with the cabinet or Emperor. They have been described as the "highest coordinating body of the state," protecting the Emperor from the crises of the period and providing essential continuity between cabinets. They embodied the informal procedures that made power so elusive in the early development of Japan and were able to evoke traditional Japanese values to preserve oligarchic rule.

The leaders of Japan had no desire to see aristocratic methods disappear, and they were prepared to subject themselves to immense stress to restrict the framework within which the new hierarchy took shape. The feudal origins of the Satsuma rebellion of 1877 persuaded them to make more concessions in the direction of participation, but these were successfully contained by other institutional changes. The Constitution of 1889 provided the structure for a parliamentary government, but it also assured the fictional rule of the Emperor (Hall, 1968). The formation of parties was discouraged, but, when they did appear, they had very similar social and political roots (Ike, 1950). Education received great care and attention, but it was in the context of the Imperial Rescript on Education of 1890 which reinforced the Confusian myths eternally fixing the relationship of ruler and ruled. Central to this continued concentration of power was the formation of an extraordinarily competent and honest bureaucracy which functioned within the paternal pattern of rule.

In 1884, a new Peerage Ordinance tried to unite the remnants of the prerestoration aristocracy and the new leadership in a House of Peers that might offset any excesses from the House of Representatives. In 1887, an ordinance established recruitment to the civil service by examination, but access to the higher civil service was quickly contained within a procedure guaranteeing the strength of the new oligarchy. Later ordinances protected the status of civil bureaucrats and prohibited the appointment of all but a few of the highest officials. Tokyo Imperial University became their training ground and the cost of higher education kept the higher posts in the hands of the upper classes. Of the 34 persons who formed cabinets in the twentieth century, all but five had backgrounds in civil or military hierarchy (Inoki, 1964: 293-296). Nearly three-fourths of the higher civil service and half the judiciary in 1937 came from Tokyo University. Thus, the new political system created a power structure which assured that the industrialization of Japan would conform to the basic political values of the oligarchy.

The articulation of Japanese values to provide the diverse institutions necessary for economic growth is remarkable precisely because such dramatic changes in socioeconomic differentiation were contained within a highly traditional concept of hierarchy. Nearly the entire population increase of 16 million persons from 1908 to 1925 moved into the cities. From the turn of the century, the rural population remained virtually unchanged, but provided both the food and taxes that supported industrialization. The oligarchic pattern of rule enabled the new institutions to be segmented and controlled, while the Emperor provided the essential symbols and the sheltered bureaucracy provided the essential expertise. Economic power was concentrated in the industrial combines *(zaibatsu)* which had close family and personal relations with the upper levels of government (Silberman, 1968). The accommodation of the immense increase in diversification and specialization was made possible by the solidarity of the ruling elite and the transcendental authority given their actions by the Imperial Household.

The fascination with Japan as a model for development has perhaps exaggerated the extent to which socioeconomic change took place prior to the resolution of basic problems of status and power in the society. A number of important decisions were made between the fall of the Tokugawa shogunate in 1853 and the abolition of the feudal lords *(daiymo)* in 1871. Even more important steps toward structuring power were made in the next two decades leading up to the 1889 Constitution. Though Japan was surely undergoing rapid socioeconomic change in the latter half of the nineteenth century, it seems possible that the basic doctrine for the definition of status relationships in the society and for the elaboration of institutional norms in the society were an afterthought. To a much greater extent than in Turkey, the modernizing elite was aware of the political repercussions of its actions and carefully transplanted in the new political system a status structure that was deeply rooted in traditions. Ike (1950: 201) has suggested that the concept of a "public" was never fully developed and noted that the primary meaning of the word for public, *ko,* is prince or duke. The new elite clearly had no illusions about the ease of combining widespread participation with the transformation of the society. Even before the Meiji restoration, each step toward the further institutionalization of more democratic politics was surrounded with new precautions to insulate the oligarchic pattern of control.

Nationalism in Japan centered on the revision of the existing culture and the adaptation of widely understood values of subordination to new circumstances, while Turkey followed a much more explicit path of aggressively asserting secular control and relying directly on military supervision of new institutions. There was not nearly the same experience in struggling with the cultural issues in Turkey, where Ottoman culture was a mosaic of diverse elements and Islamic culture had not produced institutions approaching the viability of the Confucian amalgam of the Emperor and his servants. The countries are alike in that both were determined to make rapid social and economic change by regulating and channeling institutional change, especially in order to give precedence to industrial change. Nevertheless, the underlying justification for status in Japan was more profoundly linked to the past. Until the overthrow of the system by the army in the 1930s, tradition dominated social and political institutions.

The emergence of a working ideology cannot hope to explain all of a nation's experience, but it does seem that the Japanese elite of the Meiji period were aware of the need to link the norms to political change. The Kemalist formula of state control relied on the coercive power of the army and the manipulation of nationalist symbols by a relatively small number of men, but the blend of Confucian values and oligarchic control in Japan reflected a concept of superior-subordinate relationships that every citizen understood. Thus, the Japanese elite experienced much less difficulty in achieving a coherence among institutional norms than was the case in Turkey. The force of differentiation and specialization could be harmonized from all quarters of Japanese society. This was accomplished by compartmentalizing new activity and by superimposing on each sector a notion of authority that was duplicated from the primary level of village and family to the national level of Emperor and subject.

What the early modernizers seem to have shared is their reluctance to submit the process of articulating ideological doctrine to popular forces. The explanation may be as simple as the absence of popular elements in the Turkish revolution or the Meiji restoration, but this hardly does justice to the popular commitment that both transformations engendered. A more accurate version might be that, at early stages of development, and also under less-pressing historical circumstances, leaders could more easily choose to insulate one avenue of change from another. There was little pressure for Mustapha Kemal to explain his industrial policies to the peasants, nor did the Japanese worker question major issues of industrialization policy. Institutional change could be manipulated in Japan and Turkey, though the principles on which the Japanese leaders based their political views were more clearly defined by traditional institutions. The similarities of the two countries may, thus, be based more on their historical coincidence in time and their emphasis on industrial change rather than on underlying similarities in the evolution of a working ideology. Their major commonality seems to be the extent to which finding new definitions of status was deferred in favor of rapid socioeconomic change.

POSTPONING
IDEOLOGICAL CHANGE

The comparison of the early and late modernizers has indicated that the problem of redefining status in a society is distinct, at least analytically, from the development of material wealth and increasing economic activity. Many new nations come into being and advance along the path of economic change without resolving underlying problems of status determination. The way the definition of status in political and social life takes place may not be as dependent on the level of development in socioeconomic terms as the emphasis of much of the earlier literature on political development suggests. A more accurate representation may be that societies experience growth that makes new options and alternatives available, ideological and otherwise. Having made certain kinds of decisions, they enter into a period of change where these options are not likely to arise again in the same form. The need for working ideology is affected by the development of complex institutions, but there appears to be a very high degree of latitude among nations on the amount of growth that may occur before the linkage of institutional norms to the politics becomes a pressing issue.

So many factors bear on the formation of a political system that it seems unlikely that any universal explanation is likely to be found. Japan had a very profound cultural consensus which the Meiji leaders used to great advantage to achieve a remarkable degree of structural similarity of authority across the whole spectrum of Japanese institutions. Turkey also had a highly homogeneous culture, but Kemal did not succeed in generating anything approaching the institutional similarities in the use of authority that is found in Japan. Tanzania, Algeria, and China represent more contemporary efforts to achieve a shared understanding of politics by revolutionary means. Other nations, like Pakistan, Tunisia, and Thailand, seem to vacillate between dwelling on the underlying nature of power in their societies and concentrating on the development of productive institutions. In these countries, there seem to be periodic upheavals, often led by those monopolizing sheer coercive power in the army, bureaucracy, or dominant party, when the institutional advances are brought into alignment with the more general aims. of the political system.

If no simple correlation between increasing differentiation and the articulation of an ideology can be discovered, then how are we to conceptualize the process by which the underlying moral objectives of the nation are articulated in institutionalized form? There seems, first, to be the question of whether or not the political system is established with an acceptable political culture. Where this takes place, such as Japan, the problem becomes one of the transferability of the basic definition of superior-subordinate relations to political life. Such initial consensus is, of course, more than popular recognition of government and the acquisition of legitimacy for it may relate to the use of authority in many institutions with only marginal political roles. But most developing nations do not enter into the process of change with a culturally rooted notion of authority, and some, like India, must repudiate much of their culture in order to engage in rapid change. For these countries, a very different process takes place whereby the nation must deal simultaneously with both the problem of basic nature of authority and the generation of institutional norms to organize and differentiate new activities.

Where institutionalized change overtakes the problem of arriving at a definition of status, the terms of reciprocity among individuals and the reconciliation of the norms of new and old institutions becomes difficult. Some, like Tanzania, start out to evolve widespread understanding of the entire framework within which the new government is trying to operate, often at the cost of increased differentiation and economic growth. Some find themselves in such precarious circumstances that there is no choice if they are to survive. This is probably true of Pakistan in 1947, when the new country was flooded with tens of millions of refugees, lost its major nationalist spokesman, Jinnah, and had to proceed with only a fragmentary administrative system. In most cases, however, it appears that the working ideology and its relationship to institutional norms will emerge from a continuing struggle between those institutions that are able to bring their influence directly to bear on government—often the new industries, trade unions, and commercialized farmers—and the demand of the underemployed and impoverished for a voice in national policy. The great difficulties that the developing countries have had in rapidly increasing per capita wealth indicate that these conflicts are likely to become more rather than less intense. In the absence of a working ideology, growth tends to convert the political process into a competition among groups and interests wherein the neglected and dispossessed increasingly find they have no alternative but to challenge the entire political system.

In the context of conflict among institutions, the description of a working ideology becomes manageable. The problem is not whether the government can generate norms for institutions, because, in most cases of mixed development, the institutions for promoting growth have already been given precedence. The problem is more likely to be one of whether or not the government is able to change the norms of existing institutions to achieve a degree of consistency as status is redefined in the new nation. Thus, the questions that often arise are how the Philippine government can extricate itself from dependence on large landlords and the sugar lobby or how the Pakistani or Indian political systems can combine grass-roots participation with the influence of the elite administrative corps. Under these circumstances, it is the conflict of institutional norms and the relative priority of institutions that determines whether the political system will survive. From the perspective of a working ideology, then, the problem is not simply one of insufficient institutionalization, but the distribution of institutionalized activity in the society, the relation between authority in such organizations and the government, and how great the disparities between the still formally stated principles of the system and the norms of these institutions can become before breakdown takes place. Contrary to Huntington's (1968) view, a nation may fail because, rather than being unsuccessful, new institutions have worked *too* well.

The development of a working ideology has been described as finding a shared notion of status which can in turn be applied in the institutional context in order to establish ways of sharing power and relating the use of authority to numerous activities. A degree of coherence among institutions facilitates the integration of the country's institutionalized activity and clarifies the choices involved in meeting specific needs. Many countries have great difficulty even arriving at a point where the general institutional fabric of the society is sufficiently complex to make evaluation and integration a meaningful problem, and, for them, the question of working ideology does not exist or is, at least, postponed. But, in time, institutional change raises problems of priority, equity, and coordination, especially where intensive developmental plans and programs are pursued. Most countries encounter this problem in piecemeal fashion, sometimes extolled as the "incrementalist" view. A closer look at several countries that have tried gradually to devise a working ideology in this experimental way may be helpful.

Pakistan is an interesting illusrration because it has powerful central institutions, the army and the bureaucracy, but has had great difficulties in linking individual beliefs and national values to the structure of authority. The severe dislocations surrounding Pakistan's creation put great emphasis on the necessity of social order and of performing a number of essential tasks. Out of this experience emerged the Civil Service of Pakistan (CSP), an elite administrative corps whose history began with the Indian Civil Service and British colonial policy (Braibanti, 1963). The CSP is an elite, generalist body that has remained at roughly 400 persons since independence, supported by about 3,000 other civil servants in related higher services. It remains the most influential force in a nation of over a 100 million persons. Alongside the administrative elite, and heavily interlaced with them through marriage and education, is the army. The army was also of elitist origins and heavily recruited from the Punjab, a major Pakistani province. From the mid-1950s, the army played an increasingly important political role. In 1958, an army coup took place and General Ayub Khan emerged as President (Von Vorys, 1968).

Few would disagree that the central issue in Pakistani politics has been the troublesome problem of devising a coherent and responsible pattern of authority. But every attempt to develop the framework for new political institutions has been carefully restricted to preserve the power of the administrative and military elite. Well before the military coup of 1958, Pakistan had been ruled largely under emergency powers given to the Governor General. The observance of parliamentary rule actually produced 338 days of meetings over a period of eleven years. It would be wrong to underestimate the passions and intrigue that the multiple parties and religious groups generated in Pakistan, but it is also difficult in retrospect to identify initiatives by the very influential institutions of the civil service and the army to improve political institutions.

The effects of delay and procrastination in the search for a formula to structure institutional authority became clear under Ayub. Under martial law, an attempt was made to curb the corruption of the civil service, but the military quickly learned that they could not rule without administrative support from the CSP. Ayub opted for the developmental path toward institutional change, giving substantial power to the Planning Commission and opening the way for a new entrepreneurial class to emerge in the cities. In fact, Pakistan did begin to make significant progress toward industrialization, but the new entrepreneurs were easily absorbed into the old power structure. Indeed, one can find evidence that steps were taken to further concentrate power as an economic elite emerged. The 1,500 trade associations in the country were amalgamated in 1961 into 83 organizations representing specific trades and towns, which in turn were coordinated in a federal framework under the Federation of Pakistan Chambers of Commerce and Industry (Alavi, forthcoming). The new entrepreneurial class, however, was no more accountable to the nation than were the earlier politicians, and, in time, it became clear that Ayub himself, as well as a number of high officials, had profited enormously from Pakistan's economic growth.

Ayub was also aware that Pakistan had profound institutional problems. To provide an institutional structure for the nation, he proposed Basic Democracies, a many-tiered structure of councils running from the village to the province. The aim of Basic Democracies was to divorce political activity from the influence of the politicians and to evolve more gradually forms of accountability at the local level before extending popular authority to higher levels of government. But wherever the system might prove itself at odds with the expertise of the administration—and, hence, challenge its authority—it was carefully contained. The local councils initially had appointed members to help outweigh local leaders, and there were specified quotients of officials, which effectively neutralized the elected villagers at higher tiers in the system (Ashford, 1967). Though the councils were to have a planning and development role, they obviously had no control over the allocation of funds at higher levels, nor was any special effort made to give their projects priority. Perhaps the fatal blow to the system was Ayub's desire to use it as a legitimizing agency for his own government before it had acquired respect. The 80,000 Basic Democrats were made the electors for the President under the 1964 Constitution, and from this grew much of the bitter dispute that brought Ayub's downfall.

A second country that has evolved strong central institutions with minimal ideological change is Tunisia. In this illustration, institutionalized strength has not been monopolized by a specialized group, but on a large party organization, the Socialist Destour, having a high degree of popular acceptance and an elaborate regional and local organization. Under these conditions, one might expect that the process of institutional elaboration would be more sensitive to the problems of generating new political norms as well as goals for the specialized activities of development and economic growth. The Socialist Destourian Party has a long history in the colonial struggle with France, and its leader, President Habib Bourguiba, became a national hero (Moore, 1965). A number of the internal power struggles of the party reflect the problems Tunisian nationalists had in articulating new goals for the society that would also be consistent with the supremacy of the party. In 1955, Bourguiba repelled an attack of the

Arab nationalist faction of the party; in 1956, the socialist zeal of the trade unions was successfully dampened, though it erupted again from time to time in Bourguiba's dispute with Tlili; and at various times, there have been conflicts with Tunisian youth, Baathist intellectuals, and conservative business interests closely aligned with France. In 1969, a decade of experience shaped by quasi-socialist aims was abruptly dismantled. None of these experiences, though they reflect increasing pressure to articulate Bourguiba's pragmatic nationalism, brought about a serious evaluation of Destourian values as they relate to the increasing differentiation of the society.

In the early 1960s, Tunisia was compelled to make such an evaluation because of the sheer complexity of the task of development, external pressures as Algeria neared independence, and the French attack on Bizerte. But the decision to devote the full force of the party to *la lutte contre sous-developpement* was carefully preceded with measures to centralize the party organization. The party congress of 1958 endorsed changes to reform the historic cell organization, made up largely of local notables and, hence, in some measure free of central control, and instituted provincial-level committees. In addition, the provincial administration was tightened by giving the governors extraordinary powers and making them the capstone of both the party and the governmental organization at the provincial level (Rudebeck, 1967). In effect, Tunisia reduced the institutional complexity of the political system before launching ambitious development plans and new policies.

After careful preparation by the party organization, the Socialist Destour adopted its present name and launched the country on a major development program in 1962. The program entailed a number of restrictions on privileged groups, and inescapably implied a number of basic institutional changes. A capable young Tunisian, Ben Salah, became head of a super-ministry that eventually expanded to include planning, finance, commerce, industry, education, and agriculture. Perhaps because the Tunisian elite were themselves so accustomed to centralized power, this concentration of authority was enthusiastically endorsed. Ben Salah, who was surely not free of the political ambitions of his colleagues, made very few adjustments of an institutional nature in executing his development plan, although he was firmly committed to developing a new, cooperative sector of the economy. This brought into existence an elaborate new system of cooperatives, encompassing commerce, external trade, agriculture, and retailing, and built from the top downward by officials. The new structure received additional strength when French recalcitrance led to the nationalization of the remaining foreign-owned land in 1964 and a large-scale effort was made to engage all farmers in cooperative organizations (Ashford, 1967).

In Ben Salah's hands, the cooperative organizations began to rival the scope and effectiveness of the party itself. By early 1969, the cooperatives for agriculture reached roughly a third of the active rural population and nearly all industrial and commercial activities in the cities were affected by their activities. The important point from the viewpoint of Destourian goals, however, was that the entire structure was derived from only the most rudimentary reconsideration of party and national institutions. In the five years between the Bizerte Congress of the party and 1969, Ben Salah had launched hundreds of new organizations, mobilized thousands of persons, and in effect unilaterally defined the norms for the most influential force for institutional change in Tunisia. The result was a government crisis in late 1969, when Ben Salah was removed from office. Early in 1970, he was tried for high treason and sentenced to ten years in prison. The cooperative structure was dismantled, a national organization to represent cooperatives was dissolved, and the entire governmental structure of Tunisia revised to prevent any future "distortion" of national goals. A number of factors contributed to this dramatic reversal of national policy, but certainly a key factor was the sudden realization by party leaders that enormous institutional changes were taking place without consideration of their relevance to the party structure. Seldom has there been so complete a rejection of a major effort to build new institutions, particularly in a country that enjoyed the stability and unity of Tunisia.

The evidence suggests that Ben Salah, like Ayub in Pakistan, operated with the support of the major institutions in the country, and, as in the case of the Pakistani bureaucracy, the dominant Destour Party was a formidable organization, with able leadership and a demonstrated capacity to adjust to new conditions. The experience of both countries raises serious doubts about the argument of Huntington (1968) that institutionalization somehow becomes a self-propelling and, even more, a self-stabilizing force in developing countries. Moreover, both countries tried to allow for increased demands for participation and for greater equity in the development process, Tunisia probably more than Pakistan. The answer is in part that more complex institutions in themselves are not enough to assure orderly change and that they may indeed exacerbate certain differences in a society. More directly relevant to the emergence of a working ideology, simply asserting a new institutional norm is related to the achievement of what may well be an acceptable national goal is not enough. In Pakistan, it remained clear that power remained with the military-administrative alliance. The new political institutions increased the sense of inequality dividing Pakistanis and was effectively divorced from socioeconomic change. In Tunisia, the underlying conflict in both more subtle and more obvious because the new institutions evolved almost by the default of leadership and posed an increasingly real challenge to the basic political institution of the country, the Socialist Destour itself.

THE USE AND
ABUSE OF NORMS

From the perspective of a working ideology, the elaboration of institutional norms to some measure reflects the political culture of a society. The first reservation is that the necessity evolving a coherent normative structure increases as societal complexity increases. At very low levels of development, under conditions of a highly dispersed population, and where traditional values tend to exclude national institutional forces, a working ideology is not likely to emerge nor may it be needed. Afghanistan, Iran, and Morocco, for example, have relatively little need to elaborate political values in operational form, though, as developmental changes accumulate, pressures to do so may suddenly appear. The Iranian crisis in 1953 or the Ugandan crisis of 1966 can be looked upon as the violent upheaval of organizations and groups who find the central values of the social and political system inadequate in institutional terms as well as psychologically.

If the necessity for a working ideology is partially a function of societal complexity, it must also be noted that the search for consistency between political values and institutional norms is not limited to those new activities that are explicitly political. Much of the development literature assumes that differentiation and specialization in political activity are accompanied by similar, if not proportionate, transformations in other kinds of institutionalized behavior. Experience with the developing countries since World War II suggests the opposite. Countries of highly varied ideological persuasion have had severe difficulties in transforming their doctrine into effective institutions. The basically incrementalist approach of Pakistan, the closely coordinated efforts the Tunisian one-party state, and the more doctrinaire extension of institutions in Tanzania and China have all suffered costly, often bloody, reversals.

Political institutions may or may not be joined with a fundamental concept of how status should be structured in the society. Where the definition of the terms of reciprocity has yet to emerge or remains ambiguous, whatever values are advanced as central to the political system tend to be placed in competition with the norms of other institutions. Institutionalized practices may develop to prevent, or at least forestall, an effort to compare and evaluate the relationship between institutional norms and political values. The oligarchic structure of Japan and Germany were especially adept at forestalling the clash of ideas in the political system, but, when they were subject to severe strain, their political institutions were easily subverted. The elitist governments of Latin America, Turkey, and parts of Africa have also attempted to join institutional norms to a working ideology after achieving relatively high levels of socioeconomic advancement. The result has been that political institutions, though developed in terms of their own organization, leadership, and norms, have frequently been unable to provide guidance for new institutions or to elicit the popular support necessary to service change of well-established institutions.

A more vital question to ask about the emergence of political institutions may be whether or not they are "overdeveloped." This may happen in a number of ways. The C.P.P. in Ghana appears to have become so fixed on the doctrinal aspects of Nkrumah's thinking that relatively little attention was paid to how well these ideas related to other institutions or how workable they were in the Ghanian context. A more typical form is the absorption or domination of the political process by a given institution, such as Eisenstadt (1963) suggests may happen where the bureaucracy begins to substitute itself for political institutions. There are reasons to feel that this has been happening in Pakistan and perhaps in Thailand, not to mention numerous military governments. The important distinction is that the substitution of the norms of a particular group for political institutions may preclude evolving an articulated ideology that can be understood and applied in many quarters of the society. Specialized organizations for industry, agriculture, and education are not microcosms of the political process. Institutions used to build a more complex material society must in time begin to evolve the basic tenets of morality and justice appropriate to the polity. Political institutions have peculiarly difficult problems in assessing their effectiveness and in judging how the priorities and coherence of more specialized institutional change will be determined.

Political institutions are mediators of institutional change of all kinds in a society. The clearest proponent of this view has been Eisenstadt (1964), who sees adjusting to "the continual absorption of change" as the distinguishing feature of political systems. If the elite use political institutions to monopolize power, status, and prestige, they are in effect purposefully fixing the hierarchical pattern of the society to protect their institutional base. He sees three problems resulting, all of which are closely related to the articulation of basic political values in working form. First, there may be inadequate "political aggregation," meaning that the system may not find a way of reconciling needs for performance and support. Second, protest may become increasingly intense and divorced from existing political institutions, and, third, political communications may be closed to the participants. A political system experiences serious breakdown where there is what he calls "normless competition," the inability to restore solidarity around the fundamental symbols and values of the society. Eisenstadt's concern with the maintenance of solidarity and the recurrent nature of social disintegration is consistent with the problem of devising normative links to a working ideology in the political system.

This chapter has outlined alternatives for developing normative links between concept of status found in political and other institutions. Some questions have been raised as to whether the pluralist model of competition among norms accurately represents the process of developing a working ideology and even graver doubts were raised over the possibility of using this alternative in developing countries. Among the later modernizers, more emphasis has been given to building political institutions, but, as in Tanzania, these must be evaluated in terms of the overall level of institutionalization in the society. The early modernizers do not appear to have resolved the problems of articulating their political values in ways that are reproducible today, nor do their early efforts to build socioeconomic infrastructure, often successfully, appear in retrospect to have generated political institutions that could always deal with successive changes. Last, attention was given to the relation between political and other institutions in articulating a working ideology, suggesting that more specialized institutional norms may supplant the political symbols and values of a society. A working ideology, then, reconciles the individual's perception of power and the diverse institutional norms as they relate to power. This central problem, the problem of political culture, will be examined in the next chapter.

REFERENCES

ABUEVA, J. V. (1964) "Bridging the gap between the elite and the people in the Philippines." Philippine J. of Public Administration 8, 4: 325-347.

——— and R. P. DE GUZMAN [eds.] (1969) Foundations and Dynamics of Filipino Government and Politics. Manila: Bookmark.

ADLER, N. and C. HARRINGTON (1970) The Learning of Political Behavior. Glenview, Ill.: Scott, Foresman.

ALAVI, H. A. (forthcoming) "The Army and the bureaucracy in Pakistan politics," in A. Abdel-Malek [ed.] L'Armee dans la Nation.

ALMOND, G. A. and S. VERBA (1963) The Civic Culture. Princeton: Princeton Univ. Press.

ANTON, T. J. (1963) "Power, pluralism and local politics." Admin. Sci. Q. 7 (March): 425-457.

ASHFORD, D. E. (1969) "Attitudinal change and modernization," pp. 147-188 in C. Morse, Modernication by Design. Ithaca: Cornell Univ. Press.

——— (1967) National Development and Local Reform. Princeton: Princeton Univ. Press.

BACHRACH, P. (1967) A Theory of Democratic Elitism: A Critique. Boston: Little, Brown.

BIENEN, H. (1967) Tanzania: Party Transformation and Economic Development. Princeton: Princeton Univ. Press.

BRAIBANTI, R. (1963) "Public bureaucracy and judiciary in Pakistan," in J. La Palombara [ed.] Bureaucracy and Political Development. Princeton: Princeton Univ. Press.

CLIFFE, L. (1968) One Party Democracy. Nairobi: East Africa.

CUTWRIGHT, P. (1963) "National political development: measurement and analysis." Amer. Soc. Rev. 28: 253-268.

DAWSON, R. E. and D. PREWITT (1968) Political Socialization. Boston: Little, Brown.

DEUTSCH, K. (1961) "Social mobilization and political development." Amer. Pol. Sci. Rev. 55 (September): 493-511.

——— (1953) Nationalism and Social Communication. Cambridge, Mass.: MIT Press.

DOUGLAS, L. H. (1968) "Modernization in a transitional setting: a Philippine case study." Civilisations 18, 2: 204-229.

DURKHEIM, E. (1964) Division of Labor on Society. New York: Macmillan.

EISENSTADT, S. N. (1964) "Modernization and conditions of sustained growth." World Politics 16 (July): 576-594.

––– (1963) "Bureaucracy and political development," in J. La Palombara [ed.] Bureaucracy and Political Development. Princeton: Princeton Univ. Press.

––– (1958) "Internal contradictions in bureaucratic societies." Comp. Studies in Society and History 6 (October): 58-75.

FREY, F. W. (1964) The Turkish Political Elite. Cambridge, Mass.: MIT Press.

FRYE, R. N. (1957) Islam and the West. The Hague: Mouton.

GLICKMAN, H. (1967) "Dilemmas of political theory in an African context: the ideology of Julius Nyerere," pp. 195-223 in J. Butler and A. Castagno [eds.] Boston University Papers on Africa: Transition in African Politics. New York: Frederick A. Praeger.

GROSSHOLTZ, J. (1964) Politics in the Philippines. Boston: Little, Brown.

HACKETT, R. F. (1968) "Political modernization of the Meiji genro," pp. 65-98 in R. E. Ward [ed.] Political Development in Modern Japan. Princeton: Princeton Univ. Press.

HALEVY, E. (1950) A History of the English People: The Triumph of Reform, 1830-1841. London: Benn.

––– (1947) A History of the English People: The Age of Peel and Cobden. London: Benn.

HALL, J. W. (1968) "A monarch for modern Japan," in R. E. Ward [ed.] Political Development in Modern Japan. Princeton: Princeton Univ. Press.

––– (1964) Political Modernization in Japan and Turkey. Princeton: Princeton Univ. Press.

HUNTINGTON, S. P. (1968) Political Order in Changing Societies. New Haven, Conn.: Yale Univ. Press.

HYDEN, G. (1968) "Tanu yajenga nchi: political development in rural Tanzania." Lund (Sweden) Pol. Studies 8, UNISKOL.

IKE, N. (1950) The Beginnings of Political Democracy in Japan. Baltimore: Johns Hopkins Press.

INOKI, M. (1964) "The civil bureaucracy: Japan," pp. 283-300 in R. E. Ward and D. Rustow [eds.] Political Modernization in Japan and Turkey. Princeton: Princeton Univ. Press.

KARPAT, K. (1968) "Ideology in Turkey after the Revolution of 1960: nationalism and socialism." Turkish Yearbook of International Relations: 1965. University of Ankara Institute of International Relations.

––– (1964) "Society, economics and politics in contemporary Turkey." World Politics 16 (October): 55-64.

LENSKI, G. (1966) Power and Privilege: A Theory of Social Stratification. New York: McGraw-Hill.

LERNER, D. J. (1958) The Passing of Traditional Society. New York: Free Press.

LIPSET, S. (1960) Political Man: The Social Bases of Politics. New York: John Wiley.

––– (1959) "Some social requisites of democracy: economic development and political legitimacy." Amer. Pol. Sci. Rev. 53 (March): 69-105.

McCRONE, D. and C. CNUDDE (1967) "Toward a communications theory of democratic development: a causal model." Amer. Pol. Sci. Rev. 61: 72-79.

MAGUIRE, G. A. (1969) Toward 'Uhuru' in Tanzania. Cambridge, Eng.: Cambridge Univ. Press.

MARSHALL, T. H. (1950) Citizenship and Social Class. Cambridge, Eng.: Cambridge Univ. Press.

MICHELS, R. (1915) Political Parties. New York: Dover.

MITCHELL, W. T. (1967) Sociological Analysis and Politics: The Theories of Talcott Parsons. Englewood Cliffs, N.J.: Prentice-Hall.

MOORE, C. H. (1965) Tunisia Since Independence: The Dynamics of One-Party Government. Berkeley: Univ. of California Press.

MORLEY, J. [ed.] (1968) Dilemmas of Growth in Pre-War Japan. Princeton: Princeton Univ. Press.

NETTL, J. P. (1967) Political Mobilization. New York: Basic Books.

NORMAN, E. H. (1940) Japan's Emergence as a Modern State. New York: Institute of Pacific Relations.

NYE, J., Jr. (1963) "Tanganyika's self-help." Transition 3 (November): 35-39.

NYERERE, J. K. (1968) Freedom and Socialism: Uhuru na Ujamaa. London: Oxford Univ. Press.

––– 1967) Freedom and Unity: Uhuru na Umoga. London: Oxford Univ. Press.

OLSON, M. E. (1968) "Multivariate analysis of national political development." Amer. Soc. Rev. 33 (October): 699-611.

PARSONS, T. (1966) "The political aspect of social structure and process," pp. 71-114 in D. Easton [ed.] Varieties of Political Theory. Englewood Cliffs, N.J.: Prentice-Hall.

POLSBY, N. (1960) "How to study community power: the pluralist alternative." J. of Politics 22: 474-484.

RETZLAFF, R. H. (1965) "The use of aggregate data in comparative political analysis." J. of Politics 27 (November): 797-817.

RUDEBECK, L. (1967) Party and People: A Study of Political Change in Tunisia. Stockholm: Almquist & Wiksell.

RUSTOW, D. A. (1963) "Turkey's second try at democracy." Yale Rev. 52 (Summer): 518-538.

SANSOM, G. B. (1950) The Western World and Japan. New York: Alfred A. Knopf.

SILBERMAN, B. S. (1968) "Structural and functional differentiation in the political modernization of Japan," pp. 337-386 in R. E. Ward [ed.] Political Development in Modern Japan. Princeton: Princeton Univ. Press.

SMELSER, N. J. (1959) Social Change in the Industrial Revolution. Chicago: Univ. of Chicago Press.

SZYLIOWICZ, J. S. (1966) "The Turkish elections of 1965." Middle East J. 20 (Autumn): 473-494.

TAWNEY, R. H. (1949) Religion and the Rise of Capitalism. London: Murray.

VERBA, S. (1969) "The uses of survey research in the study of comparative politics: issues and strategies," pp. 56-106 in S. Rokkan and S. Verba [eds.] Comparative Survey Analysis. The Hague: Mouton.

VON VORYS, K. (1965) Political Development in Pakistan. Princeton: Princeton Univ. Press.

WARD, R. E. and D. A. RUSTOW (1964) Political Modernization in Japan and Turkey. Princeton: Princeton Univ. Press.

WATERBURY, J. (1969) The Commander of the Faithful: The Moroccan Political Elite. New York: Columbia Univ. Press.

WEBER, M. (1930) The Protestant Ethic and the Spirit of Capitalism (T. Parsons, trans.). London: George Allen & Unwin.

Chapter VI

THE CULTURAL BASIS OF A WORKING IDEOLOGY

A working ideology has two dimensions. The emotional and cognitive meanings attached to the country's political values by individuals have been discussed in Chapter III and IV. In addition to the psychological meaning attached to values, there is also collective meaning, reflected in the norms supported by the institutions of the society, discussed in Chapter V. There is rarely total coincidence of individual and collective manifestations of values, though a number of philosophical treatises have been written to suggest how such a harmonious state of affairs might be achieved.

The evolution of a working ideology as it relates to collective behavior will be analyzed in terms of the proliferation of institutional norms in behavior which to some extent reflects the political culture. One might correctly infer from this proposition that a number of institutions might exist in society without explicitly raising the problem of political culture. This is roughly what happened in the development of many of the Western nations. The gradual decline of absolute monarchy, the institutionalization of legal principles and practices, and the later adjustment of industrial institutions to equalitarian principles contributed to a concept of political culture that is seldom explicitly stated, even in the constitutions of the industrial democracies. There are, of course, formulations of the value of human dignity, expression, and welfare in the industrial democracies, but many of these statements are summations of achievements already apparent at the time the statements became formalized.

The developing countries have been more directly confronted with the problems of devising a political culture. In some cases, there have been extended periods of self-examination, as historic empires collapsed under the power of the West—as seen, for example, in the intellectual turmoil of the later Ottoman period and the clash of ideas toward the end of the Tokugawa period in Japan. The countries that have only recently achieved independence have made even more self-conscious efforts to formulate in precise terms the cultural basis of the new polity. Many of the nationalist movements have incorporated doctrine that was meant to relate the traditional culture to new political values, but these exercises were often the abstractions of expatriots and written to mobilize support for the independence struggle. Not surprisingly, the manifestos of most liberation movements bear little resemblance to what occurs after independence. In many cases, these efforts failed because they arbitrarily tried to divorce traditional culture from the cultural element of a working ideology.

There are, of course, numerous ways by which culturally rooted institutions conflict with national aims, or may be exploited to support national aims. The Turkish village Headman helped keep rural society stable while Mustapha Kemal built the rudiments of a new state. The Pakistani *mullah* or village Islamic teacher has often generated deep resentment of the more secular, and therefore evil, urban leaders. Important as these experiences are in helping us understand the obstacles and opportunities for change among institutions, they do not represent what is meant here by political culture. The political culture should be defined in terms that can be interpreted in collective endeavor and that relate in an explicit way to the political system. The political culture of a society may, in fact, not extend to all members of the society or guide the activities of numerous institutions, a common occurrence in less developed and more highly developed countries. The political culture consists of those general guidelines that define the conditions of reciprocity in manifesting national political values. Where a working ideology takes shape, the political culture provides a restraint on the character of superior-subordinate relationships.

The usefulness of this definition is that it enables us to distinguish political culture from culture generally, which may or may not endorse behavior consistent with national values, and from institutional norms, which may or may not be consistent with the guidelines for hierarchical relationships provided by the political culture. As a society develops increasingly complex institutions, the political culture may become so submerged in the proliferation of institutional norms as to be virtually unobservable. This may be why theories of development that are derived from the experience of industrial nations give less emphasis to political culture or treat these restraints on institutions as a natural outcome of other forms of growth and development. The historical experience of both the highly and less developed countries suggests that translating values into some form of collective restraint on hierarchical relationships is no easy task, though specific institutions are sometimes transplanted with ease, and the benefits of increased differentiation in more highly institutionalized behavior may begin to accrue to the wealth of the society. Achieving industrial wealth and high levels of role differentiation does not assure a country that its political culture will satisfactorily resolve hierarchical conflicts.

An important methodological point is whether one can meaningfully distinguish collective behavior at the level of political culture from the level of institutions. An indirect answer would be that institutions closely aligned with national values—such as courts, parties, and legislatures—may exhibit high levels of institutionalization without exercising effective restraint on the hierarchical structure of society. The terms of political equality may be defined in constitutions without influencing behavior. This is as much the case for the Indian landlord who continues to exploit lower castes and impoverished sharecroppers as it is for the intricate institutional framework of the United States which still subordinates black citizens with a frequency that far exceeds the ratio of the black to white population. The Pakistani peasant whose cattle are stolen in order to influence his vote and the American migrant laborer receiving fifty cents a day are both parts of elaborate institutions, but they are effectively excluded from the political culture. These are instances of political relationships wherein the individual or group is regularly subordinated and unable as an individual or as a member of an institution to influence decisions in the political system. Subordination by default of the system is a political problem even though it may not—indeed, cannot—be discovered in the political institutions of such a society.

The denial of reciprocity in political systems at both high and low levels of institutionalization suggests the necessity of analyzing the constraints or guidelines for hierarchical structures apart from the immediate goals of more specialized collective activity. The methodological problems created are considerable, because the observations required to evaluate the range and character of reciprocity in a political system may indeed be very different from one society to another (Przeworski and Tenne, 1970). In highly complex societies, there are numerous individual rights as well as many restraints on the operation of collective activity in the form of regulatory agencies of government, review procedures for institutional practices and policies, and a variety of schemes to achieve a degree of public exposure and accountability in both public and private organizations. Thus, Almond's "participant political culture" is an adequate description of a citizenry alert to both the actions of government and their own control over the policies of government. A description of the political culture in an industrial, democratic state, then, is not just an account of the fundamental political values orienting the system, but an elaborate mosaic of how these guidelines are in fact reflected in the patterns of subordination and control throughout the mobilized population (Rosenberg 1956, 1954).

A very different approach would be needed to trace the nature of political culture in a less developed country. Most newly established citizens are enmeshed in patterns of subordination of traditional social structures, historic religious practices, or, in some cases, strongly centralized government. Because there are relatively few institutions related to the evaluation of the political system, attention must often necessarily be concentrated on those who are in fact outside the political system—i.e., those who are not encompassed by a general set of restraints derived from political values. Moreover, the early stages of institutionalization facilitate the imposition of similarly structured superior-subordinate patterns as new, more specialized forms of institutional activity multiply. Individual rights mean little to marginal peasants, landless agricultural workers, and isolated tribesmen. As a result, it is not too difficult to build new institutions that achieve growth while making relatively little change in the hierarchical structure of the society. In many cases, the hierarchical structure of political institutions becomes more exclusive and rigid.

A number of illustrations will be given below, but one of the more interesting examples of institutional proliferation in the absence of a political culture has been Argentina. Other Latin American countries, such as Brazil, seem to follow a similar pattern (Needler, 1968). While Argentina has developed some very complex and highly specialized institutions, there is no way of regulating or constraining the use of power from one institution to the next. Under Perón, the urban masses were mobilized into progressive and powerful trade unions, while the industrial elite, middle class, and plantation owners more firmly entrenched their interests. Each center of power was supreme in its sphere (Blanksten, 1953), but the *Peronista* doctrine was built on the necessity to have direct mediators between these groups. No fundamental definition of the individual or collective rights of citizens in exercising power over each other has emerged over a long period of development. One might think of Argentina as institutionally "overdeveloped," and the military intervention in 1962 and 1966 could be interpreted as the delayed, and, hence, very costly, efforts to find an acceptable, integrated hierarchical structure after institutions and classes have solidified basic discontinuities in the political system.

The severity of the discontinuities and contradictions in superior-subordinate relationships in society distinguishes political culture from the problem of legitimacy. A variety of people and institutions may support a government without sharing any fundamental principles of how hierarchical patterns in society should manifest political values. Thus, the transferability of a political culture to new social situations and new institutions is a more severe test of a working ideology's viability than simply abstaining from violence and coercion. A country may achieve legitimacy in the minimal sense without having developed operational standards of reciprocity in the political system. For this reason conflict theories of politics may be misleading. In some instances—for example, Algeria and Cuba—revolution came as a result of a totally unbearable pattern of colonial dominance. In other instances, social violence may occur once dispute on the interpretation of how hierarchical relationships are to be patterned in new institutions within a society. Clearly, the skill and foresight of the elite will be critical in making such extensions of a working ideology.

A word should be added on the relevance of the general study of culture in anthropology to the above concept of political culture. In most cases, the anthropologist is speaking of "culture" in terms of a pervasive set of values relevant to all aspects of behavior (Beals and Siegel, 1966; Schapera, 1956; Spence, 1967). However, anthropologists do tend to be more explicit about the political relevance of culture where discontinuities take on explicit institutional form. Thus, Fallers (1963: 162-163) speaks of the "secondary culture" of Buganda as ideas about the nation are derived from notions of a Buganda Kingdom, but it is difficult to see the implications of these suggestions for new institutional behavior, nor did these derivations save Uganda from a violent clash with those preferring more secular values. Another approach to the problem is represented by Gluckman (1968) and his associates, who have tried to underscore the flexibility of traditional societies. But his group has been more interested in the restoration of equilibrium than in how the principles of one group in society are interpreted to apply to hierarchical patterns in other groups. On the whole, anthropologists have been prepared to define politics, like Radcliffe-Brown, as the "control and regulation of the use of physical force" or, like Gluckman, as the "maintenance or establishment of social order." Under these conditions, political culture as defined here would be irrelevant (Easton, 1959).

A more useful notion of how values operate in subunits of society can be found in Leach (1954), whose exposure to a more diverse political situation in highland Burma led him to devise a more flexible concept of value change. Resilient as the small society may be, it also appears that there are instances where the interpretation of political values is adjusted to a variety of factors. The Kachins do not resolve their problems simply by reinforcing tribal solidarity or by finding a way of restoring endangered values, but by shifting their concepts of how to manage political relationships. The Burmese case will be explored in more detail, but does illustrate that the application of values in some traditional settings may have a certain flexibility—i.e., individuals and groups actually change their generalization about political relationships. The importance of Leach's analysis suggests that it is not that emotional reluctance or traditional values simply obstruct change, but that generalizations about hierarchical structure can redefine politics. The Kachin political system can change its terms of reference and elicit new meanings from political values under certain conditions.

Another difficulty for anthropolists is the undeniable extent to which the formal ideologies of most developing countries are superimposed on local cultures (Vincent, 1969; Cohen, 1967). With a few exceptions, the formulation of a new political doctrine is in the hands of a central elite or even a single leader, whose education and background may be quite disconnected from the lives of the citizens. Thus, Worsley (1964: 36) speaks of the "grip of Western ideology" on less developed countries. Apart from Gandhi, Mao, and a few others, the national ideology is seldom generated on concepts and values taken directly from the culture. In his discussion of socialist thought in Africa, for example, Kopytoff (1964: 58) refers to the new ideology of the African states as "social mythology." The argument that cultural homogeneity facilitates sharing ideology seems doubtful considering, for example, the turmoil of intellectual and political development in Islamic countries. The character of the traditional culture does not seem to have any single relationship to the formation of a political culture.

Social anthropologists have more directly confronted the problem of ideological change and the imposition of a new, larger framework for political action, but their conclusions are not too encouraging. For example, Mair (1967: 123) admits that tribal decision-making processes cannot provide a model for decision-making in the new states of Africa, while also noting that little of the old culture seems to be transmitted into politics on the grand scale. In the case of India, Marriott (1963) observes that there are immense problems of "culture management" in Hindu society, but the study of the Indian village does not cast much light on how cultural elements in the ideology may contribute to such a reconciliation. The problem seems to be that, in advancing anthropology to the point where it utilizes sociological concepts, a good many naive, or at least misleading, notions have been preserved about politics. If the state and ideology are viewed as the imposition of a monopoly of coercion, then the problem of how values and ideas may transform a hierarchical structure becomes a secondary question.

Like political scientists, anthropologists tend to view ideology as more or less constant across societies, because the values of the subunits with which they deal are so richly diverse (Redfield, 1960, 1953). While it may be an appropriate division of labor for anthropology to underscore the cultural diversity of the small community, the ways in which political values place constraints on superior-subordinate relationships among communities is central to the collective expression of a working ideology. For purposes of studying subunits of society in the early stages of transition, this consideration may be unnecessary because the initial changes among traditional communities are often limited and arbitrary. The new nation may require some years before its demands on the village generate patterns of reciprocity that affect collective behavior at the national level. There is relatively little mixing of community or ethnic values with the doctrine of the new state, and, in turn, the new ideology in its early phases consists largely of symbols, which may or may not be consistent with subunit symbols. In either case, the physical limitations on the new nation are generally so great that little more can be asked than symbolic recognition and little more can be initiated than minor change in subordinate social structures.

There is a vast literature in anthropology on how communities react to external factors (Swartz, 1968; Lloyd, 1967), most often technological, but relatively little on how new links to the outside world become part of a shared network of values affecting status in the entire society. The problems of integrating the community are most often phrased as problems of how the community is acted upon, not how interaction among institutions and individuals becomes a larger pattern of the society, relevant to both the subunit of the society and the entire society (Goodenough, 1963). There is an immense difference in how ideology is used in moving from Epstein's (1958) mining town, Luanshya, to Birch's (1959) Glossop or Wylie's (1957) Peyrane. It is not so much that the small communities of the modern nations are more adaptive, but that status in the communities and in the institutions extending beyond communities have important similarities. Collective action involves both individual values and institutional norms, and the working ideology contributes to both the individual beliefs and the political culture that make action possible.

VALUES, ROLES, AND CULTURE

Anthropology has found it difficult to deal with values as they operate in the large, complex social systems because of the bewildering richness of its data. The effort to adapt the discipline to changing societies, largely represented by social anthropology, tried to overcome this problem by borrowing a number of sociological concepts, particularly role, status, and social class. Without such concepts, it is virtually impossible to discriminate among factors in any given social or political problem, and, likewise, it is also impossible to attach behavioral meanings to the existence of shared values, norms, or beliefs. An argument will be made here that, by looking to sociology for rescue, anthropology sacrificed its most distinguishing characteristic—that is, the concern with how very general, shared values contribute to the integration and solidarity of social systems.

The clearest exposition of this problem has been made by Nadel (1957), whose small book presents most of the ideas to follow. How one attributes significance to values and norms in society depends on how superior-subordinate relationships are related to the division of labor in society. In its simplest terms, Nadel made a devastating attack on the Parsonian notion of role, which has been uncritically incorporated into much contemporary social and political analysis. If role is conceived in such a way that the interaction of two or more persons is postulated apart from how their expectations or shared values mediate their actions, the concept of role is easily rectified. Nadel's main argument is that some roles cannot be conceived without their incumbents—e.g., one cannot have a father without a son or daughter. In such cases, the hierarchical ordering of the roles is determined. Acting out the father-son/daughter relationship cannot be reversed, and the roles both logically and empirically must occur in a set.

Nadel called such roles "correlational" and "intransitive" as opposed to roles that may be logically but not empirically opposed. The former do not present a recruitment problem— i.e., the process of entering into the role cannot be separated from incumbency, while the latter kind of role does present recruitment problems to society. Examples of the second type of role are judge-criminal or merchant-client. These cases are "relational"—i.e., the roles being performed can be grouped into sets, and "transitive," and the status of those occupying such roles can be reversed. An individual who judges may also be placed in the role of offender, and the person who is a client in one situation may find himself in the position of merchant in another situation. Another way of stating this is that the status relationship can be validly generalized. One may speak of problems of customers, offenders, or citizens without empirically postulating the incumbents of interlocking roles of merchant, judge, or ruler. For these reasons, Nadel considered it essential to distinguish between roles where the expectations of incumbents could be considered apart from performing the roles and those where they could not.

Another way of stating the distinction is to differentiate between role and status, using role to refer to the performance of the expected behavior and status to refer to how mutual expectations are formed. Nadel is suggesting that status is not automatically determined in many of the crucial relationships of society. Hence, he defines role as the "ordering of a plurality of individuals through a relation." The conventional sociological usage of role sometimes places emphasis on the assumption that the performance is equivalent to the ordering of a number of roles, thereby confusing the disembodied act with the establishment or ordering of the relationship itself. This might be satisfactory in analyzing highly industrial societies, where one is most interested in the division of labor and the organization of highly specialized roles. But Nadel would argue that even these roles are reversible. Those occupying the employee-employer or the worker-manager roles not only have the explicit behavioral dimension of being allocated tasks in the production process, but also can, and in many instances do, act in relation to the nature of the production process itself. Moreover, the entering into these roles is made possible by a number of "publics" in the economy, such as ownership, marketplace, and legal rights. Such reference groups define the hierarchical relationship in the performance of their roles and permit the reversal of a status relationship. Nadel is arguing that the proper meaning of role should encompass status determination or, more precisely, that roles determining the relationship of a number of others are empirically very different from those roles confined by their characteristics to being acted out by only two persons.

If the expectations of one actor toward another in any given situation include the body of values, norms, and beliefs that are part of any society, then these elements in our perception of one another acquire additional significance. Our abstractions about each other no longer have the fixed meaning assigned to them in simpler concepts of role, nor is it sufficient to look upon such abstractions as only that minimal degree of common expectation necessary to performing the action involved. By virtue of the relational and transitive aspect of roles, actors are involved in relationships where their immediate behavior is influenced by experience and values that are *not* mutually assigned to the interaction. Nadel considers this a much more important characteristic of social structures and argues that even intransitive roles can become transitive in society. This is so because the ascribed qualities of age, sex, and the like are not sufficient to describe fully how people do interact. These "contingency" properties must always be combined in some way with "achievement" properties. For example, even the highly intransitive role of father-son/daughter must be circumscribed with contingency properties stating parental obligations and, in the event of disaster, describing how parental authority is transferred to other adults.

Although Nadel does not use these terms, his concept of role is triadic rather than dyadic. Action in society, except in a few very simple cases and in limited form, is always patterned around the interaction of more than two persons. There is no social behavior where a third party cannot in some form intervene, for, in the absence of such a relationship, the allocation of contingency properties would be impossible. It is through collective allocation and distribution of achievement properties in society that shared beliefs, norms, and values of society are articulated. Our abstractions about the nature of society cannot affect contingency properties of individuals—i.e., our age, sex, and so on, and the status relationship they may define in society are irreversible and nontransferable. Nadel's concept of role suggests how values have a particular significance in social structures. First, they enable us to conceptualize how properties are distributed among members of the social or political system; second, they provide means whereby new patterns of distribution may take place.

In determining hierarchical relationships, Nadel asserts that "rules of combination" are necessary. Where subordination and superiority are involved, the actors' relationship is not logically necessary, nor can the actors acquire the autonomy given actors in intransitive roles. The question of status differs from the simpler behavioral notion of role because the way in which the interaction itself occurs is subject to evaluation. Thus, not only may the judge-criminal relationship be reversed from one situation to another, but the relationship itself is reconsidered from time to time by the procedures for legal review and appeal, as well as legislation and Constitutional revision. In situations of severe value conflict—the trial of the "Chicago seven," for example—an attempt is made to reverse status instantly, thereby making the allocation of tasks totally unworkable. In a literal sense, the defendants of the trial were seeking to put the judge in the position of a criminal and to foreclose the process by which the values implemented by the judge might be subjected to review. The controversy was intensified because the defendants felt that the roles governing the immediate trial procedure were meaningless to them individually and in terms of the society which insulates the entire judicial framework from proper revision.

The fact that all roles in society, even those acquired through irremovable qualities, interlock with all other roles suggests a critical function of values and beliefs in society. Cultural values might well be defined as those values governing the evaluation of role structures—i.e., interlocking roles, and not simply the action expected by two persons. Culture involves not only the duplication of past interactions, but the "rules of combination" under which such duplication of behavior is justified and assessed. Cultural values are used to describe how qualities bearing no fixed relationship to status will be distributed in society. The sociologists' identification of role behavior with status determination has tended to blur important problems in collective action, and to oversimplify the ways in which priorities and hierarchy are determined in society. Nadel felt that problems of this kind would arise in dealing with authoritative, expressive, and service relationships. Thus, in questions of influence, aesthetics, and taste, we are constantly confronted not only with how to formulate our expectations about those we encounter, but also with more fundamental questions of whether we shall consider the existing relationship acceptable, pleasing, or adequate to our needs.

In arguing that the role structures involved in the distribution of status in society are quite different from roles involving empirically irreversible qualities, Nadel has made an important contribution to the study of cultural values and also to our understanding of how culture might be more clearly distinguished in its influence on politics. On the first question, he has suggested that cultural values are those involved in the interlocking of a number of interactions, dealing with hierarchical problems as well as with issues of creativity and gratification in society. Cultural values impinge on political systems through issues of legitimacy and loyalty. Part of the dilemma of the new states, for example, is that they must formulate and communicate values about the political system that frequently conflict with historic cultural values. The difficulties of building linkages among roles is often overlooked in establishing new institutions and subsequently it appears that the new norms are only superficially implanted, or the new institution has very limited, exclusive relationship to the society, often only reinforcing preexisting status (Wallace, 1961).

Because industrial society is a more homogeneous environment than that found in most developing countries, the links between the political institutions and political culture can be more easily illustrated. France is a particularly good example, and the marked cultural differences among the regions of France have been used to explain the instability of the French political system (Almond, 1956). While this general use of political culture helps explain the *absence* of interlocking roles in French politics, it fails to shed much light on the remarkable durability of France amid the severe failures and strains over the past century, nor does it tell us why Frenchmen remain patriotic with such severe conflict of loyalties. Nor does this argument seem consistent with the pride most Frenchmen have in their cultural achievements and educational system. There appears to be remarkable consensus in France about culture generally. Culture in the broad sense allows us to see how roles may be aggregated in less flexible ways—e.g., the prestige of age in French universities—but it fails to distinguish culture as it relates to a political system that has somehow survived the Dreyfus affair, the *Croix de Feu,* the Vichy regime, and General Salan. The most important institution through which political roles have been integrated in France has been the administration, the prefect, and the formidable *inspecteur de finance.* Those interested in major renovation of French political life quite correctly single out the administration for change, but it has been difficult to arrive at agreement on another device to adjudicate and evaluate the French system. The fascination of Crozier (1969) and others with administration in France is because it determines status, not because it is more or less efficient in doing its task.

A number of issues arise in the modern state requiring evaluation of institutional performance, and these are quite properly regarded as the most central issues of the political system. The question of reapportionment relates directly to assuring that each individual's vote carries equal weight in the electoral process. What is meant by "equal" obviously cannot be determined by the existing status structure of a society, but must be surrounded with assurances of impartiality and objectivity. Those enjoying influence are not likely to forego their power, but a fundamental value of the democratic process is that each vote should carry equal weight. The electoral process has always required protection against excessive influence of wealth, social prestige, and hereditary status. In Britain, these influences were only gradually eliminated, even the postwar Labor Government tangling with the right of the House of Lords to delay legislation. Likewise, the problems of party finance and political patronage are not strictly speaking problems of representative institutions performing their formal duties, but problems of how influence within such institutions is to be distributed.

A working ideology requires some links to values at the cultural level in this more specific sense. The general values expressed in a working ideology are formulations of how status is to be distributed. How highly developed these links must be and their degree of institutional specialization no doubt vary with the country's level of development, but, in the absence of mediating structures in other aspects of social life as well as in politics, the complexity of institutions will be limited. In both an individual and an institutional sense, persons must be able to envisage the ways in which their status is determined and changed. Because the political system is central to the hierarchical pattern prevailing in a society, its underlying values tend to be of wider cultural significance. Nevertheless, the political culture is a distinguishable and essential part of every political system and is quite different from the general cultural heritage of every society.

SUBCULTURES AND WORKING IDEOLOGY

The establishment of the linkage among political roles is foreclosed so long as overwhelming cultural differences simply obstruct socioeconomic and hierarchical change in the developing country. Unless culture is given a more specific—and, inescapably, somewhat more limited—meaning, the analysis of its relevance to other social processes is impossible. Anthropology moved closer to the social sciences by recognizing the social flexibility of tribal societies, but even this adjustment in cultural analysis does not permit us to speak precisely about values as they mediate between traditional authorities and the political process. Because our major interest is the means by which national government and the emerging political system devise a distinctly political culture, the focus in this section will not use the traditional subunits of social action, often defined by kinship, landholding, or ritual. This does not mean that the local tradition is unimportant, but only that the elements of a subculture that may or may not be incorporated in the collective values of a state.

Nadel's word suggests that the key problem is not how new tasks are performed—i.e., how increasing role differentiation takes place—but how roles are hierarchically related—i.e., how status is redistributed. The latter phenomenon does not occur until the traditional segment of society—those persons remote from the national political system—begin to acquire working relationships with the government. The complexity of the developmental process is derived from the necessity to increase specialization for productive purposes while also devising new hierarchical patterns of control and exchange in the political system. In Apter's (1965) terms, the fundamental controversy in development theory is between the reconciliation model, in which the values of the elite are preserved, and the mobilization model, in which new popular values are generated. At such a high level of abstraction, however, it is impossible to anticipate whether increasing differentiation or restructuring status is likely to create more social strain or irreconcilable conflict. Apter's own illustrations, Uganda and Ghana, indicate that either approach must be regarded as a process, rather than a solution. The traditionally based status structure must adjust to the increasing talents and mobility of its population and the more revolutionary alternative must eventually confront the problems of organizing the economy and increasing wealth, as both the Kabaka of Uganda and Nkrumah of Ghana now realize.

Perhaps political analysis has erred on the side of excessive abstraction, while the cultural analysis of the anthropologist has been caught in the mold of the subunit of society. The adaptiveness of traditional culture has been recognized, but there is little agreement among disciplines on the means by which to state the relationship between politics and culture (Cohen and Middleton, 1967). The most fruitful meeting ground appears to be the study of peasant social structure, which illustrates very nicely several of the distinctions between status and role differentiation raised above. Anthropologists have distinguished peasant societies as family-centered social units, rurally based, and organized around land-holding patterns (Halpern and Brode, 1967). Peasants have distinct lines of dependence on the external environment through their need for consumer goods and for markets. In the historic peasant societies, there were in addition established links to extract labor for state projects and manpower for the common defense.

Peasant societies are distinguished politically by the strong dislocation between the internal hierarchy of the peasant group and the status structure of the external social setting (Beqiraj, 1962). In traditional societies, both tend to be very strong hierarchies. Most thinking about political development recommends establishing links to the new political system through increasing role differentiation. The approaches to political change through land reform, rural credit, and community development are similar in that each adopts a strategy of change by enhancing the resources and productivity of the peasant group, while giving secondary importance to the restructuring of status links between peasants and the political system. In effect, much development strategy has suggested that peasant societies can be related to a national political system only on acquiring an understanding of political status as already defined in the system. But the peasant can make considerable changes in the productive relationships of his subsociety without beginning to restructure his political relationships to the system as a whole (Hunter, 1969). The failure of a number of countries to restructure status and to evolve a working ideology may account for a number of failures in rural development programs.

The peasant's ability to make substantial adjustment to change without questioning his superiors has had severe dislocating effects on many political systems. Leaders begin to assume that old patterns of control and status are adequate, even though the overall distribution of benefits may in fact be widening the gap between rural subsocieties and privileged in the cities. The potential disparities begin to be revealed, as seems to have been particularly the case in Latin America. Some of the productive links to the society, such as land-ownership, require the elite to make major value changes, perhaps even to devise a new ideology. Because land is central to the wealth of the elite, it tends to be identified with status, and governments delay reform until violent political upheaval, a direct attack on the status structure, takes place. Wolf (1955) has underlined this problem in Latin America, where he feels that the "informal alliances of families and clients (tend to) polarize wealth and power" so that even though peasants may be materially better off the dislocations in hierarchical relationships are reinforced. He makes the same point as Nadel in stressing the importance of "re-defining" behavior in which a "whole series of relations [are] evaluated and readjusted." The revolutionary experience of Mexico, for example, appears to have given her peasants a stake in the growth of the economy and confidence that the national political system could work on their behalf.

Studies of millenial movements and cargo cults (Worsley, 1957; Cohn, 1957) are extreme forms of violent reaction to the disparities, not in wealth, but in status felt by traditional peoples. In developing countries with a central power struc-ture, upheavals of these dimensions take the form of peasant rebellions and revolutionary warfare. Mao and the Brazilian elite both chose to exploit the discontinuity in status be-tween peasant and ruler, the first setting to build a new political culture, the second to erect political institutions using the existing rural-urban differences. The techniques of revolutionary warfare depend on the peasant's isolation from the political system, and as has often been observed are most effective *after* a peasant society has begun to share the rewards of a more productive society. The feeling of relative deprivation not only reflects the acquisition of wealth suf-ficient to sustain a revolutionary struggle, but also an awareness of the peasant that he is effectively prevented from participating in the governing process of the society. Johnson (1966) is correct in underscoring the cognitive changes involved in these dislocations, but the basically Parsonian view of role he adopts does not clearly make the important distinction between the peasant's desire for more income, a problem of role differentiation, and for power, a problem of status.

The generation of a national political culture can only begin when the elite is prepared to alter the values governing those key, intermediary roles of the political system—i.e., those roles governing relationships of superior to subordinate in the society. Socioeconomic change clearly plays an important part in persuading a peasantry that the society's wealth will be more equitably distributed, but unless opportunities are provided for redistributed income to have some parallel effects in redistributing influence in the society, the materialist formula is unlikely to work. The acute sensitivity to status in peasant societies does not appear to be as readily submerged as it is among more severely oppressed rural people. There is some irony that the Marxist strategists were the first to understand this and have used it with immense success in Cuba, China, and Vietnam. The irony becomes even greater, considering the large number of grass-roots development programs the United States and other democracies have sponsored in developing countries, such as *Action Communale* in Colombia and Village AID in Pakistan, without realizing that durable change in the villages requires changing political relationships throughout the system.

Obviously, peasant subcultures vary enormously from Asia to Latin America and Africa. The opportunities to find linkage between the values of the subculture and the national ideology are affected by the values of both the subculture and the emerging national political culture. Although anthropology can distinguish a number of forms of peasant cultures, differentiated largely by kinship structures, it is by no means evident that these are the crucial distinctions in devising ways of linking the subcultural to the national values. Whether a peasant subculture is segmentary or acephalous, bilineal or unilineal, and so on does not seem as critical as how, in any given subculture, the allocation and adjustment of hierarchical relationships are conceived and accomplished. In building links between traditional cultural values and a working ideology, the transferability of the status relationship in the subculture is the determining condition. The closer status relationships in the subculture are tied inflexibly to kinship, cultivation, or ritual, the more difficult it will be to introduce roles to transform status relationships. New political roles will certainly be introduced, the problem is whether or not the traditions of status in the subculture are sufficiently elastic to relate to a larger field of political activity.

Although Burma has not undertaken an intensive developmental effort, the Kachins appear to have a way of handling political relationships within their society that illustrates this characteristic. As their society is described by Leach (1954: 102-159), it appears to have several basic qualities of more extended and complex political systems. Their ideas about politics are complex and they have multiple terms and social relationships to deal with politics in the subculture. The Kachins possess a range of alternatives in dealing with political problems, spreading from a highly autocratic relationship (*Shan*) to more flexible—in some ways, democratic—relationships (*gumsa* and *gumlao*). The political values of the culture allow the Kachin to shift hierarchical relationships in confronting political problems in the society. The subculture provides the Kachins with a way to characterize political relationships and alternatives for dealing with conflict. The structural flexibility of Kachin political values suggests that links with the Burmese political system could be formed. A working ideology might be advanced which was meaningful in terms of the Kachin subculture and the national political system. The Kachins do not appear to have the rigid attachment to a single hierarchical concept that makes the introduction of more complex political roles difficult to accept and utilize.

Research on subcultural values and new ideologies is sadly lacking, but it may be fair to observe that subcultures with segmentary structures—e.g., the Ibo—and bilineal kinship—e.g., the Philippines—have shown remarkable capacities to adapt to complex hierarchical structures. How much this adaptation represents the formation of a new political culture as opposed to simple exploitation of new institutions superimposed on the society is not easy to determine. There appear to be distinct subcultural influences in a number of political systems in developing countries, but it is extremely difficult to state such influences in a way that permits cross-cultural comparison. Nor should it be excluded that the influence of subcultural patterns might contribute to instability in the political system. The dominance of a single tribal tradition, such as the influence of the Buganda or the Ashanti, is only the mechanical and rather obvious form of such conflict. Lande (1965) has suggested for the Philippine case, for example, that culturally rooted traditions in that country account in part for the difficulty in establishing enduring political organization and reliable support among political leaders. The bilineal kinship system encourages dividing loyalties and sharing obligations and may lead to only a superficial adaptation to more complex political and economic institutions, while the political culture never achieves national significance.

Although the level of socioeconomic development will obviously influence the pattern of authority in a society, it has been argued in this section that a working ideology is particularly involved with those values governing reciprocity in the use of power. An extremely poor country, a sparsely distributed population, or a badly skewed distribution of occupations between urban and rural sectors are among the factors that will surely complicate the generation of a working ideology. At very low levels of development, interaction among citizens and the impact of government will be limited. Once that happens, there will be less need for supportive linking roles and values. More highly organized or new forms of politics and influence may be introduced into a society without evolving new ways of linking political roles. A political system may undergo something similar to economic growth—i.e., increased wealth and differentiation—without development—i.e., improved utilization of resources. Such a political system may even be perceived as legitimate by the population; that is, they may accept the government's monopoly of coercive authority without being able to evaluate their country's achievements or to interpret how their own experience coherently relates to new goals.

All political systems must develop as well as grow. A political system need not only increase the total amount of influence it can exercise, but must also determine the distribution of influence and the forms of influence which are to be excluded, encouraged, or weighed more heavily. The suggestion has been made that Nadel's theory about linkage roles and the necessarily reciprocal character of complex role structures raises these questions. The working ideology provides the values and concepts which describe reciprocity and equity in the political system and may provide a way of defining the relevance of traditional cultural values to the political system. The peasant subcultures are an important example of discontinuity that often occurs in developing countries between values governing status in subsocieties and the values advanced by the new state. The values, the social organization, and the use of power in a peasant subculture tend to preserve, if not increase, the discontinuities between the peasant status structure and authority in the national political system. Some governments may find it convenient to exploit subcultures in a manipulative way and thereby preserve their exclusive, perhaps arbitrary, use of power. If emphasis is placed on simply multiplying productive rolls— i.e., role differentiation—the country may grow economically, but the political system will fail to develop reciprocity in the use of power and to create fundamental values about hierarchical relationships in the society. The failures and upheavals among developing countries are to be attributed more to weak political cultures than to their inability to differentiate and to specialize political behavior.

IMPLEMENTING A
WORKING IDEOLOGY

Essential to the concept of a working ideology is the formulation of generalizations about the acquisition and distribution of status in the society at the national level. It has been argued that a working ideology presupposes a political culture which enables citizens to understand the organization of political roles in the society. It is often difficult to distinguish between behavior related to status relationships and that related to role differentiation. Experience with development over the past twenty years has produced general agreement that technological and organizational change among rural populations is not as difficult to accomplish as once presumed. Peasants, tribesmen, and villagers are motivated to increase their income and can usually find ways of overcoming culturally rooted practices in their communities in order to increase output. Perhaps the most dramatic illustration is the introduction of irrigated agriculture into the entire Indus basin in the late nineteenth century, long before development as such was considered an international problem. The farmers learned new methods and took advantage of vast governmental schemes and technical expertise. In doing so, they changed their productive behavior radically, adopting a cash economy, regular working habits, new kinds of crops, and new methods of cultivation. But few would argue that Hindu culture in the larger sense was seriously disrupted and, in the more precise meaning of political culture, very little changed. The status structures of the society were on the whole compatible with the rule of the British *raj*, who were called the "new Kshatriyas." The remarkably effective and talented district magistrate became a broker between the diffuse status structures of the village and the totally foreign status structure of the colonial regime (Srinivas, 1962: 49-62).

The problem of the new nation is how to establish working links between village and government in matters of justice, representation, and redistribution of power. These are precisely the activities divorced from the population by the colonial regime. This is not to suggest that the colonial experience failed to stimulate reflection about political values in Hindu and Muslim culture, but there was relatively little of what Wolf has called "redefining" behavior. It is interesting to compare, for example, the persistent controversy over the role of the elite civil service of India and Pakistan with the Indonesian experience, where the Japanese occupation radically altered both opinions and practices from the Dutch colonial model. Benda has analyzed the occupation to suggest that early twentieth-century Dutch policy was shrewdly designed to exclude the cultural traditions of Indonesia, hopefully reviving *adat,* or customary Javanese law. The effects of the occupation were to reject dependence on the *priyayi,* or pre-Islamic aristocratic tradition, to make the then small nationalist movement highly visible, and to enhance Islamic structures neglected by the Dutch (Benda, 1958: 191-204). The cultural heterogeneity of Indonesia made it virtually impossible for Sukarno to extract the common elements needed to define a new political system, as suggested in Chapter III, but his awareness of Indonesian cultural values was clearly essential to his survival as a nationalist leader.

Discovering a political culture for a working ideology is seldom as obstructed by the ambiguities of the past as by the radically changed setting into which governments seek to introduce new values about status. This is not to suggest that redefining the past is unimportant, for great nationalist leaders from Ataturk to Malcolm X have found it necessary to explore how historic social structure relates to the present. The past can be shaped to current needs and beliefs and even totally rewritten, but the working ideology, much as it requires assurance and meaning from the past, is conveyed initially on a superimposed set of existing relationships between the people and the state in the postindependence period. In nearly all developing countries, the culturally rooted links between a population and the political system are fragile and poorly defined. Even in countries with rich cultural traditions such as the Muslim and Hindu societies it would be difficult to argue that cultural values have been effectively blended with working political relationships. This is not to suggest that more general and even more acute problems of cultural adjustment do not exist, but these are more often than not in the direction of preserving sub-cultures *apart* from the political system. The intense controversies about Muslim legal practices, for example, have relatively little bearing on justice and equity as reflected in the politics of most Arab states.

The political life of most rural communities in developing countries continues to be heavily influenced by kinship, lineage and age, all of which are highly intransitive relationships. Eliciting a political culture requires substantial structural change, which, in turn, often presumes increased opportunity and resources in the local community. The interdependence of these two dimensions of change is not well understood, nor are the methods for assessing the significance of change in status structures entirely adequate. Some of the best available work has been done on India, where the necessity of devising integrative relationships has been inescapable. The scale and complexity of Indian society persuaded the Congress Party leaders at an early stage in their development and planning that explicit steps were essential in order to build local leadership, to narrow the gap between village and government, and to reduce the inequalities and isolation of the lower castes. Under Gandhi's influence, the national leaders were acutely aware of the Harijans, "children of God," Gandhi's term for the lower castes. The socioeconomic plight of the lower castes was recognized in the Government of India Act of 1930, when the category "scheduled castes" was introduced. The term was preserved in the Indian Constitution of 1950, which forbids discrimination along lines of Hindu ritual status (Beteille, 1969, 1965).

In addition to being a recognized problem in India, the status structure of rural society became a central focus of government policy with the formation of the *panchayats,* or village councils, which were to provide a new institutional link between village and government. The aim was not just to proliferate political institutions, but to restructure authority throughout Indian society. Excellent case studies (Nair, 1961; Retzlaff, 1962; Marriott, 1955; Mayer, 1958; Dube, 1958), as well as the great interest aroused by this experiment, have provided a remarkably rich literature on the methods by which new political roles are introduced in traditional societies. The transformation of status involved separating the practices determining political status in the larger political system from the ritualized status structure of the communities. The critical interdependence of socioeconomic change and the restructuring of status have perhaps been most precisely stated by Epstein, who underscores the ways in which developmental change in Mysore remained structurally consonant with village structure, producing what she calls a "discrete economy" and a "discrete polity." Economic change has taken place, but linkages have not been established whereby "economic mobility may be translated into political and general social mobility" (Epstein, 1962: 159, 138).

Epstein found this to be the case in comparing two villages of very different economic structure. Wangala had been absorbed into a larger cash economy, had undergone irrigation, and had survived recent food shortages and dislocations of black markets. Yet these substantial changes were, in Epstein's term, "unilinear" within existing structures. An economically successful farmer acted through his faction as described by lineage, and factional disputes within the village were resolved around ritual events. In 1955, the government offical organizing the first panchayat elections never visited the untouchables' quarter nor did the other villagers learn of the election until a crier was sent out the night before ballotting. Nor did it appear that ritual exclusion troubled untouchables nearly as much as their exclusion by virtue of their ritual status from socioeconomic opportunities. Wangala acquired new political institutions of national significance, but cultural change did not occur.

The second village, Dalena, had roughly the same level of wealth, but had begun to undergo significant change in its status structure. Dalena is closer to a major town, has its streets clearly demarcated and lighted at night, and because it could not be irrigated has developed a diverse economy. Ritual labor exchange between untouchables and patrons has ended, agricultural labor is individually employed, and Japanese methods of cultivation are used where irrigated land more distant from the village can be rented. Although the panchayat represents lineage affiliations, the hereditary elder no longer prevails, nor does the headman have his interests concentrated in the village. He is selected for his qualities as an arbitrator, acting in formally called sessions and trying to change the conservative village faction. Though still set apart from Indian politics, the village of Dalena appears to have begun the process of building new kinds of status relationships, giving lineage and ritual relatively less influence. Moreover, this process began not because Dalena is more prosperous than Wangala, but because its economy was more diverse and its citizens began reacting to a number of external situations. A number of circumstances contributed to a basic shift in concepts and values *about* politics in Dalena.

A comparable study has been done by Bailey (1963) of two villages in Orissa, which are more directly linked to the national political system than are the Mysore communities. The first, Bisaparo, is a more impoverished and isolated village. Only in the final phases of the 1957 election campaign were policy choices mentioned and, with severe competition between the Congress and Communist Parties, selling votes was common. Bisaparo was more advanced politically than Wangala because the new medium of political exchange, voting, though not used intentionally to change the system, was converted to economic values relevant within the community. However, ritualized status was diminished as these changes took place, and the relative distance between the higher and the scheduled castes was reduced. New resources and opportunities tended to be more evenly distributed, although the villages did not yet associate their more equitable relationship at the village level with the emergence of new status relationships in the national political system.

Bailey's second village, Mohanpur, is near the district center and its residents are well informed. The villagers were familiar with legislation to enable sharecroppers to recover land, the state reorganization act of 1956, and even changes in Congress Party leadership at the state level. But, despite the higher level of development and the closer relationship to national authority, the gap between castes appeared to be increasing. The Mohanpur untouchables were even poorer than those in Bisaparo, and the economically successful freely directed their resources and energy outside the village. Village institutions and activities were more effectively insulated from change than in Bisaparo. Bailey states that the village "could easily evolve . . . secondary institutions of power into the wider society [but they] not only deliberately refrain from doing so but take active steps to see that this development does not take place through any default of their own precautions" (Bailey, 1963: 95). In a move reminiscent of many in the American South, the village elders preferred to finance their own middle-level school as they saw fit, rather than risking state support. Mohanpur was clearly differentiating behavior at a gratifying pace, but relatively little change was permitted in the political culture.

In many developing countries, access to economic status is increasing. More Indians can acquire property and resources in order to achieve economic status, but the patterns for converting such status into prestige and influence have remained relatively untouched. This is by no means uniformly the case across India. There are indications that communities in Maharashtra and Uttar Pradesh, where developmental efforts have on the whole been more generously supported and were started earlier, are beginning to enter into the full range of political relationships and not simply converting rudimentary forms of influence into traditionally approved values (Brass, 1965). Nevertheless, India may evolve into what has been called a "secular caste system," where every advance by the scheduled castes is accompanied by even greater advances by the higher castes. Lynch's (1969) study of the Javars of Agra is an excellent illustration of a group that branched into new occupations and increased their wealth, but were never able to overcome the isolation of their low ritual status. Their early attempts were confined to the ritual status system—i.e., to acquire a new caste lable, while retaining marriage within the caste. In 1944, they joined Ambedkar's Scheduled Caste Federation, but, in 1956, most followed his conversion to Buddhism, thereby totally rejecting the ritual status system, a small-scale revolutionary solution to a cultural problem.

The immense complexity of factional, communal, and caste politics at the village level creates great difficulties in aligning political forces of larger areas and in building political organizations. The discontinuities in political activity and the level of state politics, which has been receiving more careful attention from Indian scholars are most apparent (Weiner, 1967, 1963). The Congress Party has tried to keep party politics out of the system of village, block and district councils that form the panchayat system, but, in effect, this has tended to mean that political considerations have entered into local politics at the party's discretion. In fact, the decision stems from the party's policy of controlling local affairs through patronage and manipulation of district-level administration, as Brass (1965: 227) points out. This tends to leave local politics to factional alignments and personalities, whose power is derived from landholding or traditional status. The initial aspiration for cultural transformation instead of institutional growth seems to have become diluted in India as political competition at the center and state levels becomes more intense.

Although the factions are vertically organized and serve to

aggregate economic interests in localities, they have not worked to the advantage of the Congress Party, nor do they seem to open the way for increased participation. For example, the Congress Party lost control of Gujarat in 1962 with a resurgence of Rajput leadership, and lost half the state legislative elections in 1967. The discontinuity in political status, which is so easily exploited for personal motives, centers on how the factional groups link to the political system. At the level of faction, the goal may be the location of a well, title to a plot of land, or recognition of a new caste identity. These demands are concrete and specific and therefore are open to bargaining and compromise in the political system, but they are also seen by the participants within the context of the faction, an autonomous, traditionally defined unit for political action. The factional competition tends to cut the village off from state and national policy, except through the legislative elections. The national system has preferred a brokerage role in balancing out favors, benefits, and projects. There are few roles linking the faction to external politics that use the same terms of reference.

The functioning of factional conflict in India must, of course, be evaluated with relation to the alternatives, which might be intensified communal conflict. The Congress Party has tried to avoid more bitter conflict of this kind by yielding to demands for linguistic recognition and reorganizing states. As Brass (1965: 234, 242) points out, factions permit "the politicization of social and religious groups in secular terms" because "they are based upon a form of loyalty which is traditional, but adaptable to secular political institutions." But it is precisely the regulation of such adaptive procedures that constitutes the cultural link to the working ideology and describes the reciprocal roles whereby the allocation of status in the society may be changed. Whether or not India might have found a preferable way of moving toward a national political system is too vast a question to consider here, but the reliance on factional politics to link the village and district to the upper levels of the system has in a very precise way discouraged the Indian citizen from entering into new forms of political exchange. The failure of the party at the state level and the increasing use of highly arbitrary measures to prevent new party loyalties from emerging in the state legislatures reveal the growing discontinuity between the concept of status employed at the local and national levels.

In the conventional meaning of culture, India adjusted in principle, but, in the narrower sense, India has not been particularly successful in defining new structures to govern the redistribution of status in the society. Perhaps Indian leaders, like many Westerners, were preoccupied with the problems of the Harijans and tended to underestimate the indeterminacy and flexibility of caste distinctions. There were, of course, tremendous pressures to increase the wealth of the society and to stimulate economic growth after independence. The problems of poverty and social immobility direct attention to the productive capacities of the country, and, hence, concentrate on increasing differentiation and specialization. The emphasis on economic development harmonized with the Congress Party's prevailing tactic of using patronage to channel influence and to obtain support from local leaders.

As the Rudolfs (1967: 130) note, "the contradiction between public ideology and private commitment" will endure in India as it has in every other society. The reorganization of status and roles is a continuing problem in many ways more visible in the developing country than in industrial societies. The structural focus of these dislocations is more easily identified over large ranges of social differentiation and during periods of rapid socioeconomic change. Because India and China are the two most important societies in the world in the process of devising new political cultures, their experience is worth comparing. Both have retained many characteristics of their ancient cultures, but both have also made radical departures in politics and embarked on an intensive effort to stimulate economic growth. The important difference is the way by which India has tried to join the Congress Party and the process of growth, permitting, if not intending, the redefining of political status through the interaction of the traditionally structured panchayat system and the secular, more differentiated structures of state and national politics. In China, it would be most unlikely for a peasant to inquire of the Communist Party, as an Indian peasant did of the Congress Party, when he asked Nair (1961: 125), "Is Congress a man or a woman?"

The Communist Party structure of China effectively avoids consideration of status adjustment or change. At the grass-roots level, described in Chapter IV, status is converted into the citizen's economic performance and his acceptance of the ideology. This formula precludes the redistribution of status by any criteria unacceptable to the elite. China must still have to cope with the influence of lineage, kinship, and traditional patterns that persist as part of the general culture, but these forms of status are not allowed to manifest themselves as they do in Indian panchayat and factional politics. Cultural influence in the broad sense, implying self-evident discontinuities and inescapable conflict in the structuring of status, can be found in every society. The cultural links to the political system in China are monopolized by the party, and permissible participation to adjust status relationships is arbitrary. Both India and China are trying to escape the conformity of ancient cultures, wherein all measures of status tended to align individuals in the same pattern, but India tried to evolve a working ideology gradually. China is trying to build a political culture first, even at the sacrifice of productive capacity, and experiencing most severe conflict at the institutional level of politics between the party and the army.

MAPPING
POLITICAL REALITY

Geertz (1963: 64) has called ideological metaphor a way of tracing "maps of problematic social reality." His interest in the linguistic structure of ideology leads him to reject both the heavily economic reasoning of what he calls an "interest

theory" of ideology and the extremely subjective characteristics of a psychological "strain theory." His approach is not
one directed at analyzing the content and structure of roles
in society, but it clearly underscores the importance of
abstraction and imagery in the collective endeavors of the
modern state. But such maps and metaphors do not exist
wholly in literary form, and the cultural basis of a working
ideology may be considered a way of relating such abstractions to behavior. Authority in society requires formulations
about its proper and accepted use. While this can be stated
metaphorically, it must also be manifested in the power
relationships of the society, understood by the participants,
and open to adjustment as socioeconomic change takes place.

Imagery, myths, and legends abound in the descriptions of
how power is used to achieve justice, equity, and dignity.
Some, like Robin Hood, seem to survive the test of time,
while others, like the American cowboy, appear on reflection
to involve more brutality and self-indulgence than an earlier
historical period cared to recognize. But the symbols and
metaphor of ideological abstractions are also represented in
social and political organization. The extent to which an
acceptable relationship is found depends on both the social
relationships the citizen finds around him and the psychological dimensions he attaches to ideological symbols. In this
chapter, we have argued that the essential elements the
analyst attributes in describing political relationships are critically important in determining our awareness of how great or
how little such correspondence may be, and, further, that the
emphases on role differentiation and adaptation in industrial
society tend to obscure the very different nature of superior-
subordinate relationships in society.

The activity of judges, representatives, and mediators is
very different from that of workers, employers, or fathers.
Nadel has argued that social relationships involving authority,
expression, and service also involve the acceptance of generalizations about role structures. Our major concern has been,
of course, with authoritative roles in society. These roles are
distinguished by being reversible or transitive; they do not

specify in a permanent sense the situation or the link by
which two persons interact. Such roles pose peculiar problems to society because underlying agreement must be
reached on how to recruit actors and evaluate their perfor-
mances. One is not necessarily a criminal, and, in fact, justice
demands that one be considered innocent until proven guilty;
one does not automatically become a judge if he discovers a
crime. Very special guarantees and protection are needed for
those who administer justice, as is indeed the case for nearly
all professions where a high degree of authority is trusted to
officials. A political representative cannot be held personally
accountable for a law that adversely affects his constituents;
a judge bears no personal guilt for a murderer he tries; an
administrator does not pay for the electrification project that
proves inadequate.

The practices that describe such roles in society are the
cultural component of a working ideology. Although this is a
more behavioral definition of culture as it relates to politics
than has been accepted in broader studies, it by no means
diminishes the significance of culture. Nor is it meant to
suggest that those aspects of culture in the traditional sense
that involve the study of artifacts and primitive technology,
the expressive significance of ritual and myth, or the structural features of kinship and lineage are irrelevant to our
understanding of society. The suggestion is only that many
aspects of the diverse discipline of anthropology do not bear
on the manifestation of authority or on the assignment of
status in society. What is "political" about culture is the way
a society organizes activities that are reciprocal and transitive
and that define status.

Viewing the cultural component of a working ideology in
this way suggests several important modifications of our
usual ways of talking about political systems. First, it suggests that the stress on coercion and legitimacy may be
misleading. If a political system is distinguished by its monopoly on the legal use of coercion, we have by definition
excluded some of the most perplexing and persistent prob-

lems of political order. The question that torments Americans about Vietnam is not whether they are prepared to defend their country, but how the decision was made that this particular war indeed threatened the values of American society. The great doubt is by what authority the decision to intervene was made, although the entire drama has wider implications for the transformation of the use of authority in America. Political relationships are only distinguished by their monopoly of the application of coercion under very special conditions, and these are generally where the relative costs to human dignity are such that the choice is not difficult. It is the immense destructive power of modern weapons systems that has helped expose the futility of the coercion measure.

A number of other issues in American society today also suggest how the very narrow definition of political has limited our perspective, largely by arbitrarily preventing the cultural links of authority from operating. The confinement of Indians to a subhuman existence on reservations, the socially sanctioned discrimination against blacks, and the huge costs for future generations as our natural environment is destroyed are not calling into doubt the necessity of a state, but the ways in which the state operates. These issues do not question the necessity of collective authority, but the means by which authority was allocated, and often imply that the political system has, by default and negligence, been insufficiently responsive to the principles on which authority was initially concentrated in government. The immediate reaction is quite correctly that citizens must be more active, must scrutinize policies more carefully, and must, if necessary, forego or postpone some of the material benefits of modern technology and science.

Beneath these controversies is a growing awareness that we have somehow been more faithful to a Marxist logic than to our own humanitarian values. Perhaps the most articulate spokesman for this view is Dahrendorf, whose work has done much to clarify the distinction between role and status, or, in his terms, class and status. The discontinuities of cultural and political values of India are serious obstacles to continued social change, but they are no more serious than the tendency to interpret class wholly in economic terms in industrial democracies (Dahrendorf, 1959: 117-164). These terms are often used with the implicit assumption that increments in productivity, in wealth, and in economic value may safely govern the assignment of status more widely in society. Thus, the criteria of status may begin to converge, so that the highly diverse and specialized industrial society differs little in actual exercise of authority than the ritually organized Hindu village. The cultural links that make reciprocity possible, and thereby measure how well basic values are translated into action, become submerged. In this sense, the inability of the Indian peasant to examine the failure of the ritual division of labor in a caste society is no different from the inability of the economically specialized worker to relate his task to the humanitarian goals of democracy. In both cases, the symbols and metaphors have lost their validity, because status is rigidly attached to custom in the former and to economic functions in the latter.

Authority, then, essentially involves decisions about categories of interaction in society, which may occur in at least three forms. The first is perhaps most familiar to citizens of industrial societies: the reevaluation of status along a single dimension. The most obvious illustration is the adjustment of social distance, prestige, and influence among differences in income over the past century. Higher political status remains aligned with economic status, but the monetary rewards of high economic status have been diminished and the authority of low economic status has been increased by changing values about income distribution. Through labor legislation, welfare programs, regulation of business activities, and numerous additional devices, the economic dimensions of authority have been equalized to a remarkable degree. Such changes are not made possible by simply modifying the principles of economic exchange, but by establishing the importance of values unrelated to capitalist methods of production. If economic success no longer bestows authority as it did in the nineteenth century, it is surely not because industrial barons wished to see their influence diminished.

A second form of culturally determined political change is what might be called change in the permissible ways of exchanging one form of influence for another. The British Honors List always contains a number of personalities who acquire aristocratic distinction by virtue of their economic, political and artistic success. Were it not that the Honors List is prepared by the Prime Minister and not the monarch, this would be a strange case of individuals seeking to change their status into less convertible forms. Royal honors are a highly symbolic way of acquiring new forms of influence rather than becoming a lackey of the Court, as it was in the sixteenth century. But royal recognition is now for past achievements of a substantial kind and not, as was the case under Tudor monarchs, a way of conferring authority to suit a monarch's purpose. A knighthood is no longer convertible into vast landholdings, estates, and revenue. Every political system encounters conversion problems, and their regulation is essentially a cultural aspect of the working ideology—i.e., a decision about the means by which one status may be used to acquire another.

A continuing issue in democracy, for example, is how to preserve the integrity and efficacy of the voter. Mass communications have created a whole new set of problems, and the make-up man may be more critical to election than the speechwriter. The huge sums spent on elections in the United States, in turn, produce new pressures on parties to find large donors and to further their interests. The status assigned to voters by the notion of civic equality can be removed, not by any direct manipulation of voting as found, for example, in India, but by manipulating the representation of issues, candidates, and alternatives well in advance of the voting act. The cynicism and apathy that threaten participation stem from other changes in society that may effectively remove the validity of even the momentarily decisive role assured each citizen. In mass society, democracies face difficult problems of how to retain voting as a significant act.

A third problem of political systems, one that depends on transitive role relationships being established, is the definition of new forms of influence. This problem is, of course, most difficult when moving from highly ascriptive, intransitive forms of authority based on age, kinship, and ritual to more instrumental and achievement-oriented ways of assigning status. It is not simply that income has diminished significance or may no longer allow an individual to acquire social prestige or authority, but also that the meaning of wealth itself is subject to change. In the affluent society, social positions can still be ranked according to income, but income itself becomes less attractive, as many young people in industrial societies are emphatically stating. These are essentially questions of taste—one might say, aesthetic judgments about the political system—and their incorporation in new roles in highly institutionalized politics is extremely difficult.

It is in this context that the interest of Geertz and Edelman in metaphor and symbols in the identification of an ideology seems most appropriate, for it is an attempt to describe the means by which we attach validity and meaning to politics. Even the recognition that cultural symbols, in the general sense, are most important where information is incomplete or where few institutions exist is helpful because it suggests the highly fragile, abstract character of political relationships where a political culture is being formed. Where symbols fail, men cannot attach meaning to political life and, as Geertz (1963: 63, 70) states, "ideological pandemonium" may follow. A working ideology requires valid symbols as well as forms of measurement and comparison of experience. Such devices "make autonomous politics possible by providing the authoritative concepts that render it meaningful, the persuasive images by means of which it can be sensibly grasped." Without acceptable cognitive maps, we would not be able to imagine how rank, hierarchy, and authority relate to society.

The complexity of the social processes by which symbols are created is much greater than those by which their content is changed. For this reason, the "great men" hypothesis prevails, and the fascination with charisma in political life continues. There is no way of demonstrating that virtue or justice as conceived by Gandhi, Marx, or the Founding Fathers is preferable, but it is clear that these men were able to formulate ideas so that social organization changed radically. The historical circumstances may have been propitious, but, without new symbols, the implications for new ways of thinking about hierarchy in society would never have been communicated. Their abstractions enabled millions of people to redefine the justification for authority in society and to work toward the construction of new institutions to manifest reciprocity in political relationships. The cultural element of a working ideology, then, involves those activities that permit us to reformulate hierarchical relationships, as well as to evaluate the redistribution of authority in society and the acceptable forms of conversion of various kinds of authority.

REFERENCES

ALMOND, G. (1956) "Comparative political systems." J. of Politics 18 (August): 391-409.

APTER, D. E. (1965) The Politics of Modernization. Chicago: Univ. of Chicago Press.

BAILEY, F. G. (1963) Politics and Social Change in Orissa in 1959. Berkeley and Los Angeles: Univ. of California Press.

BEALS, A. and B. J. SIEGEL (1966) Divisiveness and Social Conflict. Stanford: Stanford Univ. Press.

BENDA, H. (1958) The Crescent and the Rising Sun: Indonesian Islam under the Japanese Occupation, 1942-1945. The Hague: Van Hoeve.

BETEILLE, A. (1969) Castes, Old and New: Essays in Social Structure and Social Stratification. London: Asia.

--- (1965) Caste, Class and Power. Berkeley and Los Angeles: Univ. of California Press.

BEQIRAJ, M. (1962) Peasantry in Revolution. Ithaca: Cornell University Department of International Studies.

BIRCH, A. H. (1959) Small Town Politics: A Study of Political Life in Glossop. London: Oxford Univ. Press.

BLANKSTEN, G. I. (1953) Péron's Argentina. New York: Russell & Russell.

BRASS, P. R. (1965) Factional Politics in an Indian State: The Congress Party in Uttar Pradesh. Berkeley and Los Angeles: Univ. of California Press.

COHN, N. (1957) The Pursuit of the Millenium. London: Secker & Warburg.

COHEN, R. (1967) "Anthropology and political science: courtship or marriage?" Amer. Behavioral Scientist 11 (November/December): 1-7.

--- and J. MIDDLETON [eds.] (1967) Comparative Political Systems: Studies in the Politics of Pre-Industrial Societies. New York: American Museum of Natural History.

CROZIER, M. (1969) The Bureaucratic Phenomenon. Chicago: Univ. of Chicago Press.

DAHRENDORF, R. (1959) Class and Class Conflict in Industrial Society. London: Routledge & Kegan Paul.

DUBE, S. C. (1958) India's Changing Villages: Human Factors in Community Development. London: Routledge & Kegan Paul.

EASTON, D. (1959) "Political anthropology," pp. 210-262 in B. Siegel [ed.] Biennial Review of Anthropology. Stanford: Stanford Univ. Press.

EPSTEIN, A. (1962) Economic Development and Social Change in South India. Manchester, Eng.: Manchester Univ. Press.

——— (1958) Politics in an Urban African Community. Manchester, Eng.: Manchester Univ. Press.

FALLERS, L. (1963) "Equality, modernity and democracy in the new states," pp. 158-219 in C. Geertz [ed.] Old Societies and New States: The Quest for Modernity in Asia and Africa. New York: Free Press.

GEERTZ, C. [ed.] (1963) The Integrative Revolution: Primordial Sentiments and Civil Politics in the New States. New York: Free Press.

GLUCKMAN, M. (1968) "The utility of the equilibrium model in the study of social change." Amer. Anthropologist 70: 219-237.

GOODENOUGH, W. H. (1963) Cooperation in Change. New York: Russell Sage.

HALPERN J. and J. BRODE (1967) "Peasant society: economic change and revolutionary transformation," in B. Siegel [ed.] Biennial Review of Anthropology. Stanford: Stanford Univ. Press.

HUNTER, G. (1969) Modernizing Peasant Societies: A Comparative Study in Asia and Africa. London: Oxford Univ. Press.

JOHNSON, C. (1966) Revolutionary Change. Boston: Little, Brown.

KOPYTOFF, I. (1964) "Socialism and traditional African societies," pp. 53-62 in W. Friedland and C. Rosberg [eds.] African Socialism. Stanford: Stanford Univ. Press.

LANDE, C. (1965) "Leaders, factions and parties: the structure of Philippine politics." Yale University Southeast Asia Studies Monograph 6.

LEACH, E. (1954) Political Systems of Highland Burma: A Study of Kachin Social Structure. London: London School of Economics and Political Science.

LLOYD, P. C. (1967) Africa in Social Change: Changing Traditional Societies in the Modern World. London: Penguin.

LYNCH, O. (1969) The Politics of Untouchability: Social Mobility and Social Change in a City in India. New York: Columbia Univ. Press.

MAIR, L. (1967) New Nations. London: Weidenfeld & Nicolson.

MARRIOTT, M. (1963) "Cultural policy in the new states," pp. 27-56 in C. Geertz [ed.] Old Societies and New States: The Quest for Modernity in Asia and Africa. New York: Free Press.

――― [ed.] (1955) Village India: Studies in the Little Community. Chicago: Univ. of Chicago Press.

MAYER, A. (1958) Pilot Project India. Berkeley and Los Angeles: Univ. of California Press.

NADEL, S. F. (1957) The Theory of Social Structure. London: Cohen & West.

NAIR, K. (1961) Blossoms in the Dust. New York: Frederick A. Praeger.

NEEDLER, M. C. (1968) Political Development in Latin America: Instability, Violence, and Evolutionary Change. New York: Random House.

PRZEWORSKI, A. and H. TEUNE (1970) The Logic of Comparative Social Inquiry. New York: Wiley-Interscience.

REDFIELD, R. (1960) The Little Community: Peasant Society and Culture. Chicago: Univ. of Chicago Press.

――― (1953) The Primitive World and its Transformation. Ithaca: Cornell Univ. Press.

RETZLAFF, R. (1962) Village Government in India: A Case Study. Bombay: Asia.

ROSENBERG, M. (1956) "Misanthropy and political ideology." Amer. Soc. Rev. 21.

――― (1954) "Some determinants of political apathy." Public Opinion Q. 18: 349-366.

RUDOLF, L. and S. RUDOLF (1967) The Modernity of Tradition: Political Development in India. Chicago: Univ. of Chicago Press.

SCHAPERA, I. (1956) Government and Politics in Tribal Societies. London: Watts.

SPENCE, J. H. [ed.] (1967) Contemporary Change in Traditional Societies. Urbana: Univ. of Illinois Press.

SRINIVAS, M. N. (1962) Caste in Modern India and Other Essays. Bombay.

SWARTZ, M. J. [ed.] (1968) Local-level Politics. Chicago: Aldine.

VINCENT, J. (1969) "Anthropology and political development," in C. Leys [ed.] Politics and Change in Developing Countries. Cambridge: Cambridge Univ. Press.

WALLACE, A. (1961) Culture and Personality. New York: Random House.

WEINER, M. (1967) Party Building in a New Nation: The Indian National Congress. Chicago: Univ. of Chicago Press.

――― (1963) Political Change in South Asia. Calcutta: Mukjopadhyay.

WOLF, E. (1955) "Types of Latin American peasantry: a preliminary discussion." Amer. Anthropologist 57: 465-466.

WORSLEY, P. (1964) The Third World. London: Weidenfeld & Nicolson.

——— (1957) The Trumpet Shall Sound: A Study of 'Cargo' Cults in Melanesia. London: MacGibbon & Kee.

WYLIE, L. (1957) Village in Vaucluse. Cambridge, Mass.: Harvard Univ. Press.

Chapter VII

POLITICAL INTEGRATION AND

A WORKING IDEOLOGY

The approach to ideology proposed in this volume has tried to differentiate national values that operate in ways to alter social and political behavior from those that do not. The general position from which this argument has been made is that, while ideology is used to describe any set of national values, it will remain impossible to distinguish those cases where ideology works to bring about change. This is not to suggest that those countries where national values do not significantly affect individual and collective behavior are without ideology. Every nation has at some point in the political system a set of symbols, goals, and values that represents its aspirations and justifies its existence. The important distinction is the way these values relate to individual perception of political life and to the structuring of collective endeavor. The critical first step in understanding a working ideology, then, is to realize that the dichotomy between values and behavior is a misleading assumption. In our individual responses to the political system and in our collective involvement in institutions and organizations, each of us reflects to some degree the principles on which our polity is based.

A working ideology concerns those areas where behavior and national values intersect. In some social and political systems, a good deal of change might occur without invoking a working ideology. Alternatively, one might say, a primary assumption that all behavioral change can be traced to national values would be an excessive claim for the importance of ideology. This is true whether one speaks of less or more developed countries. A country like Morocco, for example, has been steadily engaged in development for the past decade, much of it successful by economic criteria and generally accepted within the political system. But it is also correct to note that Moroccan political values have remained relatively unchanged over this period. A similar observation might be made concerning the introduction of automation in most highly industrial countries. The productive behavior of the American worker has been radically altered by the change in industry and commerce, but this change has been relatively isolated from national political values. Part of the disillusionment with ideology since the war may perhaps be traced to the relatively minor role that national values have had in some major transformations of Western societies—although many current conflicts would suggest it was presumptuous to assume that the necessity to reconcile national values with changing behavior had somehow disappeared for all time. Ideology was not ended in the United States; it was only inoperative for an interlude and had no working form.

A second general proposition advanced to delimit the problem of analyzing a working ideology has been the emphasis on the special relevance of superior-subordinate relationships, or hierarchical structure, as the focal point for identifying the ways national values relate to political behavior. Again, the reason for this assertion is that, while ideology may be relevant to role differentiation and to changing patterns of control, the concept becomes ambiguous and unmanageable without this distinction. A great deal of behavioral change in social and political systems emerges from existing social organizations and generates relatively little political conflict, particularly in highly developed nations. It has also become increasingly clear from experience in less developed countries that the peasant, artisan, and worker are not as resistant to social change as was often assumed several decades ago. The difficult problem in both industrial and agrarian societies has been finding a working relationship between the immediate setting of the factory or the farm and the larger pattern of control in the political system. The troublesome inconsistencies in both highly and less developed countries have not been that citizens resist opportunities to become more productive and acquire new skills, but that the hierarchical structures devised to distribute wealth and direct change seem to work very poorly.

Those who lamented the decline of ideology were underestimating the versatility of individuals and the flexibility of most sociopolitical relationships. A great deal of increased differentiation can be accommodated in most societies without raising basic questions about the distribution of power in society or the continued validity of the operating principles attached to national political values. The Netherlands (Lijphart, 1968) and Belgium are among the most dramatic illustrations of countries that have managed to sustain a workable pattern of political relationships and grow economically at very high rates against formidable odds in terms of the religious, regional, and doctrinal differences. The working ideology of these highly industrialized countries consists of a delicately balanced and carefully defined rules governing superior-subordinate relationships, assuring all segments of the society basic freedoms, and providing elaborately detailed procedures for compromise in the governing process. A similar phenomenon can be observed in the developing countries, though on a different scale. The restructuring of nationalist movements in the postindependence period and the stabilization of leadership in the new governments have produced much less hierarchical change than the earlier nationalist rhetoric implied. At low levels of development, it has been possible to make substantial changes in the economy without affecting the strength and scope of political control. Without diminishing the crucial significance of moving from colonial to independent status, it appears that subordination may become even more rigid and embracing.

The important departure from some earlier interpretations of the developmental process, then, is that increasing differentiation may or may not bring about change in hierarchical structures. Two further assumptions in much of the existing theory about development have been especially misleading. The first, which can be traced to the functionalist view of social change, is that, at the most general level of abstraction, instrumental or adaptive aspects of social relationships are manifested in a similar way as problems of goal definition. Though Parsonian analysis has been careful to specify that reconciliation of these two aspects of behavior is not necessarily achieved under all conditions, the interpretation of development in functionalist terms tends to combat the interdependence of these problems (Rustow, 1969). While this may have certain advantages for social analysis, so general a view clouds over the extent to which adaptive behavior—i.e., increasing differentiation, takes place within a framework of authority where political change is difficult and sometimes illusory (as Dahrendorf has argued). A second assumption, which influences Huntington's (1968) analysis, is that increased differentiation in overtly political institutions represents fundamental change in the hierarchical structure of society and politics. While these are both simplifications of complex arguments, they share an emphasis on differentiation as the key to social and political change and tend to diminish the importance of hierarchical structures in the analysis of power and ideology.

For the study of politics, the most important implication of the working ideology is that national values are difficult to study in a meaningful way so long as we think of their internalization however it may occur, as legitimacy for the state or as a permanent justification of the coercion exercised by the state. This is not to suggest that the emotional attachments of citizens to the symbols of power are not prerequisites to the existence of the state, much less that whether or not a government enjoys popular support can be empirically investigated. But the formulation of the problem of ideology in these terms treats individuals as psychologically identical, and collective behavior as conformity to some unspecified degree of necessity defined by the existing government. It evades the more enduring problem in politics of detecting whether the structure of power is changing, and, if so, what ways it is changing. A working ideology has, therefore, been defined as the way national values and behavior may change superior-subordinate relationships, not simply perpetuate order, in the society.

DIMENSIONS OF A
WORKING IDEOLOGY

This volume has been organized around what would be the major dimensions in the description of a working ideology. Before looking more carefully at the combinations they suggest, two methodological problems of analyzing a working ideology—and of many problems in comparative politics more generally—should be mentioned. The first is the importance of a time dimension. If we are interested in seeing whether the hierarchical structure of a social or political system has changed, observations over time are needed. It is the modification of hierarchical patterns in individual experience and collective activity over time that demonstrates the capacity to revise and to reinterpret national values. The ideology may take operational form, of course, while other problems or crises lead to national disintegration. Conversely, a country may enjoy economic growth or substantial social change without affecting the pattern of superior-subordinate relationships. The ways in which change takes place can only be detected by observations over time. A similar problem exists with respect to the spatial dimensions of a society. To achieve a given level of consistency in the perception and articulation of national values over a fairly small territory poses less severe problems than the same accomplishment in a large territory with a sparsely distributed population. There can be no universal formulas for making these adjustments in the evaluation of a working ideology until we better understand time and space constraints.

Chapters III and IV outlined the psychological dimensions of individual perception and interpretation of national values. The perception may be, first, highly emotional and directed toward self-gratification or self-assurance. Second, the perception of national values may extend beyond more fundamental human needs to relate national values to the motives and incentives of the social, economic, and politial circumstances of the country. Third, as the mosaic of motives and interests that are attached to national values increases in complexity, individuals may devise more generalized concepts to organize in his mind problems, issues, and needs of politics. As citizens become more selective in their political behavior and more detached from national values, they tend to devise latent attitudes or psychological rules of combination to evaluate the relevance of their experience to national values. Each of these forms of perception indicates a different way of relating behavior to values, and, in turn, has different implications for the transformation of hierarchical structures in the society and the polity.

The three psychological dimensions are, of course, to some extent interdependent. In communicating a value, the first requirement is to get the individual's attention and to arouse his interest. Once interest is aroused, the attachment, if it is to continue, needs to be reinforced and underscored in the person's memory and learning. As learning arrives at higher levels of complexity and abstraction, the person may begin to use generalizations and concepts to manage intricate communications and to order the complexities of his daily experience. Although there is such a sequential relationship in the perception of an individual, it would be a gross reification to postulate a similar sequence in the articulation and understanding of national values. The high level of abstraction, the remoteness in individual experience, and the intermittent way national values are invoked makes inferences of this kind at best misleading and at worst dangerous. However, the authoritarian personality studies indicate that, where values are perceived with a high degree of intensity, particularly where there is severe individual dependence on national values for personal identity, the accumulation of hostility toward others and fear of losing self-assurance can be shared and can contribute to rigid, compulsive behavior in social situations. Most important, where such dependence is prolonged and exaggerated, the individual may become highly submissive to authority and quick to accept the hierarchical ordering of social and political relationships that favors his emotional representation of the values at stake.

As the individual begins to interpret national values in terms of more specific interests or according to generalizations about information and experience of particular relevance to his needs, the value is articulated in operating rules, and its terms of reference are more concretely perceived. One of the most promising avenues for political research is to learn more about the kind of associations and connections made by individuals as the abstract values placed on the nation are articulated. Some basic knowledge has been acquired from the studies of political socialization, and also from cross-national survey research. Thus, the nations in the Almond and Verba (1963: 64) study vary widely in how pride is attributed to the nation as well as in the levels of cognitive skill attached to politics. While the interdependence of affective responses and cognition was not analyzed, the very high levels of pride expressed in the United States and the United Kingdom suggest that increased emotional involvement may accompany increased learning and increased information about politics. Thus, it is probably correct to claim that the increasing complexity of political relationships and institutions in the more highly developed countries does not so much eliminate emotional interpretation of national values as provide an overlay of cognitive meanings and procedural generalizations that cushion the political system against precipitous and dogmatic reactions to events and issues in political life (Inkeles, 1969).

Where national values are communicated in very shrill ways and center on distinctions that arouse personal insecurity, one might expect that the political culture, as described in Chapter VI, would be slow to emerge. The idea of increasing transitivity in hierarchical relationships might even appear threatening to individuals whose perception of national aims is highly emotional. Even in the absence of more severe forms of individual dependence on such values, highly emotional perception simplifies human relationships as a person moves from one situation to another. The shift to motives, incentives, and interests to articulate an ideology helps standardize the behavior attached to national values. Shared motives provide an opportunity for status reciprocity in different activities of the society, and may help accustom citizens to the relevance of national values to political institutions and participation. But the evidence is at best mixed, and some evidence suggests that in less developed countries reliance on the power relationships of subordinate groups and interests to define shared goals only provides additional opportunity for a small number of leaders to dominate the political process.

Very few developing countries have set out to devise a political culture by self-consciously outlining the ways in which reciprocity should be manifested in a wide range of activity in the new nation. Perhaps the most important attempt has been made in Yugoslavia, where the commune system was purposely designed to reduce the coercive influence of the state and to encourage collective decision-making in the local units of government (Mlinar, n.d., 1970). Another important example is Tanzania. The interesting common characteristic of countries that have given priority to the definition of a political culture is that they have all developed under severe handicaps, Tito under the shadow of Stalinist Russia and Nyerere under immensely unfavorable economic conditions. Thus, the viability of national values had to be promptly demonstrated if the nation was to survive. Involvement on a purely emotional level would not relieve the major threat to the nation's existence, and the measure of political equality communicated by the nation's values was an essential resource in the struggle for survival. Their broad efforts to diversify patterns of leadership and to prevent a single hierarchy from dominating all new activities have lowered the emotional content of national values. The external threat existed, but was not used to justify a rigid, uniform hierarchical structure. Though these experiments are still being acted out, the reversion to a more shrill ideology would very likely generate new constraints on the political system. A working ideology is never a static or permanent feature of a political system. Indeed, it provides means by which citizens can change the content and meaning of national values.

The psychological dimensions of a working ideology, while they may be described with surveys, do not enable us to relate individual perception to collective activity in the political system. To say that a given population is highly emotional, highly cognitive, or highly evaluative in its understanding of national values leaves us with only a distribution of beliefs, opinions, and attitudes along various modes of perception. Thus, the Almond and Verba study, which is the most ambitious attempt yet to examine these dimensions cross-nationally, does not tell us much about how perceptual characteristics are in fact related to national politics. The model used for the study indicates that persons more cognitively oriented to both the inputs and the outputs of the system will tend to be the more active participants, and implies that being more highly cognitive in perceiving the system strengthens democratic government and values. This is probably a true proposition, but does not help much in extending empirical research to the basic political question of the ways in which the manifestation of ideas itself changes. One is left with the difficulty of generalizing about the system on the basis of individually derived information. Thus, if a Mexican and an American both express pride in their political institutions, these are taken as equivalent statements. As a personal expression, this is correct, but the activities each individual attaches to this feeling and the collective activities which each might accept are no doubt different.

There are various ways of trying to adjust psychological data to system variations, as Teune and Prezeworski (1966) have suggested. One might ask as they do, that, if Mexico were to achieve a level of education similar to that of the United States, what would be the level of pride in the nation, assuming the relationship between pride and education found in Mexico at this moment endures? But this modification, while it may add something to the validity of the comparison among countries, remains a statement about the aggregate characteristics of the society in question. It is no detraction from the enormous advances that have been made in using survey data to compare the psychological dimensions of populations to point out that aggregate approaches will not permit us to analyze hierarchical features of political systems as they are indeed imbedded in various political systems. Various degrees of knowledge, involvement, and dependence on a given activity can be measured and are extremely valuable, but such findings are not statements about the system itself.

A working ideology, it will be recalled, has been conceived as the ways in which national values govern behavior in the hierarchical structures of the society. Political relationships are those aspects of behavior that define the conditions, the form of expression, and the situations where status may be changed or, more precisely, may be reversed. Democratic political systems are distinguished by the extent to which national values endorse and sanction reciprocity of status at the highest level of government. To demonstrate that democratic values had some independent effect on the activity of a given country, one would need to show that the affirmation and understanding of these values influenced the individual's behavior in a range of situations where status was involved. A possible hypothesis would be that the person accepting democratic values—i.e., placing in them a high value of reciprocity—tends to do so in numerous activities. Further, the way that these values are perceived should have some bearing on the transferability of the concept of status advocated in national political life to other endeavors. A person whose perception of national values tended to be rigid and defensive might, as some evidence from small group studies suggests, find it easier to compartmentalize his experience and to accept relatively fixed status in a number of day-to-day activities while behaving democratically with reference to the political system. Under these conditions, it would be more difficult to manifest ideology in a working form because the scope of activities related to national values would be smaller and the distinctions among various kinds of behaviors would be more dogmatically accepted.

The problem may be represented schematically as shown in the diagrammatic tabulation on values and hierarchical structure. Along the horizontal dimension might be placed the degree of transitivity in a given activity. Thus, one would expect, in a democratic political system, that a relatively wide range of activity, not only in political life but in other pursuits, would have relatively open status determination. Other activities, as suggested in Chapter VI, would have relatively fixed status relationships as, for example, the parental relationship. The vertical dimension represents the relative significance of the national values in the definition of status in the activity. While the grouping of other values influencing status under the term "parochial" is rather arbitrary, these values might be those of any organization, institution, or agency operating within the political system. They should be considered parochial only in the sense that their values do not claim to influence as wide a range of behavior in the society as those of the nation itself.

The tabulation may help in suggesting how the psychological dimensions relate to the transferability of values, which distinguishes a working ideology from a static one. A working ideology is linked to national values, but it must also have behavioral consequences in the wider determination of status relationships in the political and social system.

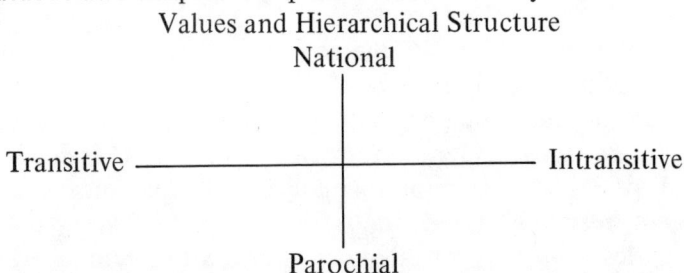

Values and Hierarchical Structure

National

Transitive ——————————|—————————— Intransitive

Parochial

National values which reinforce closed hierarchies reduce the capacity of the organizations and institutions to modify status relationships. To the extent that individuals share common beliefs and opinions about the desirability and effectiveness of more open status relationships, collective activities will be more likely to be compared and assessed as well. Hence, those psychological characteristics that discourage evaluation and comparison of how status is determined will prevent national values, assuming they advocate transitivity, from having an effect.

Democratic theory, then, is making a number of assertions about the relationship of the citizens' perception of national values and the structure of the political and social system, though they are very difficult propositions to test empirically. First, it claims that the description of status endorsed by national values will be reflected in the explicitly political institutions of the country. Second, it is suggested that the encouragement of reciprocity in political life will have repercussions on various other activities in the society—i.e., that it will be transferable. Third, the nature of individual perception of national values—i.e., whether their form is emotional, cognitive, or evaluative—will influence the development of status relationships. Which of these links is more important in achieving a degree of political stability or equality at various stages of political development is virtually impossible to demonstrate at the present state of our knowledge.

STATUS CONGRUENCE
AND INTEGRATION

Reciprocity of status is clearly both a psychological phenomenon and a behavioral circumstance. Political science has been undecided in how to reconcile these characteristics of political systems, largely because of the danger of reductionist thinking. On the one hand, political sociology has given a good deal of attention to how occupations, social mobility, education, and numerous other circumstances affect political behavior. On the other hand, survey research and political socialization studies explore how· general attitudes and values affect perception of political events and priorities. By dividing the problem of how political culture and political institutions relate to each other, the discipline has, I fear, evaded its most challenging goal. It is the infinite adaptability of the personality to various hierarchical relationships *and* the great complexity of status in working political institutions that make politics a fascinating field of inquiry. Either of these problems can, of course, be sensibly studied in isolation from the other, but the historical and contemporary complexities of politics are vastly oversimplified by doing so. Politics is about citizens and power structured in various ways. It is the existence and persistence of public authority in the minds *and* actions of men that makes politics a challenging discipline, and to concentrate on only one facet of this problem is to dilute the subject almost beyond recognition.

The full implications of this methodologically convenient division in our approach to the meaning of collective political endeavor cannot be followed through here, but its effect on our interpretation of ideology has been discussed throughout the study. In the view stressing the effectiveness of achieving political goals, ideology becomes simply another means of manipulating, if not deceiving, citizens into accepting authority. In the view stressing individual heterogeneity, political values become a sort of residue following careful conditioning in childhood and an educational experience enforced by social sanctions and rewards throughout one's life. The great pitfall of these views of ideology is that, to proceed along either path, one must impossibly simplify either personality differences or actual political life. A singular notion of personality provides a very limited notion of how the complexity of men's minds relates to politics; a singular notion of what politics is about superimposes on the analysis an unrealistic uniformity of behavior in the actual institutions of public life. In both approaches, ideology is left with very little to explain.

The concept of working ideology has been advanced in this study in order to encourage us to think more carefully about the relational quality of political life at both the individual and institutional levels. If personalities were uniform—e.g., if all citizens were suffering from unbearable insecurity about the future of the nation—the integration of the system would be quite easy. Nazi Germany illustrates this condition, stimulated and encouraged by national political institutions. If political goals were reduced to single purposes, the problem of stating national values would hardly challenge a citizen or a leader. It is the remarkable variation that takes place at both levels that makes political integration a topic of fascination to political science, and, as I have argued, a possible way of devising a more accurate notion of how ideas operate in society. A working idelogy, then, is not a doctrine or a general statement of national purpose, important as these symbols are, but the range of diversity in the citizens' interpretations of national values and, in turn, the ways in which diversity can be manifested in political institutions and behavior. I have argued that the most salient aspect of this relational problem is reciprocity of status for individual citizens and in the operation of political institutions.

Using this relational approach and confining ourselves to the role of ideas in political life, there are two important constraints in manifesting values in political life: the flexibility of individuals, and the flexibility of institutions. To assume uniformity in either respect is to reduce the study of values in politics to meaningless dimensions—i.e., to eliminate the need for a working ideology. National values relate to both individual and collective behavior in various ways, as discussed in previous chapters. How citizens and political institutions in fact manifest flexibility in the activities of the state are, if you like, the operational dimensions of how complex a mix of individual and institutional manifestations of value exist in the political system. The problem may perhaps be represented as shown on the following tabulation.

Consistency in Manifesting National Values
Governing Status Relationships

Citizens	Hi	Hi	Lo	Lo
Institutions	Hi	Lo	Hi	Lo

Though I will illustrate the combinations of citizen and institutional activity represented by the tabulation, I have not done so here in order to underscore an important point in the understanding of political integration. There are many forms of integration in political life, not just the rather dreary, passive one postulated in singular notions of legitimacy. The notion that any form of legitimacy is as desirable, adaptive, and generally workable as any other has done much to justify the charges that political science has abandoned its responsibilities. The tabulation points out that a workable relationship between a body of citizens and a set of political institutions making low demands for consistency is quite different from such a relationship existing where the requirements are substantial. Unless the values governing individual and institutional activity are examined to see how they permit, encourage, and utilize diversity, there is no way to take into account how creative or even how complex a relationship exists in establishing public authority.

In general, the political systems making minimal demands for consistency in manifesting national values at the two levels are those with high levels of participation and fairly complex representative institutions. Democratic national values are associated with these kinds of systems. In such simple form, however, the relationship is not easy to evaluate and to observe, and the extremely complicated behavior associated with status relationships in such a system raises immense methodological problems. There is no reason to assume that democratic doctrine is in fact manifested in the same way in every democratic country, as can be seen, for example, in the very different behavior and levels of interest in local elections in France (Kesselman, 1966) and the United States. Eckstein has suggested that, in Great Britain, this is achieved by deferential attitudes associated with class and group activity, though this may be an institutionally constrained way of manifesting ideology. Lijphart (1968) has outlined the intricate arrangement of explicit, almost contractual understandings that regulate political interaction and accommodate diversity in the Netherlands. The institutionalized locus of a working ideology may vary, but somehow every democratic system builds structures that enable individual and institutional diversity to interact. My only point here is that, were *either* the citizens' expectations of diverse ways to interact with political institutions *or* the institutional capacity to reconcile diverse ways of regulating authority to diminish, we probably would not recognize these systems as democracies.

Looking at the other extreme form of the relationship, one finds very substantial requirements for consistency in the manifestation of values among institutional norms and individual behavior. The values governing individual activity in Nazi Germany, for example, were rooted in racist theories that rigidly precluded reciprocity in status relationships. A single, individual quality governs the way one responds to and is placed in the hierarchical structure of an authoritarian society. Likewise, a very narrow range of diversity was tolerable in Nazi Germany in the norms governing institutions. In one sense, one might argue that ideology was of critical importance because it so accurately stated how status could be organized under Hitler. Though this is correct in an absolute sense, it is misleading in an attempt to grasp the significance of national values as an operational guide to the society. The working ideology of the Nazis was very fragile and inflexible precisely because of the severe behavioral constraints placed on citizens and institutions. The Nazi elite, as pointed out earlier, had to make a number of compromises with the industrial and military elites. More important, as Arendt (1958) has argued, the overpowering singularity of the values as manifested among citizens and institutions gradually destroyed the social fabric of the country, making violence a substitute for political interaction. In the final stage of self-destruction, there was no working ideology, because the system permitted neither deviation nor diversity in the definition and regulation of status relationships.

The intermediate cases are more interesting, for they relate to countries where national values concerning status at the normative and individual levels are imbalanced. Systemic shifts of this kind in a working ideology are typical of less developed countries, through major structural changes in developing countries may create similar problems. The tabulation is intended to point out that these shifts, or the transformation of a formal ideology into a working ideology, can occur in at least two distinct ways. There can, first, be immense diversity in individual behavior in the determination of status, while norms express more limited ideas about how status relates to national values. From an individualistic perspective, these situations might be considered something like "negative" development, for the working ideology is lagging behind with relation to political norms, while individual capacities and expectations on the transformation of status in the society are advancing. Many of the tutelary democracies, to use Shils' phrase, risk falling into this situation. The upheavals in Ghana after a long period of mobilization under Nkrumah and the vacillations of the Tunisian regime after an energetic attempt to introduce fundamental socialist reforms are symptomatic of this sort of imbalance. One-party regimes, unless they are able to keep clearly in mind the grass-roots justification of their existence, as Nyerere has attempted, are likely to fall into the situation where the citizens' ability to deal with diversity in status relationships exceeds the diversity tolerated in political institutions. In these cases, the formal ideology, or, in some instances, the sheer self-interest of the elite, replaces the task of reformulating national values to utilize the suppressed ability of individuals to deal with more complex institutions and organizations.

The other intermediate situation, increasing diversity in normative manifestations of political values while citizens are more limited in their abilities to affect status in society, is closer to the usual model of mobilization in a developing country. In behavioral terms, the Chinese experience is instructive. The regime is concerned that citizens learn to work with more complex organizations and institutions, which requires that they improve their capacities to project and transfer the methods by which status is used in complex organizations. The Schurman (1968) study, discussed earlier, is a superb attempt to portray the tensions and conflicts that may occur. In a formal sense, China may appear as a highly ideological state, though it is doubtful if national doctrine is more visible there than in many developing countries. From the perspective of a working ideology, however, China seems to be using institutional means to convey new norms to millions of citizens. The crises in Chinese politics are not those of failing to respond to a mobilized public, prepared to manifest new national values and neglected by a conservative regime, but they more nearly appear to be difficulties of reordering goals where large organizations such as the army, the party, and youth groups are unleashed to extend the ideology in rather specific, behavioral forms.

The relative nature of integration about a working ideology should be underscored. To reduce the diversity of a mobilized, articulate public and force conformity to a rigid, narrowly conceived set of norms, as in the case of dictatorships among industrial nations, is a very different matter from trying to use institutional norms to communicate new behaviors that can be attached to an ideology. The important distinction is one of scale of the system. The latter course is almost instinctively repugnant to Westerners, whose historical experience still sees the interpretation of national values as a problem of aggregating individual views. In agrarian societies at low levels of development, however, maintaining some working relationship between institutional norms and individual capacities to manifest national values may be critical to the continuity and stability of the regime. A lesson might also be drawn from the numerous developing countries which have ostensibly imitated the Western notion of attaching ideas to national activities. The bloody upheavals, the proliferation of military governments, the resistance of privileged groups to change, and the failure to acquire public confidence in many new states suggests that the effort to revise the meaning of national values during the stages of development, rather than as a sequel to development, may be critical in keeping a mobilized citizenry in harmony with enhanced and changing institutional capacities. To achieve this, the new nation must be much more self-conscious and explicit in uncovering the contradictions and obstacles between institutional performance and individual behavior with relation to national values.

CAN POLITICAL
CULTURE BE SAVED?

The burden of this study is to underscore the problem of civility in political stability and order. The experience of the developing countries, and many of the crises confronting Western democracies, indicate that political systems with relatively high degrees of differentiation and specialization (that is, with elaborate political institutions) have severe difficulties in achieving some minimal acceptance of authority and understanding of civic responsibility among citizens. The thrust of the literature on development has generally taken a pluralist stance. Huntington's work is typical in arguing that the proliferation of new political institutions will gradually permeate political life in the new nation to create a stable political system. Though he has significantly modified his basic argument (Huntington, 1971), there remain two basic problems with this theory. The first centers on the frequency with which less developed countries have dismantled political institutions, inhibited the proliferation of new institutional norms, and concentrated political power in institutions that are inaccessible to new participants. The second is the profound isolation of many efforts at more rapid political institutionalization because the national values, even where sympathetic to increased participation and the idea of public responsibility, fail to relate to the immediate concerns of peasants, tribesmen, and small farmers. Even where greed and corruption have not eroded new political institutions, the problem of attaching new institutions to an ancient culture, in the general sense, is formidable.

The concept of a working ideology that I have tried to develop in this book has separated the two problems of public authority—i.e., the institutional use of authority in a political system—and public responsibility or civility—i.e., the way citizens find national values manifested in public life. Political institutions, especially those specializing in coercion, can reach high levels of performance without extending the meaning of national values in the public at large. More specifically, the status structure of political bodies in control of a state may be unrelated to the status structure of a society. There is no compelling argument to prove that all states need such a relationship to persist, but rapid social and economic change and severe crises are likely to be distintegrative where public responsibility cannot be joined to public authority. The racial crisis in the United States, the upheaval of Northern Ireland, the splintering of Pakistan, and the failure of civilian government in Ghana are only a few illustrations of instances where institutional progress has done little to provide the underlying capacity to redefine norms and values in political life. A working ideology is one that provides content to national values at both the institutional and individual levels of behavior. Once this notion is accepted as meaningful, it is possible to see that citizens may in some circumstances be more "national" than governments. Indeed, not all political systems provide the reciprocity of status—i.e., the opportunity and capacity to redefine the way status works in the society—and there is no reason to assume that all systems need do so. In fact, it has been largely Western theorists who have imposed this sort of abstract uniformity on political systems. By so doing, we have paradoxically lost sight of the independent significance of public responsibility, which has been the major justification for the political systems we belong to. The implication for developing countries is that a working ideology may assist socioeconomic development by providing a way for public responsibility and participation to redefine and reorganize status in a society becoming more complex and more specialized.

The inability of political science to deal with these problems is not entirely due to ethnocentric bias, but also to methodological constraints. The discipline has not provided good ways of considering the individual level of interaction in politics apart from assumptions about the system itself. Our concepts are geared to authority and defined by the use of coercion at high levels, rather than by the difficulty of bringing authority and sanctions into some working relationship with individual needs and perception. Governments may lose legitimacy, but we are not clear on how they acquire it, much less able to grasp the possibility that some of more stable governments may have "excess" legitimacy (Eisensfact, 1965). Citizens acquiesce and consent to authority, but their capacity to define, and, more important, to redefine authority relationships in a political system is not very clear. In much contemporary political science, participation becomes at best an episodic and vague event called an election, and at worst a somewhat trivial and troublesome needs imposition on a passive electorate. Political sociology has done much to reveal the multitude of ways by which everyday behavior has political meaning, but it has done this by divorcing itself from the hierarchial structures that in fact provide the links between authority and participation.

The discipline's instruments for separating these problems in a different form are not impressive. The national character studies worked on the notion of a modular personality (Mead, 1951: 70-85). With its high level of generality and concentration on specific theories of personality, it has been unworkable in talking about real political systems. Survey research has tried with some success to provide profiles on public responses to authority, most notably in *The Civic Culture* (Almond and Verba, 1963). But this approach remains an aggregation of individual responses devoid of behavioral validation, and dependent on the assumption of equivalent meaning of national values and institutions across political systems. The alternative advanced here does not pretend to solve these methodological problems, but it does suggest that we are not likely to begin to do so unless the discipline distinguishes "public" from "authority." The concept of political culture is intriguing because it implies that a public has some independent significance, that it may transform authority in political life, and that it has a key part in manifesting national values. A political system without a "public" is incomplete, or at least has foreclosed identifiable avenues of change and interaction. The study of political culture, then, would appear to me to be the analysis of "publics" not just in relation to existing authority, but in order to establish their independent significance in politics. As Chapter VI argues, the inability to distinguish these concepts is, I believe, derived from the concept of "role" adopted in much social and political analysis that defines role and status in similar terms. Among sociologists, this definition has been most directly attached by Dahrendorf (1958: 45-57), who argues that many roles deal with sets of persons rather than individually responding persons, and that society as a whole constitutes a frame of reference, as well as individual interactions. The uniformity of response among publics, then, is not simply testimony to their apathy, but a relationship of considerable significance in examining whether being a member of the public affects the system. Moreover, applying this line of reasoning to politics, it is important to assess how the frame of reference provided by a political system relates to the definition and operation of status in political life. Anthropologists have been forced to confront this problem more directly because solidarity is more evident in less specialized societies, and the terms for reciprocity and exchange of status are more readily observable in small-scale situations. In addition to Nadel, whose reasoning has been outlined, Smith (1966) has raised the problem of how to deal with what he calls "corporate groups" or publics apart from "offices" or the institutionalization of authority. A working ideology has been defined as the relationship between national values as manifested in the norms of political institutions and in the values reflected in the behavior of individuals. The notion of reciprocity of status at the level of individual behavior is essential if one hopes to demarcate a public from an authoritative institution. Emphasis has been placed on the former because a working ideology cannot be manifested in a society that lacks a working relationship between status determination by individual and that by authoritative action. Nadel has perhaps been the clearest of analysts in explaining the significance of the transitivity and exchange of status for individual behavior. A political culture, then might exist without national values, if the public's concept of authority were totally at odds with governmental authority. Conceivably, following this reasoning to an unlikely extreme, there might be a political culture with no state. Many utopian views of society are exactly this—visions of self-regulating and highly transitive patterns of status definition without the imposition of institutional authority. Given the universality of violence and the complexity of modern, technological society, the possibility of a normless existence seems impossible despite its philosophical attractions.

A working ideology starts from the assumptions that political systems for the foreseeable future will have both institutions and publics. Political culture describes the degree of openness of status structures among individuals and in the relation of their behavior to national values. Political authority can be exercised in institutions with relatively open or closed status structures, which are more or less reflected by national values. The logic behind this notion of a working ideology does not exclude the possibility of high degrees of individual tolerance or diverse status structures occurring without national values endorsing openness in both the public at large and the formal exercise of authority, but it does argue that diversity would be most unlikely to occur in the absence of such values. The logic of the theory also implies that it would be most unlikely to find a political system where the political culture is based on open status structures, while authority was exercised in closed status structures. This formulation seems to me the more realistic, in that it is the interdependence of individual and collective status that is at the core of political conflict and disputes. Moreover, national values seem indispensable either where an elite sets out to generate such a relationship, as in the case of developing countries, or where a collection of individuals wishes to affect authority as a public.

Where a people begins to acquire the cognitive and evaluative capacity to interact with increasing degrees of reciprocity in the definition and exchange of status, there is almost inescapably going to be pressure for similar behavior in the activities of political institutions. Conversely, where political institutions and the elites operating them adhere to some degree of reciprocity in their norms of behavior, it is likely that citizens will be encouraged to do likewise. Thus, it is not so much the logical extremes of the theory that are important, useful as they may be in clarifying one's thinking, but the kind of balance that a political system achieves between a political culture and political authority. The argument of this book has been that, with individuals acquiring intricate and diverse psychological skills and with institutions working with equally intricate and diverse problems of status determination in society, national values have a constructive, if not essential, role to play. Not all ideologies in the traditional sense are directed toward the integration and vitalization of a political system, but, where ideas are put to work in regulating and defining the relationship of citizen to the state, they are essential to political interaction.

IDEAS AND JUDICIOUS DISINTEGRATION

Integration is most often used to refer to the degree of interdependence between two or more phenomena. In a perfectly integrated society, expectations and events would coincide. If arguments about integration are taken to their logical extreme, the result can be as fruitless as the dichotomization of ideas and action in some discussions of ideology, noted in Chapter I. There would clearly be no need for a working ideology in such a society. One might also speculate on whether there would be any change unless some device were found to alter simultaneously individual perception and social relationships. But this kind of instant harmony defies empirical treatment and, as a meaningful problem of social inquiry, seems far removed from the actual problems of reconciling perception and behavior in a political system.

A more useful definition might be the margin of permissible error between the perception of values and the manifestation of those values in society. Where ideology is being used in a doctrinaire way, to make the impoverished content with inequality or the oppressed submissive to domination, this definition does not apply. Integration even in the marginal sense is relatively easy to achieve where no change is taking place. The schematic formulation of the working ideology, however, envisages change in two directions, toward increasing reciprocity in hierarchical structures and toward more elaborate articulation of national values in political and social behavior. The simplest problem of integration would exist where there was a high degree of homogeneity in the perception of national values and a relatively unchanging relationship between superior and subordinate. As the perception of national values takes more articulate form in the concepts, generalizations, and interests citizens relate to the nation, homogeneity becomes more and more difficult to achieve. Likewise, as the hierarchical structure becomes increasingly reciprocal—i.e., as there are more channels whereby individuals may reverse their status relationship—power relationships become more unpredictable. Thus, it is not only that correspondence becomes increasingly difficult to achieve, but also that the way by which tolerable correspondence may be achieved changes. Where a working ideology takes effect, both the purposes and the content of the system are continually undergoing change.

The problem of integration where values and behavior are constantly interacting is most clearly represented in Deutsch's (1963: 98-109) observations about feedback in information systems. He distinguishes three kinds of feedback. A system may be "goal-seeking," or regularly adjusting itself to achieve a given state or target. A system may be constantly learning or adjusting its procedures to new evidence, while continuing to maximize a single goal. A system may achieve the capacity to adjust both its target and its procedures. Deutsch describes the fully adaptable system as a "conscious" system, learning from its experience about both its aims and its procedures. Goal-seeking in the most dynamic sense, then, involves being able to learn from the feedback system, to receive information about the environment and performance continuously, and to change goals as new potentials.

The paradox of the cybernetic model only exists if one insists on attributing more value to the situation at an earlier time than to the process of reevaluating and reinterpreting the situation. In terms of a working ideology, the terminal values or ultimate symbols change to the extent that the meaning attached to these values in individual experience and in institutional relationships itself changes. As earlier chapters have outlined, this can be in two primary ways. Individuals move from more emotional perception of national values toward more cognitive and evaluative modes. This does not, as has been emphasized, mean that the emotional identity ceases, but that its relative strength in interpreting national values declines. The appearance of generalizations and concepts about national values also means, of course, that skill and capacity in handling information is increasing. As perception of values is articulated, the individual in relation to the political system becomes an increasingly autonomous actor insofar as his emotional dependence on these values decreases.

In reference to collective activity relating to national values, it is necessary to be able to reorder institutional norms if goals are to be adjusted over time. The provision of reciprocity in status relationships contributes to the assessment of goals and performance both by the change within any given institution of the individuals enjoying status, and by the reordering among institutions of what kinds of activity are given priority. Just as the individual whose perception of the desirable manifestation of a given national value may become "fixed," so also does the institution whose performance cannot be influenced by external forces. The critical point in reference to a working ideology, however, is that the emergence of a set of values attached to all members of the society and the development of an open hierarchical structure enables both individual and collective behavior to be continually adjusted to new conditions, new information, and new goals. The values service, as it were, because their content is constantly changing.

An empirical demonstration of the dynamic relationship between values and behavior under a working ideology is obviously most difficult. There is relatively little comparable survey data over time that would permit more precise meas-urement of this kind of change, though historical accounts commonly discuss political change with this kind of relation-ship in mind. There have, however, been some longitudinal studies of attitudes in political systems at a single time that reveal some of the structural complexity. In interviews with Democratic and Republican leaders and followers, McClosky (1960) and his colleagues describe subjective conditions that indicate how attributed political status diverges from hier-archical norms. Many institutional pressures compel leaders in a democratic system to hold contrasting positions. The overlap between the beliefs of followers and those of leaders in the two parties did not conform to the institutionalized relationship of the parties. In an assessment of issue percep-tion, it appeared that Republican followers were more likely to approximate Democratic leaders than they were their own leaders. What might be considered incorrect perception by Republicans establishes a link outside direct hierarchical lines; integrating individuals in contradiction to party norms.

One can look upon this situation in terms of the deception made possible by national values endorsing the system, or one can consider the inconsistent division of followers a dynamic quality of party relationships in the United States. The inconsistency may be exaggerated because we are only observing two levels in the party structure. Nonetheless, it may well be that attaching different expectations to party norms makes it possible to sustain free elections and other democratic institutions in highly complex societies. Compressed within the observed responses to various issues are differences of region, economic condition, personal success or failure, family experience, and upbringing, to name only a few. The findings take on their full significance when one considers how many factors contribute to the various responses. The inconsistency represents the individual complexity that can be accommodated within the institutional structure. Such inconsistency would be truly alarming only if people were in fact identical.

There have been several additional studies that indicate how the variations, sometimes in conflict with individual and group interests, tend to overlap across various levels of activity (Stauffer, 1963; Luhberg and Ziegler, 1966; Putnam, 1966). To consider this "smothering" effect of attitudes and opinions as detrimental to the clear articulation of popular demands may be misleading. The duplication and overlap in views may act as a kind of cushion between the upper levels of decision-making and the expression of popular demands. More generally, the overlap may be very important in keeping open the possibility of changing leadership precisely because there are people with divergent "interests" who align themselves differently in terms of political norms and loyalties. Participation that combines diverse, even contradictory, intensities of feeling and information may be needed to link individuals and groups into the political system. Thus, action "against one's interest" is very like tolerance, and it is this tolerance that may produce the capacity to change leadership peacefully and to exercise reciprocity in political life.

The problems of integration in a political system are different from those in an economy or a family, and political scientists have perhaps been too ready to accept others' definitions. There are important distinctions when talking about the degree of interdependence of the individual and institutional elements of political behavior. First, the manifestation of values is extremely difficult if the degree of dependence is extremely high, because emotional tolerance of failure and uncertainty tends to be reduced. The kind of looseness found in democratic political systems makes hierarchical structures responsive and flexible and requires much less individual dependence on institutions and the goals of government. Where dependence is high, rather than low, the political process tends to become rigid, particular classes or groups tend to monopolize power, and leadership may find itself so uniformed and remote from society that only a major political upheaval can alter status relationships. Democracy may depend on individual values and institutional norms *not* being well integrated.

Politics also poses some special problems when one wishes to speak about the scope of integration. While the strength of integration refers to the intensity of the identification of any two aspects of individual or group behavior, the scope refers to how broad an impact the link among them might be. Thus, two institutions might be very tightly integrated for a narrow purpose—e.g., the oil industry in extracting tax benefits and exploration franchises from government, but very loosely integrated when interacting in numerous other ways. The same observation can be made about individuals, who may be virtually unrelated to each other in most respects while acting in concert to protect the private use of weapons or to advance a particular piece of social legislation. The more remote the values lending coherence to a political system, and the greater the effort to establish reciprocity in the hierarchical structure, the less likely interdependences of wide scope seem to appear. This is also correct about both individuals and groups. If either is totally dependent on the other, then the possibilities of exchanging status from situation to situation or from time to time are diminished.

A similar relationship holds when referring to the level of integration. If, in a sequence of status relationships, those person or persons enjoying a higher position can easily establish a high degree of domination over those of lower status, then reciprocity is unnecessary. Clearly, the more levels of integration existing in a system, the more difficult it will be to establish such a high degree of integration in any given hierarchical structure. A typical example is the controversy over local government reform in Great Britain (Robson, 1968). There exist nearly 400 units of local government, some directly related to the central ministries and others related through a sequence of local authorities. A Royal Commission has suggested that, by introducing a greater degree of uniformity in the system, the independent activities and citizen interest at the local level will increase. One might argue that, by virtue of the standardization of local government structure, the capacity of the central government to influence and to predict the behavior of local authorities will be increased, rather than the ability of local units to act autonomously. Too binding a relationship among levels would mean that the flow of information and criticism, the exchange of leadership and aims, and the range of choice exercised in the system would be diminished.

For these reasons, at least for democratic political systems, there are strong arguments favoring excess capacity. Large margins of noncoordinated behavior among hierarchical levels, in the scope and the strength of status relationships, make reciprocity possible. If the manifestations of national values rely on very narrowly interpreted or very scrupulously controlled interpretations, a high degree of integration among ideas and action might exist, but there would be relatively little room for adjustment or new learning. There is always the problem of the absolute level of performance, but the more difficult question in terms of integration involves what Deutsch (1963: 164-170) calls "uncommitted resources" that represent the difference between viability and creativity. A high degree of interdependence between national values and behavior can be achieved in totalitarian states and, on a totally different scale, in developing countries by removing national values from the imagination, choices, and behavior of most citizens. In abstract terms, the values of most contemporary governments are remarkably alike. What differ are the extent to which disparities in their interpretations can be tolerated and the ways that political norms relate behavior to these values.

In some ways, the concept of a working ideology, then, is not very different from the more philosophical form of the argument about freedom. Some freedom must be sacrificed in order to gain other kinds of freedom. But it is hoped that, by stating this classic dilemma in more behavioral terms, we will be better able to observe and anticipate the problems of putting national values to work in societies as they exist today. There is no empirical demonstration possible, at least at the present, for the advantages of individual and institutional diversity within societies (Key, 1961; Key and Cummings, 1966). But many propositions about the effects of drastically reducing autonomy can be tested and have been tested historically. The central argument of this inquiry has been that there are identifiable advantages in political life where national values begin to replace parochial values, and where transitive status relationships predominate and are supported by national values. In these terms, success in manifesting a doctrine is always relative. Where national values have little individual and institutional significance, an ideology may exist, but a working ideology would be impossible.

REFERENCES

ALMOND, G. A. and S. VERBA (1963) The Civic Culture. Princeton: Princeton Univ. Press.

ARENDT, H. (1958) The Origins of Totalitarianism. New York: Meridian.

DAHRENDORF, R. (1958) Essays in Sociological Theory. Stanford: Stanford Univ. Press.

DEUTSCH, K. W. (1963) Nerves of Government. New York: Free Press.

EISENSTADT, S. N. (1965) Essays on Comparative Institutions. New York: John Wiley.

HUNTINGTON, S. Jr. (1971) "The change to change: modernization, development and politics." Comp. Politics 3 (April): 283-322.

——— (1968) Political Order in Changing Societies. New Haven, Conn.: Yale Univ. Press.

INKELES, A. (1969) "Participant citizenship in six developing countries." Amer. Pol. Sci. Rev. 58 (December): 1120-1141.

KESSELMAN, M. (1966) "French local politics: a statistical examination of grassroots consensus." Amer. Pol. Sci. Rev. 50 (December): 963-973.

KEY, V. O. (1961) "Public opinion and the decay of democracy." Virginia Q. Rev. 37 (Autumn): 481-494.

——— and M. C. CUMMINGS, Jr. (1966) The Responsible Electorate: Rationality in Presidential Voting, 1936-1960. Cambridge, Mass.: Harvard Univ. Press.

LIJPHART, A. (1968) The Politics of Accommodation: Pluralism and Democracy in the Netherlands. Berkeley and Los Angeles: Univ. of California Press.

LUTTBERG, N. R. and H. ZEIGLER (1966) "Attitude consensus and conflict in an interest group: an assessment of cohesion." Amer. Pol. Sci. Rev. 60 (September): 655-666.

McCLOSKY, H. (1960) "Issue conflict and consensus among party leaders and followers." Amer. Pol. Sci. Rev. 54 (June): 406-427.

MEAD, M. (1951) "The study of national character," in M. Lerner and H. Laswell [eds.] The Policy Sciences: Recent Developments in Scope and Method. Stanford: Stanford Univ. Press.

MLINAR, Z. (n.d.) "Theoretical approach to the problems of structures and integration in the Yugoslav commune." (Unpublished)

——— (1970) "Education for development of personality, community, and society." University of Ljubljana. Institute of Sociology and Philosophy Reprint Paper 14.

PUTNAM, R. D. (1966) "Political attitudes and the local community." Amer. Pol. Sci. Rev. 60 (September): 640-654.

ROBSON, W. A. (1968) Local Government in Crisis: London: George Allen & Unwin.

RUSTOW, D. A. (1969) " 'The organization triumphs over its function': Huntington on modernization." J. of International Affairs 33: 119-132.

SCHURMAN, F. (1968) Ideology and Organization in Communist China. Berkeley and Los Angeles: Univ. of California Press.

SMITH, M. G. (1966) "A structural approach to comparative politics," pp. 113-128 in D. Easton [ed.] Varieties of Political Theory. Englewood Cliffs, N.J.: Prentice-Hall.

STAUFFER, S. (1963) Communism, Conformity and Civil Liberties. Gloucester, Mass.: Peter Smith.

TEUNE, H. and A. PREZEWORSKI (1966) "Establishing equivalence in cross-national research." Public Opinion Q. 30.

INDEX

INDEX

Anthropology and politics, 222-226, 233, 237, 252, 285. See also political culture, tradition and politics.
Army and politics, 189, 202. See also political participation, Turkey.
Attitudinal analysis, 23-24, 167, 291; and survey research, 271-272, 275, 284. See also ideological congruence.
Authoritarian behavior, 69-76, 86, 106, 153. See also emotional insecurity.

Behavioral change, 15, 17, 20, 30, 31, 47, 51, 57, 119, 14, 220, 241, 252, 264, 290; and ethnocentrism, 73-75.
Belief systems, 13, 75, 14, 149, 155, 172, 268-269, 290; and tolerance of ambiguity, 75. See also ideology.
Bourguiba, Habib, 240-205.
Bureaucracy, 195, 201, 202, 205, 209. See also participation, Pakistan.

Camus, Albert, 103-104.
Class and politics, 37, 44, 159, 174, 176, 254. See also social theory.
Colonization, 76-86, 222; and Britain, 78-81, 241-242.
Comparative analysis, 17, 19, 56, 122-123, 220-221, 265, 272, 275-276, 283-284; and longitudinal studies, 267-268.
Consensus, see legitimacy.

Democratic theory, 274-275, 278, 288, 290, 292.
Development, see institutional change and social theory.

Ecological analysis, 21-23, 160.
Elites, 16, 108, 178, 189, 194, 196, 203, 206, 222, 224, 236-237, 242, 250, 287.
Emotional insecurity, 28, 82-83, 89, 102-109, 268-271; and violence, 92; and childhood, 99-100.
Ethnocentrism, 73-75. See also Nazism.

Fanon, Franz, 88-90.
Fromm, Eric, 70-71.
Functionalist theory and politics, 247-248, 266. See also social theory.

Heirarchy, see political status.

Identity, national, 90-91, 136; personal, 27, 30, 49, 53, 144. See also working ideology, symbols and politics.
Ideology, definitions, 25-30, 51, 256, 285; contextual problems of, 15-19, 37, 220, 263, 289; congruence and, 53-57, 60, 75, 186, 275-278; independent effects of, 52, 58, 263, 273, 293; transformation of, 21, 24, 29, 45, 53, 279-281; affective aspect, 66-69; cognitive aspect, 125, 217, 237, 267, 271. See also working ideology.
Institutional change, 36, 52, 55, 59; and institutional norms, 60, 109, 178; in China, 97-98; in Turkey, 137-138; in Thailand, 144-146. See also political participation.

About the Author

DOUGLAS E. ASHFORD has written numerous books and articles on political development in the Third World and has lived in Tunisia, Morocco, and Pakistan. His major interest has been the relationship between nationalism and problems of institutional and developmental change. He has been particularly concerned with issues of participation and grassroots politics in developing countries, and, more recently, in Europe. He received his doctorate from Princeton in 1960 and has been teaching at Cornell University since 1964.